To my mother Bernice, for making everything possible.

Special Acknowledgments

I would like to thank my teachers at Alfred University, College of Ceramics, Alfred, New York, and Monmouth University, West Long Branch, New Jersey, for their encouragement and advice:

Val Cushing

Vincent DiMattio

Wally Higgins

Ed Jankowski

Willis G. Lawrence

William Parry

Ted Randall

Daniel Rhodes

Robert Turner

Arie Van Everdingen

Glenn Zweygardt

Contents

WHAT EVERY
POTTER
Should Know

JEFF ZAMEK

krause publications

700 E. State Street • Iola, WI 54990-0001
Telephone: 715/445-2214

www.krause.com

Please call or write for our free catalog of publications. Our toll-free number to place an order or obtain a free catalog is 800-258-0929 or please use our regular business telephone 715-445-2214 for editorial comment and further information.

Photography by Robert Tobey Fine Photography, Northampton, Mass., and Jeff Zamek

Manufactured in the United States of America

Library of Congress Cataloging-In-Publication Data

Zamek, Jeff
What every potter should know

1. Pottery   2. Ceramics   3. Crafts   4. Title

ISBN 0-87341-721-6

98-87292
CIP

Portions of chapters 4, 9, 10, 13, 18, and 21 were previously published in *Ceramics Monthly* magazine.

Foreword

When Jeff asked me to write the foreword for his book, the request caught me by surprise. I was, at the same time, flattered and a bit put off. After all, this was during summer, my slightly down time, and who needs extra work? Upon a quick collection of my thoughts, though, I realized that having this project come across my desk when I thought I had little to do was quite apropos to the theme of his book. For one of the points that comes through clearly in his manuscript is that it takes a lot of work and effort to make a go of it as a potter and there isn't much time for rest.

What Every Potter Should Know is a collection of Jeff's experiences as a teacher, potter, consultant, and technician. When his manuscript first came to my attention, I was very curious to see just what he would include and how his interpretation of the potter's handbook theme would be different from all the others. Well, in fact, it *is* different. Handbooks for the potter abound, however never before has there been one that attempts to bring together the somewhat elusive supportive elements that make a devotion to, and the practice of, pottery making complete. This is a book that I would certain-

ly have put to good use earlier in my career. Jeff has successfully put together a well-conceived package that isn't everything a potter needs to know, but really is stuff that every potter needs to know! The nature of commercial raw materials, why we as potters have to deal with apparent poor quality control, and how their variability can affect clay bodies and glaze recipes is a good example of the kind of information that we should know and that Jeff shares. How to buy supplies and how to streamline your production for the marketplace are two others.

Jeff has carefully chosen his topics so as not to bring a book to the market that would simply rehash established themes and subjects. In this effort, he has succeeded. *What Every Potter Should Know* is a unique treatment of a variety of subjects that you won't find together anywhere else. Are you serious about making ware? Do you want to expand your knowledge? This is a book for you. Enjoy it.

Steven Branfman
Newton, Massachusetts
July 1998

Introduction

Where to begin? We could begin at the beginning, when the moist clay is dug out of the ground, formed into an object, and fired in a kiln. But frankly, a sequential description of all the steps necessary to make a ceramic object has already been accomplished in many outstanding pottery books. There are also various texts on specific ceramic subjects such as salt firing, raku, low-fire ceramics, kiln building, majolica ware, etc. When I first conceived the idea for a ceramics book, the major obstacle was to avoid rewriting – probably badly – what is already on every library shelf. I hope you will find some useful information in the following chapters.

What Every Potter Should Know is meant to help potters understand the basic theories involved in clay work and to offer small pieces of sometimes unrelated information to help solve common problems faced when working with clay. It often happens with students that, at some point, a critical mass of bits and pieces of information accumulates into a more complete vision of the whole subject. After 30 years of making pots, teaching pots, and now talking pots as a ceramics consultant, perhaps I can present some new approaches to old problems in clay or just possibly explain something in a way that gives you a better understanding of ceramics.

I have assembled information from my graduate school notes, teaching lectures, workshop demonstrations, and problem-solving encounters with clients. The last category is often the most challenging and rewarding in revealing answers to ceramics-related problems. When faced with a simple problem, potters will either solve it themselves, ask a fellow potter, or devise a strategy around the mishap. As a pottery consultant, I most often hear about a problem over the phone, occasionally at odd hours (when, for example, a stubborn gas kiln won't climb in temperature or reduce properly). During the course of the conversation, often a specific glaze, clay body, or kiln problem is described inaccurately by the worried potter or an important piece of information is forgotten or overlooked. These phone calls are always exciting, with a double layer of information to be unraveled. When the initial puzzle is presented, I have to make sure I have the correct information to arrive at a fast and accurate solution.

Most of my clients are potters who make functional ceramics. While the emphasis in this book is on their concerns, in many instances the same principles apply to ceramic sculpture, the important factor being the size and thickness of the ceramic object rather than its utilitarian intent or purely artistic scope.

When evaluating glaze and clay body defects, approximately one third of the time I need to see and touch the pots. It's very exhilarating to get a box of cracked or defective ceramic objects (the UPS person always looks sheepish when delivering these boxes). As I open the box, if the problem doesn't jump out and hit me in the face, the solution to the defect usually requires some investigation and testing. The potter's written description of the defect can sometimes put the last clues in place, but at this point, unless I ask the right follow-up questions, the answer to why the piece failed is often a mystery. Evaluating the defect can be a formidable task and at times it's like a crash investigation to discover what went wrong with the clay, glaze, kiln, or potter. In more instances than I care to think about, my best efforts don't solve the problem. In such cases, I worry about what part of the puzzle I missed or what piece of information I didn't understand. On a very good day, I have just average intelligence but above average persistence, which has led me to do countless tests of raw materials and glazes in order to find out what went wrong. While this part of the business can be challenging and frustrating for me, for the potter it is something more – a loss of income.

In the following chapters, I have tried to offer a body of technical knowledge, practical advice, and just enough theory to help potters who don't have access to a ceramics expert. Often the only thing that makes someone an expert is endurance and the number of defects that arrive on their desk. The more you see, the more you know. Some types of ceramics problems don't require a vast theoretical base of knowledge – solving them comes from having seen the problem over and over on many pots. However, some problems require a detective's instinct for listening and questioning. For example, if black specks appear in a white porcelain clay body fired in a reducing kiln atmosphere, are the black specks caused by a marginal clay body formula, improperly mixed clay, clay contamination in shipping or storage, studio contamination in forming, handling, or glazing, kiln atmosphere, kiln burners, or a combination of some or all of the above? These are always the most challenging types of problem. It's often the last thing the potter says that uncovers the cause. Usually, just as they are about to end the phone conversation they will say something like, "Oh, by the way, I've been wedging the porcelain clay on the same table I use for my stoneware clay. Is that important?" It could be very important if the wedging table is contaminated with dark-firing stoneware clays because such clays contain iron and manganese particles that will transfer into the white porcelain clay and show up as black specking in the fired ware. Not all problems are so easy to solve and I still get up in the middle of the night thinking about the ones that remain a mystery.

I like tools. I especially like tools that don't have to be carried around – the ones that can be carried in your head. A tool can give you the ability to work a problem to its successful conclusion. Hopefully this book will give potters the mental tools to solve ceramics problems in their own studios. I also like the idea of learning something new. In ceramics, there are a lot of myths and so-called "unseen forces" at work. Potters often fashion little kiln gods out of their clay to sit on top of the kiln to insure good firings. Such pagan beliefs add to the excitement of firing the kiln, but I would prefer to have the tools in my head to direct the actions of the kiln and not put my trust in some clay sculpture sitting on top of the kiln. Yes, good accidents

come from combinations of clay, glaze, and firing, but they should be balanced with a thorough understanding of materials and firing techniques.

After years of teaching and traveling, it's a pleasure to work in my own ceramics studio every day. I first started making pots as a college student, then went to graduate school, taught ceramics for ten years, and for the past 16 years I have been a ceramics consultant. During my first year of making pots, I didn't realize how much my technical mistakes were delaying the learning process. There are certain advantages to being self-taught, but you only know what *you* know. A good teacher will enable you to know that and much more. I urge you to find a teacher or teachers and expand your base of ceramic knowledge and techniques.

I am still amazed by clay. In the afternoon, when my morning throwing is complete, I sometimes go into the studio just to smell the leather-hard clay. It has a warm musty smell that reminds me of other studios in the past and other potters working in their studios today. Now I am the true amateur, one who makes pots for the love of working with clay.

Since starting the ceramics consulting business, my own pots are neither exhibited nor sold. My basement is full of pots and that's fine. I don't want to be in competition with clients or show divided attention to the potters I'm trying to help. In a way, it's like going to a doctor when you're sick. If you're in their office and you see a photo of them sailing, that's fine, but if their whole office is filled with sailing photos, you begin to wonder if you're seeing a sailor who is a doctor or a doctor who is a sailor. You need a doctor who concentrates on you full-time, not one who is thinking about boats. I feel the same way when talking with potters. I'm not a potter who is a consultant, I'm a consultant who is a potter – I should be there for my clients full-time. This book is the result of being there for 16 years, hearing about and seeing countless examples of ceramics problems.

Part I

Learning About
The Craft
And Materials

Bottles fired in a soda kiln C/9/R 2336°F.

Chapter 1

A Potter's Education

Pottery, or any type of clay work, requires information, personal experience, training in techniques, and the ability to turn theory into practical application. Unfortunately, all the required skills and knowledge are not easily obtained in one location. In the past, the education process was easier – an aspiring potter apprenticed under a master potter to learn the craft or, if their father was a potter, simply learned the family business, eventually being taught everything necessary about the various aspects of producing pots. This system was in place to train potters through the ascending levels of the craft. A beginning apprentice's first job might have been cleaning the shop or digging clay. While such activities weren't exciting and often involved very hard labor, they were learned in detail. Eventually the apprentice might be promoted to wedging the moist clay and watching other potters work. After a while, they would be allowed to throw one simple shape until they became proficient in that form. In time, they would master every step of the operation.

Today, many beginning potters start making pots without the benefit of any form of ceramics education. The apprenticeship system has slowly receded, due in part to the industrial revolution that mechanized the production of pottery. Potters currently have to find alternative methods to acquire skills and master techniques. Fortunately, several sources for such training exist. In fact, many potters encounter one or more in their informal or formal search to make better pots.

However, knowing the advantages and disadvantages of each source is critical.

Ceramics in general, and pottery in particular, requires little bits of information gathered from many different sources. It is only when enough bits of information are strung together coherently that your objectives and goals as a potter begin to be realized. Determining what information is relevant and applying that information is a skill that can further your education in making pots. You need to know when a source has been exhausted and it's time to move on to the next aspect of training. This is often difficult to recognize, since the joy of making pots or ceramic sculpture prevents an objective look at technical progress or a critique of the aesthetic value of the work itself.

Listed are several widely used sources for obtaining pottery skills. Keep in mind that no one source is better than another and drawing from several educational methods at once is possible.

Teaching Yourself

Mastering any skill is time-consuming and often requires repetitive practice to become proficient. Working alone offers the capability to concentrate without the interference or unwanted criticism of other students or teachers. If you decide to go this route, don't let teaching yourself be your only method of education. You may end up wasting time and effort trying to master a new technique or discover the cause of a technical problem.

When working alone, at some point, your progress will slow or even come to a dead halt. Often ideas from magazine articles, books, or videos can get you past this universal dilemma. Since working alone and teaching yourself is a central aspect of learning the craft, it's important to recognize when you've hit a learning plateau. When you get stuck, it's time to look to other methods of learning.

The need for outside help most often arises because of a technical problem. If your plates are cracking or the handles are falling off your coffee cups, you're probably going to get frustrated enough to seek advice. Looking to other sources of information can also produce aesthetic gains in the work. Seeing how other potters place handles on coffee cups can reveal the many styles of achieving this utilitarian goal. Once new skills are discovered with outside help, it's back to the studio to practice. The main idea is to not get stuck in the studio. Why reinvent the wheel, spending your time and energy to discover what others have already learned?

Craft Centers

Craft centers have opened in many communities across the country, offering an alternative to college-based ceramics arts programs. Several centers have certificate programs consisting of studio space, classroom participation, and teacher critiques. The artist-in-residence programs in the centers can also offer unlimited studio use and the time required to develop a body of work. Many students enrolling in such programs have college degrees in fields other than ceramics. Some return to formal training in ceramics to learn particular skills or to pursue a second career as a potter. Craft centers also present workshops where experts hold lectures and demonstrations.

A craft center can make available the use of kilns, wheels, slab rollers, tools, and raw materials at relatively low cost as compared to equipping your own studio. Another major advantage is the opportunity to interact with teachers and other students and to be exposed to new techniques and concepts.

Before committing yourself to a ceramics course, talk with the instructor and several students who are already enrolled in the program. Most organizations will let prospective students sit in on a class. Take this opportunity to evaluate the teaching atmosphere. Does the teacher answer the students' questions? Do the students participate in classroom discussions? Does the teacher demonstrate techniques and monitor the progress of students during the class? Do students appear comfortable in the class? Try to find out the answers to these questions before enrolling in a ceramics program.

College Ceramics Programs

These programs are structured on the basic four-year undergraduate baccalaureate degree and the two-year graduate masters degree programs. The usual course of study in an undergraduate program is two years of basic design curriculum followed by two years of intensive specialization in ceramics. Most graduate and some undergraduate programs offer courses in art history, glaze calculation, kiln building, raw materials, and mold making. Graduate schools usually provide individual studio space for making pots that will be critiqued by the faculty. Each college offers different courses and establishes their own requirements to qualify for a degree.

Keep in mind that you are buying a commodity – a useful enlightened education. Make every effort to investigate the content of the ceramics program and try not to be unduly influenced by the degree-granting status of the institution or the amount of pottery equipment in their studios.

Both undergraduate and graduate schools require college entrance exams, portfolios of artwork, and supplemental information that varies with the college. Besides a college degree, students get the opportunity to work with other students and receive training in a formal course of study from an academically qualified instructor. However, each college has different strengths and weaknesses. Some colleges might have very strong departments in functional ceramics but lack expertise in sculptural ceramics. Always visit the college before making any commitments. Each admissions office assigns a tour guide to show prospective students the campus grounds and buildings. They can be very helpful in offering general information, but try to spend most of your time on campus sitting in on ceramics classes. Contact students who are currently in the program and ask for the names of students who have recently graduated from the program. After a few questions and phone calls, you should have a pretty good idea of whether the college offers what you need.

Other Potters

Other potters are often very good sources of information on equipment, pottery techniques, future workshops, and the location of the most reputable suppliers. Whenever possible, visit their studios to generate ideas for designing your own studio. Experienced potters have worked through many of the questions and problems you may face now or in the future. Their advice can save many hours of wasted effort and you won't have to repeat their mistakes.

Often potters will share their favorite glaze or clay body formulas. While this practice can be a good starting point in the study of raw materials, try to develop your own formulas to define your individual statement in clay.

In many communities, individual potters join together to form guilds or clubs. A club meeting is a good place to meet other potters to exchange information. Groups of potters meet regularly to discuss ideas for selling their work, future pottery fairs, discounts for group purchasing of raw materials, and other areas of mutual concern and interest. Before making a major capital investment when purchasing equipment, kilns, raw materials, or clay mixers, ask club members if they have encountered difficulties with specific items. Their comments may prevent potential trouble and expense when the time comes to make purchasing decisions. Take the time to listen carefully – advice from someone who's been there is a bargain.

Workshops

Workshops are usually held at crafts centers, schools, ceramics supply companies, or any central location that will accommodate a group of potters. They can run one day or several days and usually combine practical information with hands-on clay work. Often they are good places to learn a specific technique such as salt firing, raku, wood firing, or throwing functional pottery forms on the wheel.

Workshops can also present an excellent opportunity to meet your favorite artists who work in clay. In the United States, there are a relatively small number of artists or craftsmen who work in clay compared to the number of painters and sculptors. This means it's easier to see the significant artists in the ceramics field. Often "famous" potters or the authors of your favorite ceramics books give workshops. Attending workshops is the ideal way to meet them and discover their views on pottery. After the formal workshop presentation they often answer individual questions.

Some workshop formats allow student potters to bring examples of their work for evaluation. Having your work examined in front of a group of fellow potters might not be what most people think of as a good time, but if you can handle it, you're likely to get some good information. Critiques can answer technical questions (why handles crack) or address aesthetic concerns (my pots look just like everyone else's). Think of the workshop as a chance to step out of your normal cycle of making pots and arrive at a different viewpoint about your work. The best workshops offer inspiration and new ideas you can take back to your studio.

Teachers

Hopefully you have known a great teacher at some point during your learning process. Whether teaching a room full of students or giving a private lesson, a good teacher brings a certain joy and excitement to the endeavor of making pots. However, it's hard to distinguish a good teacher from a marginal one, especially for beginning students who simply don't know enough to judge the content of the subject matter.

The answers to several questions can raise red flags in such situations. Does the teacher make a student feel uncomfortable or dumb when asking questions? Do the students feel rushed to complete work in the lesson? Is the teacher more interested in their own work than yours? Is the teacher prepared for class? If any of these issues leave you doubtful, consider talking frankly with the teacher about your concerns. Most situations where the student doesn't feel they are getting enough out of the class can be resolved by discussing the specific issues.

In the worst or the best teaching situations, students reach a point where they must evaluate the gains they are making and decide if it's worth their time and effort to continue. Occasionally, a teacher and student cannot make a learning connection, for whatever reason. In this case, it's best to look for another teacher. More often, separating from the great teacher is harder for the student. Who wants to leave a nurturing, comfortable, supportive presence and go into the unknown? A good teacher prepares the student for this inevitable step.

Every teacher has something special to bring to the student. It's the student's job to search out different teachers for a comprehensive ceramics education. Always try to take an introductory lesson before committing to a class. The best plan is to sample a few teachers to find ones who meet your needs.

Books, Tapes, Magazines

These resources can provide information on glaze and clay body formulas, methods of firing kilns, and photographs of other potters' work. At each level – beginner, intermediate, and advanced – informative books cover every aspect of ceramics. For example, just on the topic of pottery kilns, you'll find fiber kilns, electric kilns, salt kilns, soda kilns, wood kilns, ground hog kilns, envelope kilns, tunnel kilns, and gas kilns. An advantage of using books is the ability to study at your own pace. You can read the information until you fully understand it and it's always available for your future reference.

Magazines offer topical information, photos, and articles about ceramics. Some magazines also list upcoming ceramics workshops and pottery exhibitions. They are a good source of new ideas and techniques. Depending on the magazine, different areas of ceramics are covered in each issue. Local libraries often have a selection of ceramics magazine, but having a subscription to a magazine is a low cost way to keep informed about current ceramics products and developments.

Video tapes have become very popular in the past few years. Some people feel that certain information is better transmitted by seeing the event rather than reading about it. For example, you can watch how handles are attached to coffee cups, then practice applying handles on your own pots. When viewing a tape, it's almost as if you are in the teacher's studio or attending their workshop. A disadvantage is not being able to interact and ask questions or get further explanation of technical points. If the content is well thought out and presented, tapes are still a good method of sharing information. Tapes, like books and magazines, allow the information to be presented at your own pace.

Craft Shows

Here's a great place to get practical information about selling pots. By carefully observing what other potters are doing with clay and glazes, you can learn about effective techniques as well as how to display and price pieces.

The range of shows and their entrance requirements vary considerably depending on who organizes the event. Some shows require slides of current work and entrance fees. Many shows have judging panels who grant admission by looking only at the applicant's slides. Judging any potter's work is a subjective matter. The judges' opinions should never be considered an actual criticism of your work, even though a rejection from a show can be disappointing. The best course of action is to ask a fellow potter or teacher to look over your work and make any suggestions on how to improve your presentation. Then apply to other shows.

Craft shows often have specific days for wholesale-only sales, followed by retail days. For functional potters, these shows provide an opportunity to compare the prices of your pots against those of other potters. If your coffee cups are priced at $10 and other potters are selling coffee cups at $15, maybe you should consider restructuring your prices. (The price structure also depends on factors such as labor, cost of materials, fixed and variable cost of production, wages, and the aesthetic value placed on the work.)

When your own pots are in the show, customer comments can be especially important if they concern technical issues you may have overlooked when making the pots. If your coffee cup handles are too small or have sharp edges, a customer's comment may point out the defect. Shows are also good opportunities to connect with other potters and observe how they do business. Do they have attractive exhibition booths? Are their pots selling? Does their business appear organized and efficient?

Apprenticeships

An apprenticeship is an agreement where labor is exchanged for education. Exactly what kind and how much labor for what type of education is often the weak point in apprenticeship situations. It's critical that both parties agree in advance on what is expected. Apprenticeships are as individual as the potter and the apprentice involved. In the old days, apprenticeships were the standard method of pottery education. Today, they reflect the unique requirements of both parties.

When considering an apprenticeship, find out as much as possible about the potter or organization offering the position. Knowing what's required of you is just as critical as knowing what you'll receive. A written agreement should be signed to insure that both parties know and accept their responsibilities. A trial period to see if the "fit" between apprentice and potter is working is a good idea for a productive learning experience. Apprenticeships offer onsite observation and participation in every aspect of pottery making at that particular shop. Often the techniques and methods of production you learn will be of great value in setting up your own studio.

Keep a notebook for glaze formulas, sketches of pots or sculptural forms, a list of your goals, and comments about your pots. One of my best teachers told me, "Always look for the parts of the pot that are hidden from view. If they are well thought out and finished, it's a good pot." I've kept that advice in my mind for many years and have benefited from remembering it.

Making pottery has social implications – you encounter other people while training and other people use or look at your completed pots or sculpture. Long hours alone in the studio are often balanced with classroom or workshop participation. Utilizing every learning situation at every opportunity is important. So much of working with clay is about how you view yourself in relation to others. A good education in ceramics should come from many sources. The best advice is to observe a lot, do a lot, and find your own voice with the clay.

Chapter 2
Economics and Raw Materials

In the world of ceramics, there is a constant that affects everyone from professional potter to hobbyist – the only thing consistent about raw materials is their inconsistency. With this in mind, let's look at the economic facts of raw materials.

What does supply and demand have to do with the clay used in ceramics? Everything. If you are a large-quantity user of Edgar Plastic Kaolin (a domestic kaolin mined in Florida since 1892) and need millions of pounds per year to make spark plugs (which, in fact, does happen), you probably have the clout to go right to the mines and demand a white, easily pressed, high-temperature, clean-burning clay guaranteed to have those properties with every batch. The mine management might look at your large order and agree on a specification for the clay you want, then set a price.

Potters benefit greatly from knowing that one bag of clay will be identical to the next, year after year, with consistent results. In addition to the Edgar Plastic Kaolin, other virtually guaranteed raw materials are Custer feldspar, G-200 feldspar, nepheline syenite, whiting, dolomite, flint, calcined kaolin, Kona F-4 feldspar, magnesium carbonate, and lithium carbonate, to name a few. This guarantee of uniformity, chemical composition, and quality has been forced on suppliers by large industrial demands, not by potters. Potters are the unintentional benefactors of a system that's been worked out by the large players in the supply and demand market.

Unfortunately, there is a downside to this situation which occurs when a large-user industry changes its specifications for a raw material. Suddenly a favorite body melts or bloats. Something a potter considers a horrible defect might not be considered a defect at all by a larger user, so it could be allowed into the mine's batch.

An example of a good clay for industry that is sometimes bad for potters is A.P. Green Missouri fire clay. Used mostly in the brick and steel industries, it's a perfectly good fire clay for their products, but watch out for those specks of iron and manganese that might ruin your best casserole dish. Why doesn't the mine remove the impurities before it ships the clay? Because those impurities don't matter to its industrial users. What's a few large specks in a brick? They aren't considered a defect, so why spend money adjusting or refining a clay that is acceptable to 99% of the market? Potters will always have a certain amount of difficulty using A.P. Green

The porcelain tip of a spark plug requires a consistent quality white pure clay EPK.

Missouri fire clay, Hawthorn bonding clay, Ocmulgee red clay, Kentucky ball clay (OM4), and other such variable quality clays. The probability is high that over a given period of time there will be some shift in quality.

Now that you understand that potters are on the tail end of the raw material economy, you probably also realize that it's unlikely that we'll ever wag this dog. Instead, pick and choose carefully, using "guaranteed" clays in clay bodies and glaze recipes whenever possible. You can formulate trouble-free glazes if you learn to use the supply and demand strengths rather than choosing raw materials blindly. A little knowledge in this area will produce better results.

Chapter 3

How to Buy Supplies

Typically potters believe their most important decisions revolve around aesthetic considerations such as choosing the correct glaze and clay color, temperature range, and forming method. The question of how and where to obtain the necessary materials is rarely given as much attention, but those decisions must also be made carefully.

Unless you want to mine and process your own raw materials and make your own equipment, you'll do business with a ceramics supplier. This can either be a pleasant, economical relationship or it can be expensive, unsatisfying, and time-consuming.

There are some basic factors that control the potter's quest for raw materials. Even the largest ceramics suppliers are essentially small businesses when compared to other ceramic industries. The reality is that potters buy less than 0.1% of the clay marketed in the United States. We are, therefore, using materials that are neither mined nor refined for our needs. You can't change this situation, but by knowing the characteristics of common materials, you can make informed choices. You should be aware that many materials change over a period of time, which could be as brief as the time between two purchases of clay. Before giving up all hope, consider that some raw materials do remain fairly consistent in chemical composition, particle size, solubility, melting temperature, and quality control.

The most problem-free (notice I didn't say perfect) are flint, whiting, dolomite, Edgar Plastic Kaolin, Grolleg kaolin, Pioneer kaolin, 6-Tile clay, Custer feldspar, Kona F-4 feldspar, G-200 feldspar, nepheline syenite, calcined kaolin, alumina hydrate, barium carbonate, bone ash, any of the frits, talc, Superpax, Opax, Treopax, and Ultrox. These are just some of the materials used in the paint, chemical, and paper industries. Potters should take advantage of the quality-control standards set by large industrial users. Glaze and clay body recipes should be based on this category of "guaranteed" materials whenever possible.

Conversely, some raw materials are subject to less stringent quality control. You should consider fire clays, stoneware clays, and most ball clays as raw materials that will be inconsistent. The question is not *if* the material will change, but *when*.

Fire clays contain varying levels of sand, lignite (coal), sulfur, organic matter, and other contaminants (such as iron and manganese) which can cause spit outs on

Pallets of 50-pound bags of Redart, a low temperature, high iron content earthenware clay.

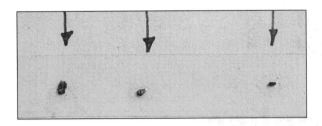

Large particle contamination found in the average bag of fire clay. (actual size)

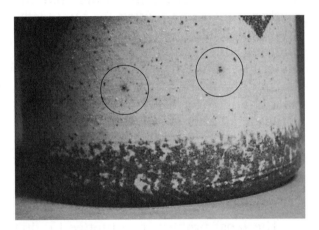

Clay body specks – green specks of copper contamination found in fire clay.

fired ware. But such impurities are insignificant to major fire clay users like the steel and foundry industries.

Ball clay can have high levels of organic material that can fluctuate from one batch to another without notice. If your bisque firing is not clean (oxidized) and well vented, black coring, bloating, pinholes, or blisters can result. Some of the most popular ball clays might keep the same name over the years even though the actual product changes or is blended with other clays. As the deposit is mined in new locations, changes take place in particle size, fired color, or handling characteristics of the clay. The mine then has to blend its clay with other deposits, hoping for a good result. All this goes on without consumer awareness of the change until something goes wrong.

Gerstley borate is also high on the list of materials that can change from one batch to the next. Some batches of Gerstley borate contain various amounts of "tramp" material that ride along with the three-mesh ore as it is ground down to a 200-mesh powder. This type of impurity can cause black specks in the fired glaze. It usually takes about 12 to 18 months for a new batch to enter the market.

What's the best way to avoid inconsistent materials? Try to cut down on the percentage of the material you need in any given formula. If this isn't possible, use two different fire clays instead of one to reduce the risk of a bad fire clay disrupting your clay body. Too expensive, you say? Too many materials to stock? Yes, but compare that to the time and effort lost on a defective kiln load of pots or sculpture.

Evaluating Raw Materials

Evaluating raw materials can be as simple or complicated as your patience, time, and money will permit. A reasonable approach is to start with screening one pound of the suspect material through a 60-mesh sieve. Note the particle size, color, texture, and quantity of the material remaining on the screen. Large particles are suspect in causing spit outs or blotches on the fired clay surface. This might be just the look you're after in a wood-fired piece, but could cause problems in porcelain. Black specks found in the sieve could indicate coal, iron, manganese, or calcium nodules in the clay, which can cause brown or black spots. As a rule, in clay bodies it's not a specific contaminant that causes a problem, it's the large particle size.

Spread all the material remaining on the screen on a moist porcelain slab. (A high-temperature white clay makes a good contrasting background.) Use a rolling pin to press the material into the clay, then fire the sample at the highest cone you typically fire to. Note any large spit outs or brown/black blemishes caused by iron or manganese. Green specks could be the result of chrome or copper contamination (found in fire clays). Also note any conical holes or half-moon shaped cracks. This type of crack is often caused by a "lime pop," the result of large particles or nodules of calcium. If it is calcium, when you peel back the clay at the crack, there will be a white speck at the bottom of the hole.

Of course, the amount of contaminants per square inch will be greater than in unsieved material but this simple test will give an indication of the worst results possible. If the fired sample looks somewhat like your own clay, only with more specks that don't disrupt or scar the surface, the probability of the contaminant adversely affecting your work is minimal.

Material Specifications

When ordering raw materials, be very specific as to trade name, mesh size, and quantity. Be aware that suppliers order the materials from a processor and sometimes there can be several processors of a raw material. This can cause a problem if each processor grinds the product to a different mesh. Whiting is an example of a glaze material that produces different effects depending on particle size. It can and does vary, depending on the plant's production specifications. In any case, a finer mesh whiting will stay in suspension longer in a glaze bucket and will melt more completely. A coarser whiting will sink faster in the glaze bucket and will tend to increase the opacity of clear glazes. Specify the same mesh on every order to insure consistent results.

Similarly, the size of flint particles in a glaze can affect results. Do you know what mesh to order? Most ceramics suppliers carry 400-mesh, 325-mesh, 200-mesh, and silica sand (coarse particle flint). As a general rule, 325-mesh flint can be used in glazes (400-mesh can help eliminate crazing although there are inhalation concerns about such very fine silica), while the 200-mesh range can be used in clay bodies. Silica sand is used in salt or soda clay bodies to promote an "orange peel" texture on the clay surface.

Metallic coloring oxides also come in a wide range of mesh sizes and various concentrations. Certain trace elements can be found in oxides, depending on the original ore deposit and method of refining. One large processing company, Pfizer Minerals, produces over a dozen types of black iron oxide for industry use. When buying black iron oxide from a ceramics supplier, would you know if it's the same type of black iron oxide you used in the past? Red iron oxide is produced in various concentrations and purity levels too.

Copper oxide, one of the most reactive of the coloring oxides, can contain various trace elements depending on how it was processed. Again, it can be very difficult to achieve consistent results in glaze color when the coloring oxide composition can change without the potter's knowledge.

A change in the raw material source (and there can be quite a few sources for any given material) can cause a shift in glaze color, texture, or opacity. A supplier might find a cheaper source of a raw material and begin selling it to customers without thoroughly inspecting the material's specifications. Only when enough complaints from potters are reported does any corrective action take place. Think how often potters don't complain, thinking they made a mistake in mixing or firing the glaze!

Smart Money

We all like to find the lowest price for everything. In today's consumer market, it makes us feel that even if we're not beating the system, we're not getting taken too badly. This mindset might get us the best price on a car or television, but careful analysis is required when purchasing ceramic materials, clays, glazes, tools, and kilns.

Buying a premixed clay to save a few pennies per pound is not a true savings if the clay is improperly mixed and ends up ruining a whole kiln load of pots. Quality control, good raw materials, and a knowledge of clay-mixing procedures cost money. A professional clay-mixing operation might charge slightly higher prices to cover the costs of producing better premixed clay. If you are now using a ceramics supplier's premixed clay and have had good results, you should probably look for cost savings in other areas.

Another false economy is "free" material. For example, a potter with a source of cheap wood (a broom handle factory located just three feet away from the wood kiln) decides to fire with wood to save fuel costs. Firing a wood kiln is time-consuming at best and at worst requires constant physical effort to gain temperature. After a few wood firings, how much energy do you think you'll have to load your van and drive to the craft show?

In short, it's more important to think smart than to think cheap. Buying proven clay bodies and well-designed equipment, which might cost more initially, is actually less expensive in the long run. Quality equipment lasts longer, makes work more efficient and less tiring, and has a good resale value when you want to expand or upgrade. The more overall planning you do to save labor, the more time you'll have to concentrate on the process that really counts – making the work. Your labor is the most limited resource you have.

Liability

One of the largest areas of misunderstanding between customer and supplier involves raw material and clay body problems. The ceramics supplier accepts limited liability – a fact that is usually stated in the catalog and on clay shipment boxes or raw material bags. When a clay differs from the mine's general analysis of the material, the mine will replace the clay for the ceramics supplier. This involves sending samples of defective clay back to the mine for testing. If the mine is at fault, it will replace the material but won't pay for any subsequent damage caused by the material. This policy is then passed on to the supplier's customer who received the bad clay.

If you purchase a defective bag of dry clay or moist premixed clay that causes the loss of a whole kiln load of pots (perhaps even melting all over the kiln shelves), in most cases the ceramics supplier will replace only the clay and that's only if you can prove the clay was defective. If you mistakenly fire a premixed cone 06 1830°F clay to cone 9 2336°F, don't expect a refund. The markup on moist clays and raw materials is not high enough to allow the supplier to invest in quality-control procedures. Consequently, many problems with materials end up being passed on to the customer, which doesn't seem quite fair.

If you remain in the ceramics field long enough, it's just a matter of time before you purchase a defective load of clay or encounter a raw material that is contaminated. To avoid significant down time, test clays and materials as soon as possible after delivery. When you find a problem, call your supplier at once. Speed and accuracy are essential in obtaining a refund, exchange, or credit. The supplier might ask for a sample of the defective material, so be prepared to send it along with the date of purchase, bill of sale, quantity purchased, and any other pertinent information. Don't try to use a material after you have encountered a problem, as this act can constitute acceptance as is. Call your supplier to discuss options.

Premixed Moist Clay

Most ceramics suppliers carry a line of premixed moist clays, ranging from low-temperature, white casting slips to dark stoneware for throwing. Specialized blends of clay are frequently available for salt/soda firing, raku, midrange porcelain, and slip-casting applications.

The supplier may mix such bodies in-house or buy them from a larger clay supplier/manufacturer. In most clay-mixing operations, the dry clay is placed into a large mixer and water is added in the correct proportion. Once mixed, the batch is fed into a pug mill, which will compress and de-air the clay, extruding a well-blended pug.

The usual packaging consists of 25- or 50-pound blocks of clay, each wrapped in a plastic bag. Always look for a heavy-gauge (three mils) plastic bag to protect the moist clay from drying out due to rips or punctures in the packaging and shipping process. Moisture can also evaporate through a lightweight plastic bag over a period of time.

Some clay manufacturers mark the box with a date or number code that indicates production information about batch size, recipe, etc. Look for this code on your clay shipment box and save it for future reference. If a problem develops with the clay, the code number will be useful in helping the supplier isolate the questionable clay batch. At this point, the supplier should investigate the cause, making sure to test the suspect product before selling it to other customers.

A private recipe is a mixture of clays, feldspar, flint, and grog or any other ceramic materials, which has been developed to meet the specialized needs of a specific potter. It is sometimes assumed that having your own clay body is superior to a stock clay, but keep in mind that a supplier's stock recipes represent high volumes used by a variety of potters under various studio conditions. If it were not

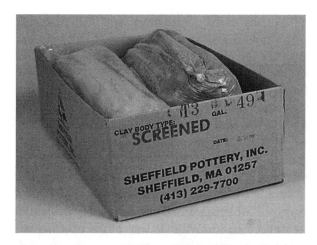

Most ceramics suppliers package moist clay in two 25-pound plastic bags. Suppliers with reliable quality-control procedures will list the clay body name, date of clay mixing, amount of water used in mix, and any special blending of the clay body (for example, the fire clay component of the clay body was screened to remove contaminants).

consistently successful, it would no longer be sold. A private blend of clays is fundamentally only as good as the knowledge of the person who developed the formula and the person who mixed the recipe. If you're just starting in clay or your technical knowledge of ceramic materials isn't extensive, stock clay bodies are time and volume proven, low-risk alternatives to a private blend.

Choosing a Supplier

A retail store location and showroom that displays equipment, tools, books, and supplies is characteristic of a full-service supplier. This is usually the place to find an extensive line of commercial glazes and a wide range of pottery tools and equipment. Expect slightly higher prices on some items (kilns, slab rollers, wheels), but also expect good customer service, efficient repairs on equipment, and technical information on materials and equipment. If you're a novice in ceramics and need product information, a full-service store will probably prove more helpful than a discount supplier.

A discount ceramics supplier might not have a retail store location or an extensive range of ceramics products. Some operations are run through a post office box or business phone number. While the inventory may be limited, low overhead generally results in lower prices on the items that are stocked. Repairs on equipment, return of defective products, and specific technical information might be difficult or impossible to obtain from this type of operation. However, if you have better-than-average knowledge of manufacturers and their products, a limited service discount store might serve you well.

Before ordering from a ceramics supplier, find out the policy on returns of goods or raw materials. Is there a restocking charge? Does the pottery equipment carry the manufacturer's warranty? What is the procedure for repair or replacement of defective products?

When you order 12,000 pounds of clay, will it be delivered to your front door? Will the delivery person help you stack the shipment in your studio? Is there an additional charge for this service? Also read the supplier's catalog carefully in regard to placing an order, back-order policies, taxes, shipping charges, and terms of payment.

Does the company have a good reputation? Ask other potters if they have received good service. Are they made to feel it's their fault that the fire clay caused blisters and spit outs, or is the problem clay replaced without delay? With every business, a reputation develops – good or bad – that can guide the actions of the customer. Find out how the company is regarded by the potting community, then act accordingly.

Try to visit the clay-mixing facility. This is more likely if the clay is mixed on the same premises as retail sales. Always ask to visit at a time that won't interfere with business operations and don't stay long enough to hinder production. During your visit, take a look at the clay storage and mixing areas. Are they reasonably clean and well organized? Do the people mixing clay appear competent and knowledgeable about their jobs? Are the pug mills and clay mixers kept clean? Are any special cleaning procedures enacted when mixing white clays or porcelain? What quality-control measures are taken when different clay body recipes are mixed? You don't have to test the pH of the water or request a maintenance service record for the pug mill, but a few commonsense observations will reveal how seriously a ceramics supplier regards clay mixing.

Find out if there is someone on staff with technical and practical knowledge of raw materials. Can you reach this expert when a problem or question arises? A certain percentage of customer problems occurs when the product or raw material is used incorrectly. We've all been in the studio mixing up a batch of glaze, only to run out of Custer feldspar. What's a good substitute? Can your ceramics supplier tell you what other potash feldspar is likely to work?

Are the salespeople knowledgeable? Do they show an interest in helping you find the right tools and materials for your individual needs? Do they know the advantages and disadvantages of each type of kiln? There are over a dozen electric kiln manufacturers in the United States – can the salespeople tell you which ones have the lowest incidence of repair? If not, to make a cost-effective purchase, you will have to find this out for yourself.

Always try to buy raw materials and clays in their original bags. When you receive a shipment, make sure each bag is properly marked. Each time a ceramics supplier has to take a 50-pound bag of flint and repackage it into ten five-pound bags for resale, the chance of mislabeling increases, along with the price per pound. Obviously, buying 50 pounds of tin oxide at one time would be too expensive, but purchasing flint, whiting, dolomite, clays, and feldspars in 50-pound lots shouldn't be too costly because most clay body and glaze formulas require them.

Keep accurate records of your purchases. Note any irregularities as soon as the shipment arrives (make sure your order of manganese carbonate is not magnesium carbonate or that the nepheline syenite is 270-mesh, not 400-mesh). If a problem does occur with an order, it makes replacement easier when your records and delivery date are available at the time of the complaint. Once the complaint is stated, give the supplier a chance to make an offer of compensation. If there is not an offer or you think the response was not adequate, speak to a higher authority in the company. Keep in mind what you believe constitutes realistic compensation. If you are not satisfied with the response, small claims court is always an option.

If you plan to pick up materials, call ahead to give the supplier enough time to assemble your order. While there, double check each bag label and note any irregularities. This is the time to ask if that plaster is fresh (plaster has a shelf life of about six months) or if that bag of black powder is manganese dioxide or black iron oxide. Discovering you have the wrong material back in your studio can be expensive and definitely time-consuming.

Always test new shipments of raw materials before committing time and effort to a production run, whether you're making 100 coffee cups or a single sculpture. Having said that, I fully realize that it's sometimes difficult to do the testing when you should. It is a risk, though, and the longer you allow yourself to use untested materials, the more likely it is that a problem will develop. Try to think one or two steps ahead in the production process. When you're down to the last half of your clay shipment, order a new batch and test it along with your current production. In this way, you allow time to adjust the clay or complain to the ceramics supplier about the problem and get restitution.

Establishing a good business relationship with your ceramics supplier is important. Jumping from one supplier to another in search of the lowest priced clay, wheels, or tools only provides a short-term gain. When you're considered a valued customer, you are likely to receive benefits like having clay delivered and unloaded inside your studio rather than on a nearby sidewalk. Returning defective equipment or raw materials is also easier. It might not be fair, but it's human nature. While most businesses have specific policies on the return of defective goods, the interpretation of defective may depend on how long the customer has remained loyal to the company and how much business he/she has generated.

Chapter 4

Raw Materials – Be Careful and Specific

At some point in the process of working with clay and making glazes, you'll need to reorder raw materials, increasing the potential for problems. When a raw material changes sufficiently, it can produce variations in clay bodies or glaze formulas. Several factors might have changed since you ordered your last bag of clay or feldspar. It's not that raw materials stored in your studio change over time (except soluble materials), it's the possibility that recently ordered materials have changed, which can produce problems.

Why is reordering so likely to cause trouble? Because companies that mine or manufacture materials can change a raw material's particle size, chemical composition, or availability without notice. Also, ceramics suppliers can use another manufacturer's product with the same generic name but with different critical specifications. Some potters don't know the chemical composition and mesh size of the raw material currently in their studio and the new batch of materials may or may not match. When a raw material can no longer be obtained, manufacturers may make substitutions. If a raw material changes in particle size or chemical composition, the consumer or ceramics supplier might not be aware of the "new" product with the old name. Some changes take place over years; some occur from bag to bag. Often variations in a glaze aren't caused by inaccurate weighing of materials, kiln firing mistakes, or glaze application faults but rather by a raw material changing over its

production life. Glaze and clay body problems are most prevalent when new batches of raw materials are brought into the situation.

What can you do to offset the fact that potters don't control or dictate raw material specifications, quality, or availability? To increase the chances of getting what you require for glaze and clay body formulas, it's critical that you order precisely. If the ceramics supplier doesn't have the exact material, at the very least, you may learn that a raw material has changed or is no longer available. This knowledge is the first step in preventing many potential problems.

More than 200 raw materials (including different mesh sizes of many materials) are available to construct a glaze or clay body formula. Fortunately, you don't have to know every characteristic of all materials to proficiently develop a glaze. Overall, combinations from two to 15 of the same raw materials are found in more than 80% of all base glazes. Some common raw materials found in glazes are flint, Custer feldspar, nepheline syenite, dolomite, whiting, talc, frits, E.P.K., Kentucky OM#4 ball clay, tin oxide, zinc oxide, lithium carbonate, and magnesium carbonate. The metallic coloring oxides, stains, opacifiers, suspension agents, and gums make up other materials that can be added to the base glaze for color, opacity, glaze suspension, and raw glaze hardness characteristics. Knowing this interesting statistic makes the job of learning about raw materials manageable.

Your next goal should be to obtain the exact raw material in every shipment from the nearest reliable source. Below are several factors to consider before placing an order for raw materials.

* **Choosing the correct ceramics supplier makes everything easier**. Finding and patronizing the best-run and most reliable ceramics supply company is the first step in avoiding potential raw material problems. The ideal supplier would be next door to your studio and run like a Fortune 500 company. Find a reputable ceramics supplier as close as possible to make small convenient purchases and to save shipping costs on large amounts of material. On large dry clay orders, the cost of freight can equal the cost of the clay. Always ask questions. Find out if the supplier has a good reputation with other potters. What is their return policy on materials? When purchasing less than a full bag of material, is the bag accurately weighed and labeled? Does the company have a knowledgeable and helpful technical person on staff? Are the storerooms and clay-mixing areas clean and well arranged? Do employees offer pleasant fast service? The answer to these and similar questions will lead to the most appropriate supplier for your raw material needs.

If paying the lowest full-bag price for a raw material is your objective, any supplier will work, but most potters combine their purchases with less than full-bag orders and other supplies or tools. In the end, staying with the most reputable supplier for all your raw materials will pay off because, sooner or later, a glaze or clay body defect will be caused by a raw material. Ceramics suppliers have limited liability on raw materials and under most conditions they will only replace the defective material. The time, labor, pots, or damaging effects of the defective material won't be covered. All things considered, long-term loyal customers will still get the best possible resolution to their problem. Choosing a supplier based only on the lowest priced materials can be false economy. Well-run professional businesses with knowledgeable staffs have higher costs of doing business and might charge more for goods and services, but paying a small increase now with the right supplier is better than suffering potentially high losses through inefficiency and bad business practices with a questionable supplier.

* **The availability of raw materials will always influence the reordering process**. The most logical consideration before ordering raw materials is one of consistent supply. If your goal is to produce a reliable, uniform, consistent glaze or clay body formula, basing your formula on a material that has gone out of production isn't logical. Occasionally, the ceramics supplier will have a stockpile of out of production material and won't find out the material is no longer available until they try to reorder from the mine or manufacturer. Don't put yourself in the position of developing a whole set of glaze or clay bodies only to discover one or more of the raw materials in the formula are out of production.

As mentioned before, most raw materials used by potters aren't developed or mined for potters. Large industrial markets dictate how long a material stays in production. Oxford and Kingman feldspars (potash feldspars) were once very popular and used in many glaze and clay body formulas. Both feldspars are no longer being mined. Does this mean the feldspar mines are exhausted? No, both feldspars still exist but further production is no longer economically viable because large companies no longer purchase the quantities necessary to make mining them profitable. The demands for specific feldspars or raw material are not generated by potters, but by large industrial users.

Favorite feldspars or raw materials can change or the supply can be depleted. How can you avoid this situation? Have the ceramics suppliers do their homework. Ceramics supply companies receive notices from the mines and are regularly visited by salespeople and company representatives who are excellent sources of information about the availability of their products. Other potters might also have information about unreliable raw materials that can save you time and effort.

* When and how can you substitute raw materials in glazes and clay bodies and obtain good results? We have all inconveniently run out of a material needed in a glaze or clay body formula or tried to reorder a raw material that is no longer available. If the raw materials are no longer in production, what material can be substituted? Often a substitution can't be made precisely, but by knowing what group the material falls into you have a better chance of making an exact or acceptable match. Clays, feldspars, and other raw materials are grouped together by chemical composition, refractory qualities, and – as often happens with clays – particle size and shape, among other distinctive characteristics. Choosing a substitute from the same group of materials will produce a better chance of matching the original material.

For example, in most instances Custer feldspar can be substituted in clay body formulas and glazes for G-200 feldspar (both are potash feldspars) with good results. Custer feldspar can also be used in place of Kingman or Oxford feldspars, both potash group feldspars. In glaze formulas, E.P.K. can be substituted for #6 tile clay (both are plastic kaolins). When using opacifiers in glaze formulas, a high degree of matching can be achieved by substituting superpax for zircopax, as both are zirconium silicates and either one will produce opaque white in glazes. In most glaze formulas, flint 325x-mesh can be substituted for flint 200x-mesh without a noticeable difference in the fired glaze. Each situation requires a thorough knowledge of the materials involved and how

they react at different temperature ranges. Always test a possible substitute material before committing yourself to large quantities of materials and labor.

* Know the materials before ordering – the consistent and inconsistent and how to tell them apart. Increased knowledge of materials leads to decreased material-related problems. Strive to know the individual characteristics of each raw material in your clay body and glaze formulas. Learn how they react together at different temperature ranges. Some materials are variable by their nature, which means that even though the name on the bag stays the same, the raw material in the bag can change. Gerstley borate, a calcium borate, can have chemical changes over a whole production run or change from one bag to the next. Fire clays and some stoneware clays can also shift in particle size and level of contaminants. Grog can be made from old hard brick, some of which might be contaminated from its original use in smelting or other heat treatment operations. Such grog can cause green spots or irregular blemishes in the fired clay surface. If stability and consistency are important for a reliable glaze and clay body, choose materials that have a good record of reliability. The ceramics supply company should be able to provide information on problem-causing materials.

Certain groups of raw materials are almost guaranteed to be uniform in consistency with every bag. Since large industry decides the qualities of clay and glaze materials, they give the mine a set of clay specifications. The mine then finds materials that meet their specifications. These companies are large customers who want many thousands of tons of premium clay a year and potters can take advantage of such situations by using these materials in their formulas. It's in the best interest of the mines to keep the materials the same every year, not for potters (who make up a small segment of their market), but for the large company. Whiting, feldspars, and clays are all used in ceramics but the big consumers of the materials are paint, cosmetics, and foundry industries. Other raw materials and clays fall into this pattern as well. Potters should learn which industries use ceramic materials and use the same materials in their clay and glaze formulas whenever possible.

Soluble materials found in glazes or clay bodies are always areas of potential problems. Whenever possible, use materials that are insoluble or don't break down in the water system of a glaze or clay body. Soluble glaze materials (Gerstley borate, colemanite, borax, soda ash, pearl ash, magnesium sulfate, boric acid, wood ash, and to a much lesser degree, some soda feldspars) can take on water in storage, causing an inaccurate glaze weight. As the soluble material is mixed with the glaze, it dissolves in the water and when extra water is poured off the glaze, some soluble material goes with it. Soluble materials also cause problems when a glaze dries on the pot. The high areas of the pot or edges are more likely to get an unequal concentration of glaze materials as water evaporates off the wet glaze and the soluble material moves to the pot's ridges or high areas. The concentration can cause dry areas or bubbles in the fired glaze.

Soluble materials in a clay body formula break down, causing the moist clay body to become rubbery and soft or hard and rigid, depending on the particular soluble source material. At low temperatures, a very small amount of soluble material in the clay body can cause the development of a white granular powdered surface (scumming) on the bone dry or fired ware. When fired to higher temperatures, the concentration of soluble materials in the clay body formula can act as a body flux, causing an uneven melt. Consider using soluble materials in a glaze or clay body formula only when the oxide contained in the soluble material can't be obtained in the insoluble form.

The mesh size and amount of melting are two related factors in choosing materials for a clay body or glaze. The finer the mesh (smaller particle size), the greater the surface area exposed to heat and other fluxing materials, all of which cause a more thorough melt than the same material in a larger mesh size. Keep in mind that ceramic materials all appear as white, off-white, tan, or brown powders in the raw state and the specific mesh size of a material might not be readily noticeable. Always use the same mesh size in clay and glaze formulas for consistent results. In some glaze or clay body formulas, a coarser or finer mesh might not make a significant difference, depending on the individual formula and the raw material. However, to produce reliable results, find out the mesh size of each raw material and specify it on every reorder, then check the label on the new raw material bag when it arrives at your studio.

For example, Atomite (a brand name for whiting) is a very fine mesh calcium carbonate used in glaze formulas. Snowcal (another brand of whiting) has a slightly coarser or larger particle size. Both materials in the raw state look like fine white powder. When used in a glaze, the coarser mesh whiting sinks to the bottom of the glaze bucket as a thick mass, while the finer mesh whiting stays in suspension in the glaze bucket. Another dramatic result occurs when the fine mesh whiting is used as part of a clear glaze formula. The results are a clear gloss fired glaze but when the same amount of coarser whiting is substituted in the formula, the fired results are a semiopaque gloss glaze. The mesh size of raw materials can cause changes on many levels. In this instance, the finer mesh whiting stays in suspension longer in the glaze bucket and produces a greater degree of melting in the glaze due to its smaller particle size.

* The trade name, mesh size, chemical composition, and the mine or manufacturer of the material are critical

points to state every time you order a raw material. Apart from testing materials before doing large quantities of work, potters should know the mesh size, chemical composition, and if possible, the manufacturer or processor of the material. Safety data information (MSDS safety data sheet) and chemical analysis sheets (typical analyses) should be available from ceramics suppliers upon request. List every raw material used in your clay and glaze formulas and place your next order for materials using exact specifications. For example, specify a 50-pound bag of Flint, 325-mesh SIL CO SIL, US Silica Corp.

* **Raw material costs are nothing compared to your time and labor**. The cost of any raw material should be the last consideration when placing an order. Letting cost dictate the purchase or use of a raw material is not an accurate criterion for reducing potential problems or increasing savings. Apart from a few raw material exceptions (tin, cobalt oxide, cobalt carbonate, and bismuth subnitrate), the most expensive part of making ceramic objects is your labor. This is the most important factor in cutting any cost in production. If a moist prepared clay is two or three cents less per pound and mixed incorrectly, the result will be loss of time, labor, and the ceramic piece. If pots have to be fired again or remade because of material or clay-mixing defects, the loss will be greater than any small saving from purchasing inexpensive clay.

Any variable quality material that doesn't give consistent results must be carefully considered before using it in a clay body or glaze formula. Is the special effect caused by the variable quality material worth the risk of an unusable firing defect? Can a more reliable material achieve the same result? Conversely, any material that is consistent in chemical composition, particle size, and availability will reduce the problems caused by raw materials. For reliable results, use as many guaranteed raw materials in clay and glaze formulas as possible. Sometimes the highest-priced best-quality material might save money if it produces fewer defects than a less expensive problem-prone material.

What Works?

Producing ceramic objects, whether it's pots or sculpture, is never a problem-free enterprise. It is impossible and unrealistic to think all ceramics-related problems can be solved, but some can be isolated and made less frequent. Raw material related problems can be decreased by following a few simple ordering procedures. The raw materials used in ceramics never stay the same. Think of raw materials as trains that are in constant motion. They can move fast or slow but never stay in one place. Sometimes the trains move slowly, with slight or almost unnoticeable changes and sometimes they move fast, causing drastic and damaging results. Potters can't stop this movement, but they can control one part of the process by ordering raw materials carefully and to specifications.

Gaining a detailed knowledge of materials used in clay body and glaze formulas is the fundamental long-lasting solution to changing materials. With increased knowledge of how raw materials act alone and in various combinations, you will be well-equipped to formulate new strategies for the constant inconsistency in ceramics. Understanding the materials will also give you more options for obtaining a specific result. Once you can analyze a glaze or clay body by temperature range, texture, light transmission, color, and the kiln atmosphere it will be fired in, you'll see that many different raw materials can achieve the desired effect.

All temperature references to cones are based on large Orton pyrometric cones heated at 270°F per hour.

Chapter 5

Preventing Common Problems

Anyone who plays with clay long enough will have something go wrong. It's not a question of if, but when. Knowing what you're up against can go a long way in preventing problems. The raw materials in clay bodies and glazes can subtly shift over time or change instantly. Forming techniques and kiln firing cycles all have the potential for producing countless variables, upsetting the finished piece. Once you start to realize the scope of unpredictable results, you'll be amazed that *anything* works on a regular basis.

Yet, over the centuries hundreds of thousands of potters have produced durable ceramic pieces consistently. Why? Probably because a tradition of master potter and apprentice was in operation. The master potter was a storehouse of practical day-to-day knowledge of materials, techniques, and trade secrets used to produce ceramic objects. He had gained this information from his teacher and, in turn, passed it on to his apprentice. Most unproductive results were weeded out and useful information was shared with a new generation of potters.

Today, this system is no longer in place and the results are evident. New potters left to themselves or learning from other new students repeat and pass on inaccurate information and faulty techniques. Ignorance of how ceramic materials function does not often lead to good pots or sculpture. At present, there is no viable ceramic forming heritage to learn from and most potters are forced to reinvent the wheel.

Some problems can't be reduced to know-and-avoid situations, but there are many problems that can be solved or avoided just by learning from the mistakes of others. This is information the master potter would have shared, but since you weren't alive a few hundred years ago, you may have missed it. Just knowing about the most common problems enables you to complete a project with less wasted time and effort. Why repeat somebody else's mistake? This is not to imply that all problems have a simple clear solution. It's unrealistic to assume this in any field. Some types of problems, once known and understood, need not be repeated. Just think about all the mistakes that can be avoided.

Forget the Masterpiece Method

The goal of making a perfect pot or sculpture has been fostered by the current culture where immediate success is expected to be easily obtained in any endeavor. While this might not be the first problem caused by ceramic materials, it is the first misconception potters often bring to the craft. Pottery requires practice. The cycle of wedging clay, forming pots, trimming, bisque firing, and glaze firing has to be repeated many times to increase specific technical skills in each area.

Every pot or sculptural piece has a technical learning curve. Don't box all your time and energy into making one piece. Assuming that you'll make a perfect piece without a technical or aesthetic problem is unrealistic. The myth of producing a perfect piece from a single attempt dies hard (it would have been pounded out of anyone working in a master potter's shop). Working with a series of pieces or in a multiple mode produces the best results and allows your aesthetic ideas and technical knowledge to grow with each piece. If a glaze runs or a pot blows up in the kiln, another piece is ready, hopefully with a better result. Spread the risk, learn with each piece in the series, and get a better result.

Order Specific Raw Materials

The specific raw materials required in a glaze or clay body can come in different mesh sizes or grinds, the chemical composition can vary depending on what plant or mine produced the product, or it contain other impurities not listed on the bag label. All these situations can occur without your knowledge.

An example of this potential problem is flint. Flint is produced in different mesh sizes that all look like the same white powder. What does mesh size matter? In a glaze, a coarser mesh flint can cause the glaze to sink in the bucket. In some clear glaze formulas, a coarser grind of flint can bring about opacity in the fired glaze. Generally, a larger particle size doesn't melt as readily as a small particle size. Find out the mesh size of every raw material in your glaze and clay body formulas to prevent potential raw material problems.

Some whitings are produced with more magnesium carbonate tagging along with the calcium carbonate. While the small percentage of magnesium doesn't seem to affect glazes, in other raw materials the type and amount of impurities can throw off a glaze result. The point is, just because it's called whiting in the ceramics supply catalog doesn't mean all whitings are the same. Whiting is a generic term

and it's your responsibility to investigate exactly what you're ordering. A ceramics supplier could change to another source of whiting without informing their customers. Will this new whiting have the same chemical composition and mesh size as the previous one? This kind of variability or loose labeling of raw materials can affect every material used in clay bodies or glazes.

When ordering any raw material or clay, state the exact mesh size, chemical composition, and trade name of the material. If you don't know this information about the materials you're now using, find it out from the supplier. When the time comes to reorder, state the exact specifications and try to purchase materials in their original bags (you'll pay a lower price per pound this way too). This will eliminate potential rebagging mistakes. The ceramic field is full of uncertain events, ordering raw materials precisely is one thing you can do to cut down on the unpredictability.

Check Availability of Raw Materials Before Testing

When considering a material that's no longer being mined, ask yourself if there is a long-term advantage in mixing up several great glazes using a material that you can no longer get, even if you have a good supply in your studio. Another common situation occurs when potters don't check beforehand to see if glaze materials are still in production. Many potters put hours of hard work into testing and developing glazes only to discover that a feldspar, clay, or other raw material has been discontinued. They assume that if a certain feldspar is in their studio storage container, it is still being mined and distributed. Don't waste time on this problem – check the availability of materials before starting to develop a new glaze or clay body.

Avoid Glaze Materials that Cause Problems

Some glaze formulas require the use of soluble materials and frequently, part of a soluble material dissolves in the water component of a glaze. When excess water is poured off, it changes the actual glaze formula. When a pot is glazed, soluble material in the glaze water can leach into the interior of the clay. When the glaze water on the pot begins to dry, the soluble material in the glaze water moves to the exterior higher surfaces of the piece, causing a different chemical composition glaze on the pot's edges or high ridges. The nonuniform distribution of glaze materials in the dry raw glaze can cause numerous glaze defects when fired.

If a glaze contains Gerstley borate or colemanite, it will eventually cause a glaze problem. Both calcium borates are soluble and take on water in storage. With high amounts of either material in a glaze, it looks and feels like oatmeal and is about as easy to apply. Gerstley borate and colemanite can change chemically from one batch to the next, causing problems in fired glaze texture, color, and opacity. The fact that they work a great deal of the time and are listed in many glaze formulas unfortunately leads potters to use these two high-problem glaze materials. Gerstley borate and colemanite both have found a place in raku glaze formulas because raku glazes are mixed in small batches and variable qualities are desirable in the fired glaze result.

Borax, soda ash, and pearl ash are less commonly found in glaze formulas but when used, can cause problems because of their solubility. Often a frit can be utilized in place of the soluble material, which helps because frits are uniform in oxide content and relatively insoluble.

When possible, choose insoluble glaze and clay body materials in formulas. The ideal situation is to have little or no breakdown (leaching) of raw materials into the water component of the glaze. Soluble materials used in clay bodies can migrate to the clay surface during drying, eventually causing a thin film or disruption on the fired clay surface. They can also cause the moist clay to become very hard or very soft and rubbery. In clay bodies containing the wrong frit (partially soluble frit), leaching can cause a drastic change in the moist clay body's handling characteristics. Even a slightly soluble frit oxide will cause either hard or soft moist clay, depending on the specific oxide in the frit that's leaching. Changes in the moist clay's consistency can occur in as short a time as two to four days after the clay batch was mixed.

Prevent Glaze that Sinks or Dries Dusty

Glaze application problems are common in ceramics. Before you can apply a glaze, it often settles too fast in the glaze bucket. Settling is prevalent in glazes containing high amounts of dense material such as flint, feldspar, dolomite, and whiting. Since the same dense materials are found in most high-temperature glazes, settling can be a major problem. Low-temperature glazes that rely on frit as the major flux also encounter a glaze settling problem due to the heavy weight of the frit. High amounts of metallic coloring oxides in a glaze can also cause the glaze to settle in the bucket.

Traditionally, 1% or 2% bentonite (a very plastic, small platelet structure clay) was used to float or suspend the heavier raw materials in the water medium. Epsom salts, 1/2% to 1%, also helps keep a glaze in suspension. However, a more effective suspension agent is VeeGum T, a magnesium, aluminum silicate. VeeGum T is more potent than other types of suspension agents.[2] VeeGum T can be used from 1/2% to 2% based on the dry weight of the glaze. VeeGum T should be weighed out dry, then mixed in water until it is completely dispersed. The mixture should then be added to the glaze. It can't be mixed into the glaze materials dry or it won't disperse correctly.

Glazes containing high amounts of clay or light density material such as magnesium carbonate frequently crack or become dusty to the touch when drying on bisque or raw clay surfaces. This causes several problems, one of which is a fragile glaze surface. The raw glaze surface flakes off in handling and makes for a difficult kiln loading.

A more common defect is crawling, where the fired glaze seems to roll or peel back on itself, showing bare patches of clay body. Crawling can occur when a dried glaze doesn't make and maintain contact with the clay body during firing. A dusty glaze can act like microscopic marbles or balls, preventing a uniform bond with the clay underneath. VeeGum CER, a mixture of VeeGum, magnesium, aluminum, silicate, and medium viscosity sodium carboxymethyicellulose, causes a smooth hard raw glaze surface that mechanically bonds the dusty glaze to the pot. VeeGum CER can be used in amounts of 1% to 1-1/2% based on the dry weight of glaze. VeeGum CER should be weighed out dry and mixed with water and all of the mixture should be used in the glaze. Always pass the wet glaze through an 80x-mesh sieve to completely blend all glaze materials.

A 35-cubic-foot electric kiln.

Choose the Correct Kiln Size

Ideally, we hope to never outgrow a kiln. However, the best potters can expect is to choose a kiln size that will serve them for a few years. A large kiln will cost more, but doesn't have to be loaded, unloaded, and fired as often as a smaller kiln. Your own labor and time are the most valuable commodities, not the relatively small cost difference of a larger kiln. After the kiln is in use, most potters complain that they could have used a larger kiln. Think carefully about kiln size before building or purchasing this important piece of equipment.

Kiln size should be determined by the amount and size of your work. Production pottery and large sculpture will require greater kiln space than ceramic jewelry. Choose a kiln size that will allow for a reasonable production cycle. Production potters might want three- to five-week cycles of making, bisqueing, and glaze firing pots. Many production potters fire gas kilns between 20 and 60 cubic feet. Large sculpture might require a three- to five-month cycle and the kiln size can range

2.   VeeGum T and VeeGum CER can be purchased from R.T. Vanderbilt Co., Inc., 30 Winfield St., Norwalk, CT 06855, PH: (203) 853-1400. West Coast: 6279 East Slauson Ave., Los Angeles, CA 90040, PH: (213) 723-5208

A gas fired 26-cubic-foot catenary arch kiln.

A gas fired raku car kiln.

An 18-cubic-foot wood fired kiln.

Studio kilns: a 20-cubic-foot updraft gas kiln (right) and an electric kiln (left).

from 40 to 120 cubic feet. Keep in mind that if the cycle is too long, staying interested can be hard and if the cycle is too short, you will spend a lot of time loading and firing the kiln every day.

When considering kiln size, it's easier and less expensive in the long run to opt for a larger size than needed at the time of purchase. The time to find out there is not enough kiln space is before, not after, the kiln is built or purchased.

Don't Assume the Electric Kiln Shut Off Device Will Work Every Time

It's amazing how many people sleep peacefully, depending on their kiln sitter bar to come down on that cone and shut off their kiln. In this case, ignorance is not bliss. Even with backup kiln timers, things can go wrong. While pyrometric cones are made to exact standards, they do not deform under temperature perfectly every time. A cone can bloat or melt in such an irregular shape that it will cause the shut off bar to get stuck or the shut off mechanism itself can malfunction. And posts or kiln shelves can shift during the firing, blocking the shut off device.

What are the chances of such events happening? Often enough – and the disastrous results include the loss of pots, warped kiln furniture, burnt-out heating elements, and over-fired kiln bricks. This is a very expensive gamble that can be eliminated by simply being present when the kiln turns off "automatically." If your schedule doesn't allow you to be present at the end of the firing, try preheating the kiln on low the night before the firing. Doing an overnight preheat and turning the kiln up the next morning will cause the kiln to reach temperature sooner on the firing day. I don't think most potters would run the risk of an automatic kiln shut off failure if they really knew the odds against them.

Don't Fire the Kiln Too Fast

Firing the bisque kiln too fast can result in a very dramatic effect called "instant shards." Chemical and mechanical water, when heated, turns to steam. If steam cannot travel through the cross section of the ware at a comfortable rate, an explosion or crack will take place. Many potters assume that just because a pot is bone dry, all the moisture is gone. Remember, pots can "dry" in the studio for months and still contain the moisture content of the studio and chemical water as part of their structure. When in doubt about how fast to fire the bisque kiln, remember that longer firings can't harm the pots and can only improve the firing outcome. The very slight increase in firing cost is insignificant compared with just one pot that blows up or cracks.

The rate of heating in a bisque kiln depends on many factors. Small kilns tend to heat and cool faster than larger kilns. Another factor is the size and mass of the ceramic pieces being heated in the kiln. Larger pieces with thicker cross sections take longer to heat and cool because the thermal mass of the object being heated dictates the rate at which a kiln can be fired. Closely related is the amount of work per volume of kiln space. If the kiln is densely packed with pots or sculpture, a longer kiln firing can result.

The clay body composition can also determine the rate of heat increase within the kiln. Clay bodies that contain large amounts of inert materials (grogs, sand, molochite, and kyanite which changes to mullite when heated) and relatively small amounts of fine particle materials such as ball clays, can be heated and cooled faster. Inert materials (having been fired already) will allow the clay body to heat up and cool faster. A slower firing schedule is needed with clay bodies containing fine particle clays with greater surface areas which are surrounded by water in the moist clay forming stage. When the clay body is heated, mechanical and chemical water need time to be driven off the clay without causing cracks and stress. A slower firing time is recommended to allow for this process to occur safely.

For average size functional pottery (pots or sculpture up to 16" high and 1/2" in thickness), the bisque firing should take 10 to 11 hours to reach cone 06 or 1830°F, which does not include preheating the kiln. In electric kilns, one or two elements are turned on low overnight for preheating. In gas kilns, one burner is turned on very low overnight. If the ceramic objects are larger and/or have thicker cross sections (over 1/2" in thickness), a longer preheat and longer firing time are necessary. Tiles also need longer drying, preheating, and firing cycles. It might take two or three times longer to reach dull red heat with forms that have large surface areas and/or thick cross sections. However, when dull red heat is reached (approximately 1100°F), the firing can proceed at a normal rate of temperature increases.

Firing glaze kilns too fast is another common mistake. A whole list of glaze and clay body defects can result from this error. Glazes can pinhole, bubble, craze, fire dry and/or opaque – all from firing the glaze kiln too fast. A more subtle problem occurs when the clay body is immature.

This "soft" body looks hard but, in fact, is often not dense or vitreous. Fast firing doesn't allow enough time for substantial glass formation within the clay body, which will strengthen the fired piece and decrease absorption. One cause of glaze crazing is an immature clay body. Ceramic materials found in clay bodies and glazes need a certain endpoint temperature to melt and the time it takes getting to that temperature is critical. The longer the time to temperature, the greater the melt. A guideline for heat increases that will insure proper maturing of clay body and glaze materials at stoneware temperatures is: after 1830°F there should be a 60°F to 65°F heat increase per hour until the end of the firing. Ceramic materials do best with slow steady heat increases and decreases. Firing and cooling faster can increase clay body and glaze defects dramatically.

Special Considerations for Tiles and Large Pieces

Flat tiles and large scale ceramic pieces have a few things in common. Both will blow up or crack in a fast-firing kiln. Tiles and large ceramic forms are often treated the same as functional pottery in drying and bisque firings. This misconception will cause problems starting with the drying process. Both tiles and large ceramic pieces require even drying, which doesn't necessarily mean slow drying. The tile or sculpture should change color (indication of drying) not just from the top down, but the drying should occur over the entire surface area of the object. If large pieces are not dried evenly, cracking can result due to the greater surface areas that are subject to stress. When water evaporates from clay, it causes shrinkage. The larger the piece, the greater the stress on drying. Stress due to shrinkage has to be evenly dissipated through the entire piece or cracking can take place.

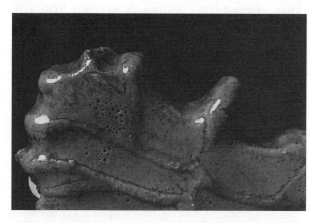

Glaze pinholes occur when the glaze kiln is fired too fast and the molten glaze doesn't have enough time to settle down and smooth itself out at maturity.

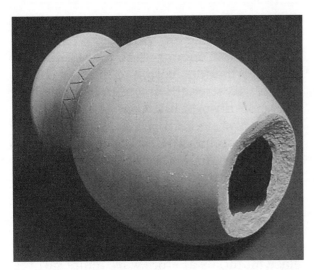

Moisture in the clay body produces steam during fast bisque kiln firing, causing the bottom of the pot to blow out.

As ceramic objects increase in scale, drying and firing problems increase. Often the problem encountered with firing tiles and large pieces is that the same firing cycle, or rate of heat increase, is used as when firing functional pottery. Large ceramic objects have greater surface areas and thicker cross sections which require increased time to temperature. Tiles also have similar characteristics and problems. A slower heat increase enables the ceramic objects to release moisture and steam at a slower rate. If this rate is exceeded, the piece can blow up or crack.

How slow should the kiln be fired? Taking weeks to dry properly is common for large sculpture pieces and these pieces might take days to fire. When in doubt, go slow. There is no danger in slow firing, but a total loss can occur when fast firing the kiln.

Understand Reduction and Why It Can Be a Problem

Reduction takes place when carbon monoxide is present in the kiln atmosphere during the firing. Carbon monoxide is a colorless, odorless gas that is oxygen hungry, which means it can take an oxygen molecule away from ceramic oxides. However, metallic coloring oxides (copper oxide, chrome oxide, iron oxide, rutile, manganese dioxide) will show a heightened color or texture reaction to a reduction atmosphere. In white stoneware or porcelain clay bodies, a blue white color is achieved. In white firing clays, there can be trace amounts of iron which can cast a blue tint to the clay body fired under reduction.

Aside from changing the clay body and glaze color, a reduction atmosphere can increase the fluxing action in the clay body and glazes. Clay bodies can become tighter with less absorption due to the fluxing or melting action of the oxides within the body under reducing conditions. The interface (the layer where the clay body ends and the glaze begins) is usually better developed in reduction due to the surface fluxing action of the clay body as it binds with the above glaze layer. The glaze itself can become glossy or drip due to its oxide content being fluxed by reduction atmospheres.

Such atmospheres can be achieved by introducing a greater ratio of fuel (natural gas, propane, oil, wood, or any combustible fuel source) than air into a situation where combustion is present (such as a kiln burner). A byproduct of a reducing kiln atmosphere is black smoke and the

A cross section of over-reduced clay (dark gray/ black clay color).

An over-reduced cone 10 porcelain clay body. The gray color is from trapped carbon in the clay body during the kiln firing.

smell of unburned fuel, but reduction or carbon monoxide can occur in the kiln without such obvious indications. A reducing flame at the burner tip is yellow/red in color and can be described as dirty with black wisps of smoke at the flame edges.

An oxidation kiln atmosphere occurs when the ratio of air exceeds the fuel present for combustion (this condition always takes place in electric kilns under normal firing conditions). The flame at the burner tip is clean and blue, much like the burner flame on a gas hot water heater. In a neutral kiln atmosphere, the fuel and air ratios are balanced. The opportunity to change clay body and glaze colors in the kiln by both types of atmospheres can offer many areas for exploration. Reduction kiln firing offers many potential virtues which can turn into glaze and clay body defects if you don't know how to control fuel and air ratios in the firing process. Remember that the amount of reduction/oxidation and its duration can also affect oxides contained in clay bodies and glazes. In this regard, firing with a fuel source that can be turned into carbon monoxide can generate bad or good results depending on your knowledge of the firing system.

Problems occur when you over-reduce or under-reduce your kiln. Over-reduction, a subjective term, can lead to a variety of clay body and glaze problems. High iron content glazes can become matte metallic or bubble when over-reduced. Clay bodies can become brittle and lose strength when too much reduction is present in the kiln atmosphere. There is no definite point where over-reduction starts, it depends on the clay body, glaze, and kiln atmosphere factors. Some low-iron content clays and glazes can take higher levels of reduction than high-iron clays and glazes. When the degree of over-reduction increases past a certain point, clay and glaze defects are more prevalent.

Clay bodies and glazes that are under-reduced tend to look washed out and muted. A high-iron clay can look pale and cream-colored when there is not enough reduction present in the kiln atmosphere. Glazes frequently look pale and dull, with glazes containing copper going toward green instead of red. Under-reduced glazes can also lack highlights and variation normally obtained through reduction. Some glazes can look immature, having dry surface textures due to the increased melting effect of a reduction atmosphere on certain clay coloring oxides found in clay bodies and glazes. Many times, there's a spotty effect of oxidation and reduction present in the kiln, causing pots to be reduced on one side and oxidized on the other. Such a firing can indicate too much fuel pressure and/or too much air pressure, causing plumes of reduction backed up against plumes of oxidation in the kiln atmosphere. The fast-moving rivers of different atmospheres are reflected on the surfaces of the ware. Lowering the gas and air pressures in the kiln allows for a slow languid rolling atmosphere in the firing kiln which is more effective in evenly distributing the reduction effects to clay bodies and glazes.

Learning how to fire a reduction kiln can be accomplished in many ways. In an ideal situation, you would have time to read all the available books on reduction firing while watching experienced potters fire their kilns. Unfortunately, not everyone can arrange to learn in such a comprehensive way. Most potters use the system of reduction firing they were taught without knowing the principles behind the methods. This rote way of reducing the kiln, whatever the method, doesn't allow for variables in raw materials found in the clay body and glazes. In addition, kilns and burners can change over time, producing inconsistent results.

At this point, potters need information on reduction – what it is and how it happens – so they can learn how to cause reduction atmospheres in any kiln. They will then be able to apply the basic reduction principles in any firing situation, with any kiln. Without genuinely understanding the principles behind reduction kiln atmosphere, simply replacing one reduction firing cycle with another without knowing what's actually happening, a problem will inevitably develop. When this occurs, it's time to get educated on this important part of kiln firing.

Don't Put All Your Trust in the Test Firing

Often potters fire a glaze in a small test kiln. If the results look good, they mix a large batch of glaze and apply it to a whole kiln load of pots, which they load into a large production kiln. Sometimes things don't go as planned and the resulting glaze can look quite different from the same glaze fired in the small test kiln.

Why? One of the reasons is that kiln size can play a critical role in the fired glaze results. Test kilns are useful because they provide knowledge about how a glaze or clay body will react under temperature, but at some point, testing glazes in a large production kiln will become necessary for accurate results.

Small test kilns heat and cool faster than larger kilns due to less thermal mass. Gloss glazes are the least affected

by a fast-firing curve, but no type of glaze is immune from this effect. Satin matte and matte glazes can show the most change when fired in small versus large kilns. Glaze opacity can also be affected. A faster heating and cooling cycle can increase the opacity of a glaze. Any glaze, when fired fast enough, can be made to appear opaque and have a dry surface texture. Fast firing can cause a glaze to craze in a test kiln and fire without crazing in a larger kiln.

Ceramic materials react not only to endpoint temperatures but to the time it takes to reach that temperature. A small test kiln might reach the correct glaze temperature but it will also heat up and cool down fast. Increasing the time to temperature and slow cooling in any kiln will cause a greater degree of glaze melting and better clay body vitrification, which increases the chances of a noncrazed glaze and a stronger clay body. A large kiln will heat up and cool slower because of its increased thermal mass. The larger kiln contains more bricks, posts, shelves, and pots, all of which take on and hold heat longer than a smaller kiln with less mass. Matte glaze results in a small test kiln might fire to a satin matte in a larger pro-

A small electric test kiln can have extremely fast heating and cooling cycles which can produce inaccurate glaze tests.

duction kiln because of the thermal mass effect.

Small test kilns are useful tools when used correctly and the glaze results are interpreted accurately. Test kilns can suggest new glazes that might work well in a larger kiln. A good procedure is to use the test kiln to get "in the ball park" results and then try them out in the larger kiln. After you produce a good test glaze, do intermediate testing then place that promising glaze in a large production kiln and see how it fires. Intermediate testing (repeating a good test result in the actual production kiln) is one of the most important areas to understand. Most potters get a good test glaze and then mix up a large production batch. Usually the results are successful, but don't take such a chance with every test glaze or inevitably a bad glaze will result, causing lost labor, damaged pieces, and sometimes ruined kiln shelves. Knowing a glaze well before committing yourself to mixing up a large quantity is critical. Train yourself to read the test tile results from the kiln firings so you can move to intermediate glaze testing with a better knowledge of what to look for in test tiles. Reserve a certain percentage of kiln space in every large kiln firing for test pieces. If you don't have enough time for intermediate testing, you increase the risk of potential glaze problems in the large production kiln.

Another factor that can throw off a test result is the shape and size of the test piece. Some glazes, when applied to horizontal test tiles, settle very well when molten, but the same glaze on a vertical test tile might run down the side of the tile, pooling on the kiln shelf. A similar situation occurs when a small test piece with a limited surface area is glazed. A glaze might do very well under such conditions but when applied to a larger surface area might move under its own weight when molten, causing sheets of glaze to slide off the pot. The amount of surface area to be glazed and its relative position to the hor-

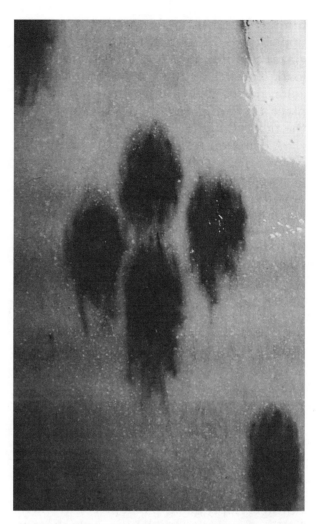

A vertical test tile with white glaze and cobalt blue underglaze. The bleed edge of the blue design is caused by the glaze running when molten. The test tile was fired in a larger kiln with a longer heating and cooling cycle, causing increased melting in glaze.

izontal kiln shelf can affect fired glaze results.

A variable result can occur when two different glazes are placed next to each other in the kiln. This can cause glaze fuming during the firing, most often when glazes containing chrome oxide are placed next to glazes containing tin oxide. A pink blush can develop on the fired glaze surface. Several raw material combinations can cause color shifts. One or two firings in a small test kiln will not cover all the possibilities. Most color changes due to fuming occur in regular production situations due to the higher number of different glaze combinations in a particular kiln load. The best advice is to recognize the color defect when it happens and don't place the two glazes near one another in the next kiln load.

A common test piece variable happens when a glaze dries on a small test tile. The glaze can look perfect, but on a larger tile or a differently shaped test tile, the same glaze might crack or pinhole after drying. Different size and shape surface areas on greenware or bisqueware can change the drying characteristics of a glaze. A tile's thickness plays an important role in how it absorbs a glaze application. A thin-walled pot will take on water in the glaze differently than a thick-walled pot. The water in the glaze penetrates the thin wall, causing the opposite unglazed surface to become saturated with water. A glaze application on this surface is not possible until it dries. Thin-walled pots might also become saturated with water faster, preventing a sufficient glaze buildup.

Glaze application methods can also play a part in how the glaze fits a ceramic surface. Apply glaze to test pieces in exactly the same way you plan to apply them to production pieces. For example, if you dip test tiles, count on dipping the production glaze for the same result. Spraying or brushing the glaze might produce a different effect than dipped test glazes. If the production pots will be once-fired, the test tiles should be once-fired to get an accurate glaze result. The glaze thickness and method of application can affect the fired glaze result. All testing should be designed to duplicate the glaze application methods you plan to use on the real pots.

The atmosphere inside the kiln during firing is another significant factor in changing glaze color, surface texture, opacity, and molten viscosity. Electric kilns produce the most consistent results in glazes, clay body colors, and textures. Electric kilns produce an oxidation atmo-

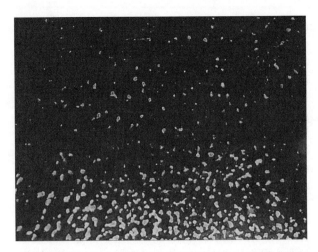

Small crystal growth in the glaze upon cooling (devitrification). This causes the glaze to change from glossy to crystalline.

sphere. Gas, wood, oil, coal, and other fossil fuels can produce a wider range of glaze and clay body colors because the kiln atmosphere can change during the firing. A reduction, neutral, or oxidation atmosphere can be introduced at any point in the firing, causing a reaction with the clay body and glaze. When testing, keep the kiln atmosphere the same in every firing to produce the same results in clay and glazes.

A glaze can also change color by breaking up into mottled or streaked patterns. This type of variation can be caused by glaze application thickness, kiln atmosphere, or the rate at which a glaze kiln cools. A glaze application that is thick or

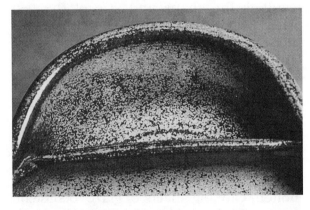

A dense field of small crystal growth causes opacity in the glaze color (devitrification).

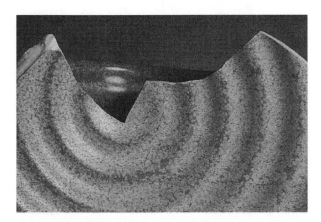

A dense field of small crystal growth causes opacity in matte glaze color (devitrification). Shown in the background is the same glaze unaffected by crystal growth.

heavy will produce the true color and surface texture of that particular glaze. Glaze color can be dulled or lost completely by a very thin glaze application. A reduction kiln atmosphere can bring out highlights or streaked patterns in glazes containing iron, rutile, titanium, and other metallic oxides. Every kiln cools at a different rate (also called reoxidizing) because air (oxygen) enters the kiln when it cools. During specific points in the kiln cooling cycle, crystals can grow on a glaze. The process is devitrification and it can cause large silver-dollar size crystals or very small crystals. Very small crystals can make the fired glaze look opaque. A small test kiln will have a different cooling rate than a larger production kiln. Will this effect the

Large crystal growth pattern in glaze.

glaze colors? Predicting it is impossible. It all points back to placing a few test glazes in a large kiln along with the rest of the regular production. To further complicate matters, different parts of a kiln can cool at different rates, causing a glaze to grow beautiful crystals in one part of the kiln while not showing any crystal growth in other parts.

One glaze applied over another can also produce surprising results in glaze colors, textures, surface conditions, and viscosity. Some glazes will bubble, change color, or run off the pot. Each glaze might react well by itself but some combinations of glaze oxides don't melt well together when overlapped. A glaze can also "break up" over throwing lines or sharp edges on the clay. Fired glazes may become extremely sharp to the touch. Showing enough information in just one firing is very difficult for one test piece. Overall experience with a glaze in many firings (especially reduction firing situations) is the best method to insure a good result. Let the repeated glaze results over a few firings indicate when to mix up a large glaze batch.

With experience, each test tile will tell you more about the potential for the glaze. Experts are good at telling people what can go wrong but don't let anyone take away the mystery of opening the kiln door and discovering that exciting new glaze or clay body. Things can and do go wrong but that shouldn't keep you from trying new clays, glazes, and kiln firing techniques. While many clay and glaze combinations produce unexpected results, they can be very informative in supplying knowledge for future projects.

Repair Cracked Pots

There's a saying that proves true more often than not – "Cracks stay the same or get worse." Every potter has tried to repair

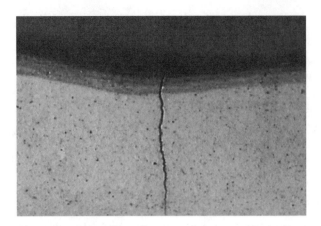

Crack repair is often labor intensive and unsuccessful.

a pot that has cracked in the forming, drying, bisquing, or glaze firing process. Your first impulse is to try whatever it takes to smooth over or fill the crack and the results of such efforts are often disappointing. The crack can get wider, stay the same, or the patch never seem to match the surrounding clay or blend into the glaze.

Ceramic objects shrink when drying due to loss of moisture and they shrink further when firing due to vitrification of the clay. It's very difficult to repair or fill cracks because of the dynamic quality of the clay body when drying and/or firing. It's rare when a patch or filled-in crack shrinks at a rate compatible with the clay body. A perfect unblemished repair is not the norm. Most successful repairs are accomplished on clay in the wet to leather-hard stage rather than on bone dry or bisqueware.

For every successful crack repair, ten attempts will fail either during repair or at some point after the firing. While this might seem like bad news, it can give you a pragmatic idea of what to expect. A more efficient use of your time might be to make another pot. Often this is the only realistic way to solve a crack problem. Start making pots and sculpture in series or multiples so that if one piece fails you can continue working with the next piece in the series.

Even after this dire conclusion, many potters will still attempt to fix a crack. Do so, but don't lose valuable time in the effort. Try to keep any repair jobs under five minutes.

Choose the Correct Clay Body

Just as the foundation is critical to building a solid house, the correct clay body is critical to making a successful ceramic project. The clay body is the foundation for the structure and the support for any glaze. An important criteria for choosing any clay body is temperature. Choose the appropriate clay body for the highest temperature it will reach, be it in bisque or glaze. Most clay bodies have a two to three cone range at which they will mature. If the clay body isn't dense enough at temperature, the covering glaze can craze and the strength of the fired piece can be compromised. If the clay body is too dense, thermal cracking, bloating, excessive warping, and melting can take place. While both situations represent different ends of the spectrum – the black and white possibilities – most problems occur in the gray areas.

A porcelain bowl warped due to an over-fired clay body.

A body on the edge of failure due to the glassy phase of unglazed clay areas. Over-fired and/or over-fluxed clay bodies can warp, shrink excessively, or stick to kiln shelves.

For example, if a clay body matures too early in the firing, the only indication might be that the fired piece warps or sticks to the kiln shelf. Is this clay body being over-fired? Yes, but it is right on the edge of working or not working and any variable can cause it to have real problems. If the kiln takes longer to reach temperature, more melting in the clay can take place, causing bloating or complete melting of the clay into the kiln shelf. It is often the case where small subtle indications in the ware can indicate larger problems about to be encountered.

Another example of an "almost" good clay body is one that has a very high iron content, either from iron oxide or high iron bearing clays. The dark high iron clay might work well for many firings in a slightly reducing gas kiln. It might take only one firing with a little more reduction to cause the clay to bloat and/or become brittle when cool. When clay bodies with high amounts of iron are over-reduced in a kiln, bloating and brittleness are the two most common defects caused by the excessive fluxing action of iron in a reduction kiln atmosphere.

How can you prevent clay body failure? One recommendation is to use a ceramic supply company's stock clay body and fire it within its stated temperature range. The stock body is produced in large amounts and many potters use it, hopefully with good results. However, it's always a good practice to find other potters who are using the stock clay body and ask about their experience with the clay. The main disadvantage in using a stock clay body is that most ceramic supply houses don't release the clay body formula to their customers.

As always, test a sample of the stock clay in your own kiln. Place samples of the clay with your glazes in several different locations in the kiln. This should show how the clay will react under different temperatures (since no kiln fires exactly even throughout) and glaze options. Keep in mind that different clay bodies can change the color, texture, and fit of a particular glaze. Inherent in each clay body formula is the rate at which it will shrink based on its raw materials, water content, and other factors such as the method of mixing and pugging. Pugged clay forced by mechanical screw through a de-airing chamber will show a slightly lower fired absorption rate. This can be attributed to the compacting of clay platelets. The same body without the de-aired pugging and without the extra packing of platelets might be 1/4% to 1/2% more absorbent.

What factors determine shrinkage and absorption in clay bodies? First, a discussion of terms is required for a complete understanding of what takes place in clay/water structures when forming, drying, and after firing.

Shrinkage is the decrease in the size of a piece of clay that takes place through air drying, bisque firing, and glaze firing. Clay bodies shrink due to loss of mechanical, chemical water, and vitrification (glass formation in the clay) during the firing process. The shrinkage rate of any clay body depends on the clay body formula, kiln atmosphere, firing temperature reached, and the time it takes to reach that temperature.

The absorption rate for a fired clay body is based on how much moisture will be contained in the body after it's immersed in boiling water and wiped dry of remaining surface water. One method for finding the absorption rate is to place the fired clay bar in boiling water for two hours, remove it, and wipe each side down to remove any surface water. To arrive at an absorption rate, use the following formula: the fired weight of the bar wet minus the fired weight of the bar dry divided by the fired weight of the bar dry times 100 equals the percent of absorption. Like the shrinkage rate, the absorption of the fired clay will be affected by the clay body formula, firing temperature reached, and the time it takes to reach that temperature.

Make at least six bars of clay when doing shrinkage and absorption testing. The bars shouldn't have any indentations or scratch marks on the surface that will trap water during an absorption test. If the bars aren't smooth, water will collect in the recessed areas and give a false reading of the amount of water the fired clay bar is absorbing. When the bars are fin-

Test at least six bars for an accurate shrinkage and absorption rate of the clay body fired in your kiln under your own firing conditions.

ished, place them in several locations in the kiln. Every kiln has hot and cold spots – by having several test bars, you can get an average shrinkage and absorption rate and thus more precise information about the clay. After the bars are fired, test each bar and calculate the average test results. In this way, a greater degree of accuracy can be obtained for shrinkage and absorption rates.

The average fired shrinkage rate for stoneware clay bodies cone 6 to cone 10 (2232°F to 2381°F) falls between 12% and 14%, with highly plastic and vitreous porcelain clay bodies in the 13% to 14% range. The more plastic a clay body (plastic clay body formulas have greater amounts of small platelet-sized clay), the greater the dry and fired shrinkage. Each small clay platelet is surrounded by water in the moist clay state; when the piece begins to dry it has greater shrinkage than clay bodies with coarser or larger platelets. Clay body formulas with increased amounts of small platelet clays (ball clays, bentonite) have greater shrinkage rates due to the increased amount of water required for plasticity. Clay bodies with high plasticity and shrinkage warp more in drying and firing. Drying cracks are also more likely due to the high amounts of small platelet-size materials in the formula. Cracks are often found where knobs or handles join the main section of the pot.

The average fired shrinkage rate for earthenware clay bodies cone 010 to cone 04 (1641°F to 1940°F) is between 5% and 7%. Earthenware bodies are not characteristically as dense and vitreous as high-fire stoneware clay bodies. One factor is the low amount of glass formation in earthenware clay, resulting in a lower fired shrinkage rate. A higher shrinkage rate would indicate increased glass build-up in the clay and a denser fired clay body. Or it could indicate a higher plastic clay content in the clay body formula, causing increased clay shrinkage. Earthenware clay bodies can be fired higher but bloat-

Bloating in the clay body causes small bubbles in the clay due to over-firing.

ing, warping, and excessive shrinkage can occur long before reaching stoneware temperature ranges. Excessive iron, low amounts of alumina, and high amounts of fluxes confine earthenware clays to low temperature ranges. Typically, earthenware clays have a very narrow maturing range (the temperature range at which the clay is the most durable and achieves its maximum physical fired strength).

High shrinkage rates can also suggest a dense, vitreous clay body. During body maturation, glass formation in the clay will cause shrinkage due to sintering where platelets of clay fuse. At this point in the heating cycle, absorption begins to decrease as more glass is being formed in the clay body. The fired strength of the clay increases due to vitrification. Over-firing a clay body can produce bloating and slumping and cause the clay to stick to the kiln shelf. If fired high enough, the clay body can become a glaze, depositing itself as a molten puddle on the kiln shelf.

A clay body that is too plastic will cause cracking and shrinkage problems. When developing a clay body, use only the amount of plasticity required for the formula. Throwing bodies require a greater degree of plasticity than tile or sculpture bodies due to the forming process on the wheel. Tile or sculpture bodies don't require much plasticity and accordingly, should contain fewer plastic materials. Plasticity in a clay body formula is nor-

mally obtained from bentonite, ball clays, and stoneware clays. Clay bodies with too much of these small platelet-size clays have a rubbery feel when being worked in their moist state. Too much plastic material in a formula can cause the moist clay to accumulate on your hands after pulling up a form on the wheel, and the form is likely to wobble when thrown. Tall forms can sink back in on themselves after a pull up on the wheel. All these characteristics indicate a formula that is too high in plastic material. Small platelets of clay and/or small particles of raw materials are sliding past each other, not gripping and locking together as would occur with a balanced clay body formula of small, medium, and large platelet structures.

Other than the clay body formula, the biggest factor in choosing the right clay body is absorption and shrinkage, both of which affect potential glaze fit. Shrinkage and absorption can change depending on your kiln and firing cycle. Ceramics supplier percentages for absorption and shrinkage, even at the temperature you plan to use, should always be taken as estimates. True shrinkage and absorption rates can vary 2% above or below the stated rate. For greater accuracy, test the clay in your kiln. The most workable solution might be to test a few stock clay bodies at one time. Find a clay body formula that meets your requirements and test it again to build your confidence in the clay. After a few firings, it should be apparent what the clay can and cannot do in your kiln. Keep in mind that the same clay body might fire differently in another kiln. Take nothing for granted when choosing a clay body or glaze. Always test under the same conditions as in your regular production cycle.

Developing Your Own Clay Body Formula

Before developing your own clay body formula, learn about the raw materials, clays, fluxes, and grogs that will be used in the formula. Try to find out if their supply will be stable and reliable. It doesn't make sense to mix a formula, only to discover one or more of the clays are no longer being mined. Learn the characteristics of each material in the formula – its melting temperature, what it feels like when mixed into a moist consistency, how it reacts with other raw materials. This information is available from analysis sheets of the raw materials, experience from past tests, and trial test body formulas.

Often the easiest way to develop a clay body is to start with a known formula and make small adjustments. For example, if the initial clay body is "short" or not plastic, add 5% to 10% ball clay to increase plasticity. If the clay body doesn't have enough "tooth" or can't stand up when formed into a shape, add 5% to 15% grog to improve the flabby clay body. Adding some large particle size clays (fire clays, some stoneware clays) will give the clay body more standup ability when being formed.

Adjusting a known formula or starting from scratch and developing your own formula requires knowledge of the raw materials and a subjective evaluation of what the clay body should accomplish. Knowing what each raw material does alone and in combination with other materials is imperative. Knowing what the limits are for each raw material in a formula is also important. Excessive amounts of low-temperature clay in a stoneware formula can cause bloating, warping, and melting of the clay body. Too much grog can cause the clay body to be short and not plastic enough for forming. The clay can become gritty with a rough surface texture. The type and amount of raw materials in a clay body formula are determined by the firing temperature, kiln atmosphere, forming process, fired color, texture, and durability of the finished piece.

The best clay bodies have small, medium, and large particle and platelet sizes.

Platelet sizes can be chosen from various clays. Large platelets are found in fire clays, medium platelets in stoneware clays, and small platelets in ball clays and bentonites. Particle size variations are found in grog, silica sand, molochite, flint, feldspar, talc, wollastonite, and other non-clay materials. The small, medium, and large sizes and shapes found in clay body materials can greatly increase plasticity and the ability of the clay to stand up when moist. Grogs offer an irregular particle shape and can be obtained in different mesh sizes that make an ideal addition to most clay body formulas. Overall, clay handling properties are greatly improved by the interlocking of particle sizes and shapes. Grog also has a stabilizing effect that causes moisture in the clay body to be released at an even rate when drying.

Feldspars, flint, and talc have round or oblong shapes. They are considered nonplastic and don't have the same handling characteristics as clay when moist. Round or oblong shapes act like ball bearings in a clay body, rolling past each other and causing a loose feel as the moist clay is being formed. While these nonclay materials don't make for a good mechanical fit in a clay body, they are needed for vitrification, glaze fit, and dry shrinkage functions. A good clay body formula will have the correct ratios of round, oblong, irregular, plastic, and nonplastic materials.

On a mechanical level, the various sizes lock together, causing a better clay/water ratio. Less water fills the voids between particles composed of small, medium, and large sizes. Any open spaces in the clay structures fill with water, so larger spaces between clay platelets hold more water. This causes more shrinkage and increased cracking in the clay body upon drying. When the water is taken away through evaporation and/or heating, the clay platelets are left hanging, not touching each other, causing a crack. Achieving the ideal mix of materials is not practical or possible for every clay body, but some degree of particle size variation should be considered when developing a clay body.

Saving Money – False Economics

Everyone wants to save money and cut costs. The profit margin in producing pottery is very small, so any savings is critical. The challenge is to choose effective cost-cutting methods. Each cost-cutting idea should be carefully considered before implementation. You may save a little by driving to the ceramic supply company to pick up raw materials and clay instead of having them shipped to you, but the savings are quickly offset by the loss of a day's production in your studio and the expense of traveling to and from the shop. The first and most important priorities are your time and labor.

Whenever possible, purchase the best grade of equipment, kilns, tools, supplies, and materials. Their durability and reli-

A used 70-cubic-foot car kiln in need of repairs! A lower purchase price when buying used equipment can be an expensive price to pay in your time and labor for repairs.

ability over time will save money. Your tools (anything required to make pots or sculpture) should make the production and handling of work easier and more efficient. If they don't, you are fighting an up-hill battle to produce the work and get

A wood kiln firebox.

The remainder of the wood pile after firing the kiln.

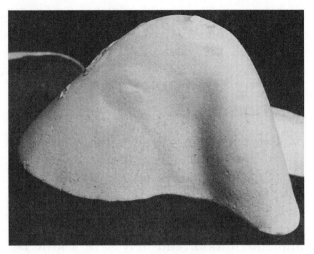

Firing the kiln too fast causes dry, dull, surface texture in the glaze.

past any poor design characteristics of the tools. Purchasing a used kiln without knowing how to build or repair kilns can be an expensive way to save money. Money spent on efficient equipment is always a savings if the equipment increases production.

Building a wood kiln because a low cost supply of wood is available simply will not work as a cost-cutting method. The money saved in cheap wood fuel will be more than used up by the intense labor required to fire the kiln. At best, after all production costs are calculated, you might find yourself working for a few cents per hour. Again, the cost of clay, equipment, supplies, burners, and glaze materials (except tin and cobalt) is secondary to the cost of labor.[3]

If you mix a gallon of glaze (that doesn't contain tin or cobalt) that doesn't turn out, it's often less expensive in terms of time and labor to start over than to try to adjust the bad batch. The time you save can be used for making more pots. The same time-saving principle should be applied to mending cracked pots – the time you spend trying to fix it would be better spent making more pieces.

In some production situations, making your own clay may seem like a cost-cutting option but once you calculate the cost of clay-mixing machinery, labor, and clay storage, it becomes apparent that purchasing premixed clay might actually be less expensive. If mixing your own clay is still important to you, first consider what is involved. Every minute you spend making clay is time away from making pots.

Firing fast or at lower temperature to save fuel is not effective if the glaze pinholes or has a dry surface texture, both common consequences of fast glaze firings. If a pot has to be refired, you've probably lost money on it. Think about it – you unload the kiln, reload and possibly reglaze the defective pot, and refire the

---

3.   As of this writing, cobalt oxide costs $38/lb. and tin $11.45/lb.

kiln. The refired pot will take the space of another pot waiting to be fired.

Look for ways to cut production steps. Ask yourself if the piece can be once-fired (no bisque firings) or if you can use two or three glazes instead of eight (less time spent mixing different glaze formulas). If the answer is yes, you can realize a real savings in time and money.

Some potters wash their pots after the bisque firing to remove dust and keep the pot from absorbing too much glaze. This step can be eliminated simply by covering the bisque pots when they are removed from the kiln. Firing the bisque kiln one or two cones higher will cause the glaze to build up more slowly on the bisque pots. It costs too much time and labor when each piece has to be washed. Your studio should be arranged so all work flows smoothly from one area to the next. Remember, the more times you handle each pot, the more money you lose.

Learn and Remember

Apart from the actual making of ceramic objects and the techniques of construction, glazing, and firing, you should also be continually acquiring a storehouse of basic knowledge about why things happen.

Learning the whys of a bad kiln firing will give you a broad serviceable base of knowledge and keep you from trying a quick fix that sends you onto the next firing. This is especially true when firing reduction kilns. Many potters learn one technique for firing and use it successfully until something changes. At this point, the potter must have a complete knowledge of what causes reduction atmosphere and how to achieve it in any kiln. A broad and comprehensive base of knowledge will help reduce the time spent on unsuccessful attempts to correct defects. Many pottery students – once they find a successful technique or aesthetic – stay within the comfortable confines of making "good"

pots. True understanding of clay occurs outside the safe areas that produce whole kiln loads of "perfect" pots. Clay, techniques, materials, and kiln firings have to be pushed to the limit and beyond to acquire increased knowledge.

Gather information from many sources: books, workshops, formal courses, personal experiences, and other potters' experiences will increase your knowledge. Aside from the actual construction phase, making successful pots or sculpture involves little bits of information about the process. It is only when enough bits are strung together that the problems in producing ceramic pieces start to diminish. Unfortunately, there is no one text or reference for all the potential problems and corrections that occur in the course of making ceramic objects, but several problems come up frequently in many potters' experiences with clay.

Knowing why a problem happened and how to correct it is one base of knowledge you can gather. Knowing the principles that support clay and glaze formulas, raw materials, forming methods, and firing procedures will give you an expansive, adaptable base of knowledge. This knowledge can then be applied to problems or situations that aren't listed in a text book. Both types of knowledge, along with personal experience, are critical.

Any student of ceramics must be willing to suffer through running glazes, pots that slump or fuse to the kiln shelf, and any other technical pitfalls that might happen. There's a lot of truth to the old saying, "It takes more than two dozen firings to know a kiln." Potters must take the time and make the commitment to learn their craft. Producing good pots or creating sculpture is not easy. When trying to solve technical problems in ceramics, having a flexible approach for gathering information is most important. Finally, the tool most needed is the ability to gather and use all forms of information, wherever you find it.

Chapter 6

Avoid Potential Problems Selling Pots

Several situations can cause financial difficulties for potters trying to make money in the field of ceramics. While some problems are technical and can be solved, other problems are based on ignorance of common business practices. If the process of making and selling pots isn't thoughtfully organized, it can become a very expensive hobby. The most perplexing problems arise when you have a high level of sales but find that profits are slowly being eaten away by "hidden" production costs. A common complaint is, "I'm working harder every year and making less money." Why do many potters find themselves in this scenario? The answers can be found in some recurrent situations present in each failing pottery business.

Organized studio dry greenware ready for bisque firing.

A professional pottery booth display for craft show wholesale/retail sales. (Bob Woo Potter)

You probably started selling pots because there was joy in making pots. At the entry level, selling pots to friends, family, and the public is easy because it seems everyone has an affinity with handmade objects and wants handcrafted coffee mugs. At this stage, the pottery market has low barriers for entry. Expenses for starting your business are low and you are selling your work with little effort. With the income generated from even modest sales of pottery, you can purchase equipment, kilns, raw materials, and supplies. Unfortunately, at some level, producing more pots will not necessarily translate into making more money. If selling the pots isn't producing a profit, selling more pots can eventually cause increasing losses.

After the easy entry phase, the next stage of selling involves more business knowledge than pottery skill. What started as an enjoyable nontraditional escape from the commercial market turns into a business, competing in the commercial market. To profitably sell pottery, the potter must develop skills to run a business that just happens to make pots.

In profitable pottery businesses, several characteristics are usually present. It often helps to understand the commonalties of profitable enterprises and then plan your own business with this knowledge. And there are several potential problem areas that should send up red flags if making pots for profit is your business goal.

Start with a Basic Business Education

In many communities, college and adult education courses are offered in accounting, marketing, economics, and other basic business-related skills. While sitting in a classroom might not be the first thought that comes to mind when deciding to make pots, it might be the way to get the skills needed so you can keep making pots.

Other useful information can be found in the many books published for craftspeople who want to start their own businesses. Often professional potters who have remained in business for a period of years can offer advice and specific information on how to stay in business. Every type of business is different, but a potter who has been successful might just be the person to offer valuable nuts and bolts information on running a profitable business. It's easier and less costly to learn from other people's mistakes. Oddly, college ceramics and art programs are sadly lacking in the rudimentary business courses many of their students will need after graduation.

Develop a Business Plan

A business plan is a requirement for any commercial bank loan application and many times you'll be asked to explain your product and its sales potential. Even if you aren't borrowing money from a bank, the plan is still an important tool to organize a blueprint for your plan of action.

Among other things, your business plan should include advertising and marketing information about how your work will be sold A complete financial breakdown of the direct and indirect costs of production, hourly wages for yourself, and profit margins will give a clear picture of the business. The plan should also include a timetable to reach short- and long-term goals and a listing of primary and secondary markets for your pots. Be prepared to review the plan at regular intervals to decide if the objectives are being met.

Keep Accurate Financial Records

Accurate and up-to-date financial records are often the first indicators of difficulty. Many failed pottery businesses didn't realize the nature and extent of their problems until it was too late. In these cases, the potters were exclusively focused on the day-to-day requirements of making pots and didn't make the everyday business decisions that are necessary for survival.

To Thine Own Self Be True

Make pots based on your own aesthetic, not what you think will sell. This is often the easiest advice to give and the most difficult to follow. Making pots is hard work and it is doubly hard if you end up not liking the work. Choose pots that are fun to make and express your own aesthetics. Then you will find the market. Chasing the market with the popular glaze color of the month might produce short-term results, but it will slowly become just another job, making objects that will become devoid of real imagination or meaning.

Many potters make a compromise and produce objects they know will sell. Once they've finished the "guaranteed income pots," they make pots they enjoy producing. Try to maintain a balance of so-called guaranteed income pots and pots that express your aesthetic statement.

Use Reliable Materials and Equipment

Don't make production pots with clay body and glazes formulas that have narrow margins for successful results. Often potters find a unique glaze or clay body that looks good but doesn't consistently produce acceptable results. Plan carefully before making sample pots to show potential customers. A key element in producing pottery for sale is the ability to duplicate the clay and glaze colors ordered by your customers. Choosing a clay body or glaze that matures at a specific cone or exact temperature places unrealistic expectations on any type of kiln. Most kilns have hot and cold spots generated by the firing cycle, kiln design, stacking arrangement, and other variables. Not all kilns fire exactly evenly throughout their interior space. It's best to choose clay bodies and glazes with at least a two or three cone range to produce an acceptable result. Reliability and consistency should be the basis for choosing clay body and glaze formulas for production ware.

Another complication of generating work on demand is the inability to fire reduction kilns. You should understand the theory and practice of reduction firing so the atmosphere inside the kiln can be re-

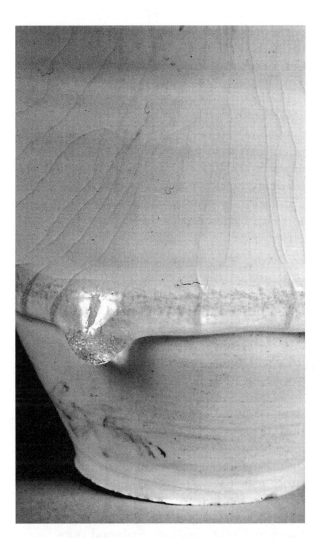

Limited maturing ranges of glaze can cause glossy, dripping, over-fired glaze surfaces.

Limited maturing range of glazes can cause dry, dull, bubbled under-fired glaze surfaces.

liably controlled. For example, a gas kiln atmosphere allows the manipulation of metallic coloring oxides found in clays and glazes; it can also produce inconsistent results when fired incorrectly. Using gas, wood, coal, oil, or any combustible material as a heating source raises the possibility for countless variables in atmosphere and temperature that will produce different variations in clay and glazes. Having many options to control the atmosphere of the kiln and its subsequent effect on clay body and glaze results increases the chances of turning out ware that is under- or over-reduced.

Keep the tolerance range of clay bodies, glazes, kiln firing atmospheres, temperatures and decorative techniques as wide as possible. If a favorite glaze depends on a precise amount of kiln reduction atmosphere and your kiln cannot consistently produce a good result, consider using a more reliable glaze. Some glazes are more sensitive to thin glaze applications and will look radically different when a thicker coat of glaze is applied to the clay surface. Such glazes have to be applied to a precise thickness every time to insure the correct color, adding yet another variable to the process.

Avoid clay body and glaze formulas that are extremely sensitive to kiln atmosphere conditions until you have developed procedures for reliable kiln firings. Every kiln fires differently and it's unrealistic to assume the first firings of any new kiln will be perfect. At some point, if you aren't making progress at firing your kiln with consistent results, look for someone who is firing a similar kiln and ask for help. Take the time to know your kiln before committing yourself to full-scale production. Often communities have ceramics programs that offer courses in kiln firing. Don't start a pottery business until you have educated yourself in all aspects of turning moist clay into finished pots.

Firing a gas kiln that yields unreliable results offers no advantage if customers are waiting for specific orders that you can't produce. If you are thinking of selling your work on a wholesale basis, remember that prospective customers are usually looking for a close or exact match of the pots displayed as samples. Often the number of reorders will depend on how faithfully you can reproduce the sample pots. When starting out, choose clay bodies, glazes, kilns, equipment, and any other elements of production that will work under a wide variety of conditions and still produce a consistent product.

Electric kilns have a better chance of producing reliable clay and glaze results than gas or wood-fired kilns. But electric kiln firing produces different results in clay bodies and glazes than gas kilns, so it's very difficult to duplicate the results of gas firing in an electric kiln. The electric kiln's oxidation atmosphere can (with experimentation) produce unique clay body and glaze results. Choose the type of kiln that will be the easiest to fire accurately for the line of pottery you produce.

Keep clay body and glaze formulas simple, using as few raw materials as possible. Many simplified versions of clay body and glaze formulas produce the same fired results as formulas that contain many individual raw materials. The actual raw material amounts used in a glaze or clay formula can be rounded off to the nearest whole number. For example, if a glaze formula requires 45.3% flint, use 45%. Coloring oxides, stains, opacifiers, dyes, binders, or suspension agents are the exception and the exact amount should be weighed out. Fewer raw materials in the studio and easier weigh-outs translate into a savings of time and labor. Glaze and clay formulas with fewer materials also mean simpler ordering and less money tied up in raw material inventories.

For example:

C/06 Satin Blue

Ferro Frit #3134	59.7	=	60
EPK	20.2	=	20
Nepheline Syenite	14.6	=	15
Flint	5.4	=	5
Cobalt Carbonate	3.2	=	3.2
CMC Gum	1.5	=	1.5

Buy Supplies From Someone You Trust

Your list of raw material and clay suppliers should be kept short. A good reputation and a history of customer service should be your first considerations when choosing a ceramic supplier. Preferably, the supplier should be close to your studio. While shipping costs and long supply line problems are always present with distant ceramics suppliers, the real concern is buying from a ceramic supplier who doesn't offer good service or reliable products. Buying premixed stock clay or custom mixed clay from a supplier who doesn't know or care how to mix clay properly is always a losing situation.

Don't let a supplier's bad business practices become your business problems. Late clay deliveries, low supply of stock items, and incorrectly mixed clay body formulas should all be the supplier's concern, not yours. Your main focus should be on producing salable pots. Any problems originating with ceramics suppliers should be corrected by ceramics suppliers. Don't waste time trying to fix or work around a problem caused by a supplier. The fastest, least expensive fix to this problem is to use a different supplier.

Keep Your Designs Simple

Don't design or make pots that are labor intensive or rely on decorative techniques that have to be exactly executed. Making pots is labor intensive. Time-consuming decoration, forming processes, firing cycles, and handling all use up labor. Design the pots and all aspects of making the pots so each element carries its own weight contributing to the eventual sale. An overglaze painted flower design might look very good on a coffee mug but the

A dinnerware set.

time and effort required to paint the design might drastically increase time and labor costs. Make some mugs without the design and compare the sales of both. It's possible that the shape of the mug is the selling feature, not the design. Forming techniques, design elements, kiln firing cycles, finished pot handling, and packaging all must be as efficient as possible. Think of your business as a lifeboat in the middle of the ocean – any part of the business not pulling its own weight has to go over the side.

Defective pots and seconds with small imperfections don't contribute to maximum profits. A failed pot that has to be made again takes up time in making and increases labor in loading and unloading the pot from the kiln. Replacing a failed pot causes multiple losses in time and labor.

Limit the line of pottery produced to a select range of well-planned functional items that allows for less complicated production and less potential for forming, glazing, and firing problems. Good technique in all forming operations is easier to achieve if you don't have to learn or execute varied and diverse forms. A small production line with a wide price range will insure a balanced opportunity for sales. Every pot in the line should stand on its own and produce a profit. If you

A set of six small bowls.

need to expand your line, consider making sets of bowls, cups, plates, goblets, etc. as the number of pieces sold will increase along with profits.

Calculate Costs Before Pricing Your Pieces

Make it your business to learn all the production costs before setting wholesale/retail pricing. Include an hourly wage and a profit margin on each pot in the total selling price. Many potters only include a profit margin in the selling price and after all the hidden costs take effect, they are actually working for a few cents per hour. Carefully calculate the time and labor required at every stage of the production operation.

Cut cost wherever possible but weigh how the cost reduction will affect the whole process. One potter's idea of cutting cost was to build a wood kiln because free wood was available. While the wood was free, the increased amount of time and labor to fire the kiln was not, causing a labor intensive lesson in pottery production. That potter now uses a gas kiln which requires only a turn of the valve and the time previously spent cutting, stacking, and firing the wood kiln is now spent making more pots.

Maintain Quality and Correct Problems

Closely monitor quality control in production and fix technical problems. Track pottery defect rates from all causes, whether a pot is dropped on the way to the kiln or cracks in the firing. The total defect rate from all causes should average less than 8%. Higher defect rates indicate a problem that should be addressed immediately. Keeping a close watch on defects and their causes is an early warning system that problems are developing.

Consider this scenario: After throwing several large platters, the potter noticed that they had cracked upon drying. Each platter had an S-shaped crack at the bottom. He tried covering the platters with plastic and slowing the drying time, but it didn't solve the problem. Unfortunately, he didn't realize that the cause of the cracking was an improper centering technique. Slowing the drying time only delayed the onset of cracks and lost valuable time.

Identify the problem, find the cause, correct the problem, and get on with the work. High defect rates and the lack of accurate technical corrections result in major losses.

Explore All Markets

Don't rely on only one or two markets for sales. Wholesale and retail craft shows are the most widely publicized markets for pottery sales but they represent only a small segment of the market. Entry fees, exhibit booth fees, shipping, and traveling expenses all reduce profit margins. Poor sales at one or two shows can reduce your income significantly.

Successful potters have a diversified approach to marketing and selling their pots. Build a mailing list of previous customers and use it to generate sales through private shows and kiln openings in your studio. Often people like the idea of visiting a potter's studio to see the pots come out of the kiln. Many potters have used this idea of direct studio sales with great success. Selling pots through this method can save time and money. Otherwise, packing, traveling, setting up a display, or shipping pots decreases profits. The overall strategy should be for you to touch the pots as little as possible once they are fired.

Steer Clear of Custom Orders

Don't make custom pots to order. Turning down a request for a personalized plate or bowl is often difficult and almost every potter has been placed in this situation by family, friends, and customers. It can be arduous and labor intensive to produce a pot based on another person's idea of color, shape, and design characteristics. Allowing the customer to design the work and to evaluate the finished piece is always a risk.

If you must do custom work, show samples of what the customer can expect and don't stray from the sample options. If the first piece doesn't meet the customer's requirements, making a replacement usually eliminates any potential profit.

Often a customer will want a replacement pot for a set that's no longer in your production line. Or worse, the customer will want you to match a pot made by another potter. Don't fall into this costly and labor intensive trap. Changes in raw materials, firing cycles, glazing techniques, and other variables make it difficult to reproduce a pot exactly to match pieces made in the past by yourself or others. Avoid this problem by making extra pieces for the set during the original production run. While storing and handling the extra pieces will be an inconvenience, having a few extra on hand will eliminate the larger loss of time and effort required to exactly duplicate pots made in the past.

Making Pots, Making Money

After surveying all aspects of making and selling pottery, the one factor that dominates all others is labor. While buying handmade objects has an appeal for a certain market segment, the actual number of people who value handmade pottery is small. Also, the culture of functional pottery in the United States doesn't regard pottery as a high art form. By comparison, sculpture is considered a high art form and sells for higher prices.

The potential pottery buying market is modest and the price you can reasonably ask for a piece of functional pottery has a limit. You are squeezed from both sides – high labor costs at one end, low retail prices at the other. You also have to contend with buying low quality-controlled materials (clay) and trying to produce defect-free objects (pots). The effort to reduce your time and labor cost in the production process while maintaining handmade quality is a constant struggle. Every time you unload the kiln or in any way touch or move the pots, your profit margin narrows.

While the potential pottery buying market is small, it still exists and it's a good business practice to locate the customers within that market who will be attracted to your pots. The great temptation is to produce a copy of someone else's glaze, throwing style, clay body, or ceramics aesthetic. This tactic can generate limited success in terms of selling the pots, but it will eventually lead to frustration and exhaustion from not following your own ideas in clay. As a long-term approach, it's better to struggle with your own ideas and techniques while searching for the market that will appreciate what you have to offer. Looking for the people who will buy your distinctive pots based on your own aesthetic about clay and glazes is time-consuming but you can develop a following of loyal customers who will likely buy more pots in the future.

A vital part of any endeavor is the ability to evaluate each aspect of the business periodically. A flexible approach and the ability to drop unprofitable items or production activities can mean the difference between overall profit or loss. An example of that kind of examination would be a potter who throws only coffee cups. That potter must ask himself if he's making a true profit on every coffee cup sold. Would other functional pieces such as covered jars sell for a greater profit? Many potters think that because they sell many coffee cups, they are doing well, but a thorough accounting of the sales might reveal they are making a small or nonexistent profit selling coffee cups. Don't let brisk sales lead you into thinking a net profit is guaranteed. Always calculate the actual expenses incurred in making the pot.

Since we all have a limited amount of time and energy, always plan in advance how your efforts will return a profit. Making pots eats up a lot of time and labor so any wasted or inefficient activity will impact the bottom line to a greater degree than in other less labor intensive businesses. One potter spent so much time applying for shows, photographing pots, building display booths, packing pots, sitting with the pots at the show, and repacking the pots for the return trip home, that it was not worth the total effort expended. Sit down every few months with the records of sales and expenses and figure out how much profit you are actually taking home. One solution to this labor trap is to develop a mailing list of people who have bought your pots in the past, potential customers, friends, and other potential markets, and invite them to a kiln opening of your finished pots. Visitors can see where and how the pots are made while you sidestep any of the costs involved in taking the pots out of the studio. The optimum result is for the customers to buy pots right out of your kiln.

Any time spent learning about other small pottery businesses will pay off. Learning what makes a pottery business viable will save you from making countless mistakes of your own. Most potters who have been in operation for years have specific methods you can adapt for your own operation. A profit-making "model" for your pottery business can be a very valuable resource. Learn from others whenever possible and listen to their advice with an open mind.

One professional potter recommends not shipping out too much stock on consignment. Why give the shop a free inventory of your pots? In consignment situations, you must rely on the shop to protect your pots, keep accurate records of sales, and issue timely payments. Duplicate this scenario with a dozen or more shops and you end up in a situation where everything must work perfectly in every shop – not a realistic expectation in any business.

As with any successful business, many individual elements contribute to the total profit margin. Business skills, which include product development, marketing, advertising, accounting, and sales all have to be mastered and executed to sustain any selling organization. I realize many potters with successful pottery businesses do the exact opposite of my recommendations (such as making pots for individual custom orders). Clearly, those potters have developed a method to turn a potentially negative situation into an area of profit. The point is that they didn't accept someone else's structure and limitations on their business. Challenge any ideas, no matter what their source, about what constitutes a successful business. Carefully evaluate what will work in your individual situation and think it through from beginning to end before getting caught up in the process.

Acknowledgments

I would like to thank professional potters Bob Woo of Shutesbury, Mass., and Michael Cohen of Amherst, Mass., who generously gave their time and advice to make this chapter possible. Both potters are making exceptional pots and are still in business.

Part II

Clay Bodies

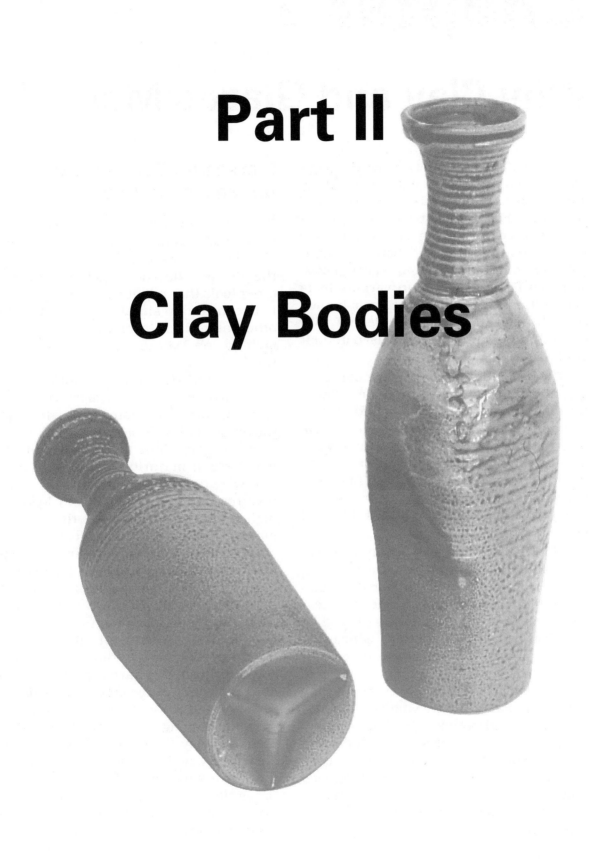

Chapter 7

Why Clay and Glazes Melt

Producing ceramic ware is generally not a difficult endeavor. Many people create excellent and satisfying pots and sculpture. For the most part, the principles involved in making pots are readily understood by potters. There's a great body of information about clay, glazes, and kiln firing available in various texts and potters further increase their knowledge through their own experiences with the techniques and materials used in their studio.

The basic information of forming, glazing, and firing isn't hard to understand – the difficult part is getting the information all in one place. This isn't likely to change and potters interested in learning more about their craft should gather knowledge from whatever sources they can find. The following information is presented to provide you with a few more bits of information.

Working with heat is required in ceramics – some form of heat treatment is essential to melt a clay body or glaze into a durable object. Therefore, the way heat affects clay and glaze materials should be a critical part of every potter's education. Understanding how heat works on ceramic materials is the first important piece of information necessary to correct firing problems, which will inevitably happen if you use a kiln long enough. How effectively the problems will be solved will depend on how much information and knowledge you bring to the situation. Therefore, let's examine several important factors that influence ceramic materials and kiln temperature.

Increasing Temperature Increases Melting

This is probably the most easily understood and practiced part of firing pottery. If it doesn't look done, fire higher. While the idea is valid and does work, there are other tools that might be more appropriate to use in certain situations. Knowing what other factors are involved in raw material melting can lead to a more efficient solution.

Through trial and error and observation, most potters have learned that increasing the kiln temperature increases the amount of melting. We have all experienced a glaze kiln firing that somehow didn't reach maturity, resulting in glazes that were dry or off-color with dull surface textures. Firing the same kiln load to a higher temperature caused the glazes to mature and have a glossier look.

Increasing the temperature in a glaze kiln brings the clay body to a greater melt. Most stoneware clay bodies have a three-cone range at which they are considered dense and vitreous. When a clay body is over-fired, it can warp, shrink excessively, bloat, or stick to the kiln shelves. Some clay body formulas have very short maturing ranges – they go from under-fired to over-fired in a very short temperature span. Increasing the temperature will also increase clay body shrinkage and decrease clay body absorption. One reason that stoneware clay bodies and glazes look "integrated" or blend so well is that the clay body/glaze interface is well developed. The interface is the area where the clay body and glaze fuse under temperature. As temperature increases, the interface becomes more developed, resulting in greater glaze melting and a vitreous clay body.

Time to Temperature

Often when the bisque kiln is fast fired, if the pieces don't blow up, trap carbons, or crack, there will be very little difference in the fired pots. The exception to this rule is when fast firing increases the glaze absorption rate of the bisque pots. Here the glaze absorbs quicker on a fast-fired bisque piece because the clay body hasn't had a chance to get harder (less absorbent) which normally takes place with a longer firing process. Fast firing in a glaze kiln can lead to glaze or clay body problems. A forming crack can occur when a thin cross section of clay joins a thicker cross section of clay. The different rate of shrinkage between the thick and thin cross sections causes the crack. A fast bisque firing can reveal the crack but the problem essentially starts when the pot is formed. Unequal drying of tiles can also cause cracking which can be caused by too fast a heat increase in the first stages of bisque kiln firing.

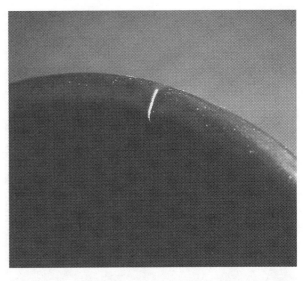

Round edge glaze cracks occur during forming, drying, bisque firing or anytime before glaze application.

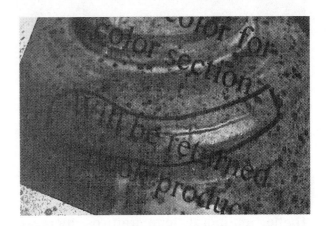

A forming crack. The round edge glaze crack occurred where the bowl had a thin cross section.

Fast bisque firing. The round edge cracks (fired glaze rolls back from the edge of the crack) indicate that the pot was cracked before glaze application.

A round edge crack formed due to unequal drying of the tile.

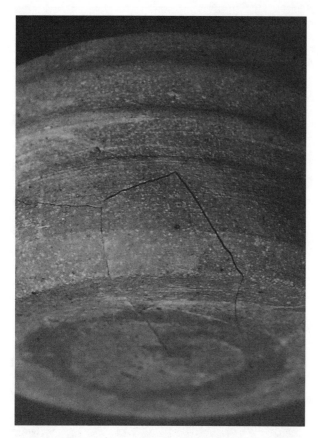

Fast cooling of the glaze kiln can cause a sharp edge hair line.

example, if a glaze kiln is being fired to cone 9, it should take eight to nine hours to go from cone 06 to cone 9. Will this firing schedule produce a perfectly fired kiln? Nothing is perfect in ceramics, but there is a greater chance for a good maturation of clay and glaze using a slow per hour heat increase. Is this the only way to fire a glaze kiln? No, there are many glaze firing schedules that work. This one seems to work well with many sizes and types of kilns. Clay body vitrification, or glass formation develops between 1000°F and 2300°F. Going too fast through this temperature range will result in lower fired strength and higher absorption rates to the clay body. High absorption rates (more than 3%) can cause glaze crazing. The fired ware may not be able to hold liquids because the clay is porous. Physically, the pots will not be as strong and durable if fast fired and they often produce a dull thud when tapped instead of a pleasant long resonant ring.

Firing too fast through the cone 06 to cone 9 temperature range can produce a whole array of glaze defects. This is because all glazes need time to settle down and smooth out in their liquid molten state. The first and most prevalent glaze defect caused by fast firing is a dull, dry, sandpaper glaze quality. In matte glaze formulas, the fast-fired glaze can almost look like dry cracked powder. In gloss glaze formulas, fast firing can result in opaque glaze surfaces or bubbles suspended in the fired glaze layer. Glaze pinholes, blisters, rough areas, and glaze color variations are found in a fast-fired kiln. Dull or bleached out glaze colors are also due to fast rates of heat increase.

Many potters fire their kilns fast and report good results. Other than the potential problem of the clay body not being as mature and durable as it could be if fired at a slower firing rate, they have found glazes that work with a fast rate of heat increases. In most situations, however, a slower firing during the cone 06 to cone 9

Before describing the defects, it's important to understand that ceramic materials need endpoint temperatures to melt. Higher endpoint temperatures increase melting and the longer it takes to reach that endpoint temperature, the more melting occurs. The time to temperature is often overlooked or not recognized as an important factor in the vitrification of clay bodies and glazes. Ceramic materials used in clay and glaze formulas react well with slow increases and decreases of temperature. The potential for clay and glaze defects increases as the kiln is fired faster and cooled faster.

How fast is too fast? Let's use a cone 9 (2336°F) glaze firing as an example. Excluding preheating and temperatures up to cone 06 (1830°F), after cone 06 the temperature should raise about 65°F to 70°F per hour to the end of the firing. For period is the most likely way to reduce clay body and glaze defects.

The Smaller the Particle, the Greater the Melt

A smaller particle size produces a greater surface area than the same material in a larger form. The smaller size enables the heat to work faster and more efficiently to cause melting. A smaller particle size also allows for the material to come in contact more with other substances that cause melting in the clay or glaze formula.

Slight differences in glaze texture and opacity can be traced to changing the mesh size in a glaze material. When ordering raw materials, always specify the mesh size. Using the same mesh size in raw materials every time insures uniformity in the fired glaze. Particle size can also determine how long a liquid glaze stays in suspension in the glaze bucket. Coarser size glaze material will sink to the bottom faster than finer mesh materials.

Silica or flint is found in almost every formula, whatever the temperature range, texture, or color of the glaze. Silica can be used in several different mesh sizes. The coarser mesh sizes of silica won't mix into a glaze melt as readily as finer mesh sizes. As an example, try adding 10% silica sand 60-mesh into a glaze. The fired result will be a glaze with sand particles sticking out on the surface. The same addition of 10% silica with finer 325-mesh will be taken into the viscous molten glaze, resulting in a smooth glaze surface. Smaller particle sizes will be absorbed into a molten glass faster than larger particles of the same material.

There are several different mesh sizes of whiting (a calcium carbonate), all of which are sold as whiting by ceramics suppliers. A finer mesh whiting in a glaze formula might produce a transparent gloss glaze. The same amount of coarser whiting in the formula can produce a semiopaque white glaze. The coarser grades of whiting don't dissolve as thoroughly in the molten glaze, leaving the fired glaze white, opaque, and clouded. Both mesh sizes of whiting look identical in their shipping bags, so you must know exactly what mesh size is used in the glaze. Every ceramics supplier should have the mesh sizes of the materials listed in their catalog. Get this information and keep it in your records for future orders.

When fine particle size clays are used in clay body formulas, you'll notice the difference in the handling characteristics of the moist clay. Using a high percentage of fine particles makes the clay body rubbery or like cream cheese. While the terms are subjective, these fine grain bodies tend not to have tooth or standup ability when moist. Occasionally, they can warp from high drying shrinkage. Drying cracks are also prevalent in high clay content, high fine particle size clay bodies because the many small particles are encased in water to make the clay plastic. When the water leaves the clay body, some particles can be left hanging in midair, causing cracks. The increased amount of water required for plasticity can cause increased dry shrinkage. The best clay bodies have small, medium, and large clay platelet and raw material particle structures.

Rate of Kiln Cooling

Ceramic materials in clays and glazes don't react well to fast cooling in a kiln. Fast cooling can damage a clay body and increase the chances of glaze crazing. When the endpoint temperature is reached in a glaze firing, most glazes are completely viscous and molten. However, some glazes need more time at this molten stage when the last of the gases and bubbles from the breakdown of oxides and carbonates are traveling up through the molten glaze. A sudden drop in the kiln temperature will cause the molten glaze to freeze, leaving behind surface craters or glaze bubbles in the finished ware. A clear glaze frozen or fast cooled can look opaque because of the many tiny bubbles suspended under the glaze surface. Many matte glazes, if fast cooled, have a dry surface texture. In both kinds of glaze, slow cooling or holding the glaze in its maturing range longer produces a greater degree of glaze development.

Holding the glaze kiln near or at endpoint temperature is called soaking. By soaking, you can extend the glaze maturation range. Often, glazes in small test kilns can't be duplicated in large kilns because the small kiln's faster heating and cooling cycles can't be accomplished in a large kiln. Soaking the small kiln can sometimes compensate for its lack of thermal mass, but for best results, satin matte and matte glazes should be fired in a larger kiln. In a large kiln with lots of bricks, shelves, posts, and pots (increased thermal mass), soaking and very slow cooling are often not required. The larger the size and mass of the kiln supplies, the longer it takes to change temperature (the bricks, posts, shelves, and pots take more time to heat up and cool down). Not every glaze or clay body needs to be soaked or slow cooled to achieve good results.

Slow cooling and, to a greater extent, soaking in the glaze firing, allows a clay and glaze to stay in the maturing range for a long time. Increasing the firing time in the maturing range can increase clay vitrification, causing a stronger more durable fired clay body. With glazes, more time in the maturing range gives the molten glaze a chance to settle down further and complete the glass formation process. The clay body and glaze now have a better chance of fitting when cool. Glazes that haven't been allowed to cool slowly often appear to have surface bubbles or popped open volcanic-looking craters. Some gloss glazes have dry areas from fast cooling. Many glazes can be refired to the same temperature with a good result. When the glaze is given more heat treatment, it increases the existing glaze melt. However, sometimes refiring won't do well because of the repeated melting of fluxes within the glaze. Remelting some fluxes can cause a boiling effect, producing pinholes or blisters in the glaze.

Think of a glaze firing as a curve on a graph, with temperature increases as a line going up and temperature decreases as a line going down. If the top half of the curve is rounded or even flat, the chances of good clay body and glaze results increase. If the firing curve looks like a sharp spike with a point on top, the chances of good clay body and glaze result decrease. Does this rule work for every clay body and glaze situation? No, but it works for most.

Kiln Atmosphere

In a glaze kiln firing, the presence of reduction, salt, or soda will cause increased melting compared with a kiln fired in an oxidation atmosphere. Reduction, salt, and soda act as a fluxing agent on clay bodies and glazes. All the oxides residing in clay bodies and glazes are subject to these atmospheres. The metallic coloring oxides such as iron, manganese, copper, chrome, cobalt, etc. are visibly changed by reduction. As an example, heavy reduction in a high iron content glaze can cause the glaze to run off the pot because the iron is fluxed more than it would be in an oxidation atmosphere. High amounts of iron in a clay body can cause the clay to bloat or bubble in a reduction atmosphere due to its fluxing action.

Firing with wood as a fuel can produce a reduction kiln atmosphere along with the wood ash, which is another strong flux. Wood ash at cone 10 (2381°F) and above can form a glaze and act like a flux if it falls into an existing glaze or an unglazed clay surface. Salt, soda, and wood ash can cause a faster, inaccurate melting of pyrometric cones due to the fluxing action on the cone's surface. The cones should be shielded from the kiln atmosphere whenever possible to insure an accurate cone reading. Sodium from regular salt or sodium carbonate will cause a fluxing action on glazes and pyrometric cones in the kiln. Sodium vapor in the presence of an exposed clay body develops a sodium, alumina, silicate glaze surface. The fluxing action of sodium vapor is confined to the surface, unlike the more penetrating atmosphere of reduction that can flux the oxides in the interior of the clay body.

Glaze Application

The thickness of glaze application can affect the glaze melt. With a thin glaze application, the fired glaze is more likely to melt if all other factors are equal. The thin glaze layer is subject to heat radiated from the clay body and heat from the kiln firing. A thicker glaze layer takes more time to react and melt. Often this factor isn't a major consideration in the kiln firing because the large thermal mass of the kiln, bricks, shelves, pots, and posts hold and radiate heat, causing a glaze layer of any thickness to melt. In small test kilns with less thermal mass and faster heating and cooling cycles, glaze application thickness and subsequent melting can be critical.

A thin glaze application (especially in a reduction kiln) will sometimes melt to a greater degree because the clay body/glaze interface is closer to the glaze surface. (The interface is the area where the clay and glaze meet.) Under reduction firing conditions, a thin glaze application is likely to look brown because of the brown color of the clay body underneath the glaze. Porcelain or white clay bodies don't take on a brown color in reduction, but can turn gray in heavily reduced areas. With any glaze, the true glaze color

Thin glaze application in a reduction kiln can cause glazes to appear brown due to the dark color of the clay body underneath the thin glaze layer.

will be more apparent with a thicker glaze application.

Interface with Clay Body

The interface can play an important role in how a glaze develops. In low-temperature clay bodies, this area is not well developed, causing many low-temperature glazes to look like they were painted on the clay body. At higher temperatures, the clay body and glaze fuse to a much greater extent. High-temperature clay and glaze almost look like they are melted together, having a more integrated look and feel.

In some glazes, a greater degree of glaze melting can be achieved by combining the glaze with a particular clay body. Because of a higher amount of glass formation within the clay bodies, they fuse with the glaze, bringing the glaze to a greater melt. This happens to an extent with most stoneware-range clay and glazes, but some combinations cause a greater intensity of glaze melting in the interface area. The effect of greater glaze melting is most evident in porcelain clay body and glazes. Porcelain clay bodies are very dense, almost glass-like in vitrification, and the fired glaze seems to blend into and become part of the clay. The opposite effect is often seen at earthenware temperatures (cone 010 1641°F to cone 04 1940°F) where there is less fusion of clay and glaze (less development of the interface). At low

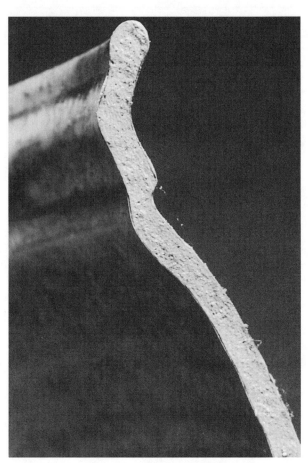

On high temperature clay bodies there is more integration of the clay body and the glaze layer (interface).

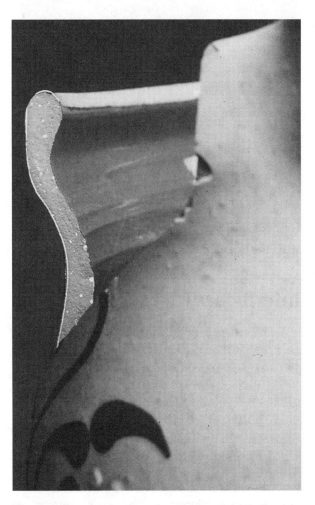

On low-fire clay bodies the glaze can look like it's riding on the surface of the fired clay.

temperature ranges, the fired glaze appears to be riding on the surface of the clay.

Metallic Coloring Oxides

Each metallic coloring oxide can be grouped as a flux or refractory agent. Red iron oxide is one of the most common metallic coloring oxides used in glazes and sometimes in clay bodies. If used in high percentages, iron oxide can be classified as a fluxing oxide in clay bodies and glazes. It can act as a flux, causing the base glaze to go into a greater melt. In reduction, this effect is greater because of the further fluxing effect of the reduction atmosphere. Increasing the amount of iron

A high iron content clay body that is over-reduced in the kiln firing can cause bloating (bubbles in the fired clay).

oxide will increase its fluxing action in a glaze. The finer the particle size, the greater the degree of dispersion in a molten glass. Smaller particles melt faster than large particles because there's more surface area exposed to heat.

High amounts of iron oxide in clay bodies or high iron bearing clays can flux the body, causing brittleness, cracking upon cooling, and over-fluxing (over-firing). Never use more than 2% red iron oxide powder in a clay body because of its strong fluxing action. The safest way to introduce iron oxide into a clay body is through high iron content clays. Black iron oxide has a stronger fluxing action and shouldn't be used in clay body formulas. In clay bodies, particle size does influence melting and large chunks of iron oxide in a clay formula will cause a melted brown spot in the clay. A finer grind of iron oxide dispersed through the clay causes an overall darker color clay when fired.

Keeping in mind each metallic coloring oxide has its own characteristics, depending on many factors. Learn what each oxide does alone and in combination with other coloring oxides.

Glaze Formulas

The amount and type of flux used in a glaze formula determines the melting characteristics of the glaze. For every temperature range there are appropriate fluxes that can be used to cause melting. Starting at the cone 06 1830°F to cone 04 1940°F temperature range, most primary fluxes will be frits, colemanite, Gerstley borate, lead, or combinations of these materials that will be used to bring the silica to a glaze melt. Once a primary flux is chosen, the amount used to cause the glaze melt is critical. Too little flux and the glaze can have a dry or matte surface texture. With too much flux, the glaze can blister or run off the pot when fired.

Feldspars are the primary fluxes used in the cone 6 2232°F to cone 10 2381°F temperature range. Most feldspars fired alone will melt into a semiopaque crazed glaze after cone 6. There are three basic groups of feldspars used in ceramics: potassium, sodium, and lithium. Within each group there are many different feldspars. As an example, a sodium feldspar may contain calcium, potassium, alumina, and silica but the predominant oxide besides silica and alumina is sodium.

A few individual soda spars are nepheline syenite, F4, Mins spar 200, and Kona C-6. Some of the most common potash feldspars are G-200 and Custer. Lithium feldspars in use today are petalite, lepidolite, and spodumene. Feldspars can affect overall glaze melting, with soda feldspars melting 100°F below potassium and lithium feldspars. As in low-temperature fluxes, choosing the correct feldspar and using the right amount in a glaze can be critical. Too much feldspar in a glaze can produce a glossy runny glaze, too little can produce a dry matte glaze surface texture.

Primary fluxes are used to bring secondary fluxes and alumina and silica to a melt. They make up the backbone of the fluxing action in any glaze. Silica by itself will not go into a melt at temperatures reached in current kilns. It's the job of the primary flux and secondary fluxes like calcium, magnesium, or lithium to bring the silica to a melt.

Every raw material in a glaze influences the maturing range, texture, and color, but choosing the appropriate primary flux plays an important part in a successful glaze result. One problem area with many glaze formulas is the use of an inappropriate flux for a specific temperature range. Often a high-temperature glaze will contain a low-temperature flux. Depending on what low-temperature flux is used and the amount in the glaze formula, several problems can be encountered. Low-temperature fluxes will go into a melt at high temperature, but they can also boil off, causing pinholes, blisters, or craters in the fired glaze. This effect can happen the first time the glaze is fired or in the subsequent firings. Often, some variable (thick glaze application, different clay body, longer glaze firing, more reduction, etc.) kicks in to cause this reliable glaze to produce a bad result. This situation is often found in high-temperature glazes containing Gerstley borate, colemanite, and certain frits, which are essentially low-temperature fluxes.

Sometimes the wrong flux is used for a glaze. An example of this is Gerstley borate in a high-temperature glaze (above cone 6 2232°F). Gerstley borate is a low-temperature flux and can cause problems in a high-temperature glaze. Such problems can range from glaze blisters in the fired ware to glaze pooling or running of

Glaze blisters and runny glaze due to Gerstley borate (a low temperature flux) used in a high temperature glaze.

the vertical surfaces of the clay. Conversely, feldspars aren't the correct flux for low-temperature glazes cone 06 1830°F to cone 04 1940°F because they don't melt below cone 6 2232°F. When developing a glaze or clay body formula, always research the correct group of flux materials available and use the correct amount for optimum results.

Eutectic Effects of Materials

A eutectic effect occurs when two or more materials combine and cause a melt at the lowest possible temperature. The most common example of eutectic principles at work is between lead and silica. Lead oxide melts at 1616°F and silica at 3110°F. If a glaze is mixed with 50% lead oxide and 50% silica, it should melt at the halfway point (2363°F). However, this mixture would melt at the much lower temperature of approximately 1472°F. This is a eutectic effect at work.

There are many other single and multiple combinations of materials in clay body and glaze formulas that can produce a similar lower melting point effect. The specific raw materials used will determine the eutectic characteristics of the clay or glaze formula. Since silica and alumina are found in every clay body and glaze formula and are very refractory, they will most likely be combined with feldspars, frits, boron compounds, lead, or other low-, medium-, and high-temperature fluxes. Eutectic combinations help bring the maturing ranges of clay bodies and glazes down to practical firing temperatures. When choosing a flux, the main criteria is whether the flux is suitable for the temperature range the clay or glaze will reach. A low-temperature flux that forms a eutectic with materials in a glaze or clay body won't function properly if the clay or glaze goes to high temperature.

A common but unwanted eutectic effect can occur when a glaze overlaps or

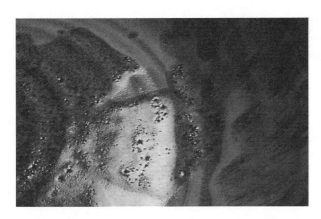
Incompatible overlapping glazes cause blisters.

partially covers another glaze. In one or both formulas, there is a raw material that causes extreme melting to take place at the overlap. The fired overlapping section of glaze can run off the pot or bubble with craters, all caused by an over-fluxed glaze area. Reduction kiln atmospheres can intensify the effect because it can cause increased fluxing of any metallic coloring oxides found in either glaze. Test each combination of raw materials in both glaze formulas to find what materials cause such a eutectic.

The melting point of the flux and its eutectic reactions with the formula have to be taken into consideration. Most of the common combinations of flux, materials, and eutectic properties can be observed by looking at batch formulas of a glaze or clay body. For example, after looking at the batch formulas of cone 9 2336°F clay bodies, it can be inferred that feldspar may be the major flux reacting with the other materials in the clay body. Most formulas will use between 5% to 20% feldspar to achieve a dense, vitreous, mature, clay body at cone 9. It's not necessary to know exactly what eutectic combinations come into play, only that they work. Other fluxes and different temperature range formulas can also be viewed in this manner.

Many factors control the melting of ceramic materials. No one factor dominates – several forces compete, compound, and occasionally neutralize ceramic mixtures as they heat in the kiln. There are many variables that result in a clay body or glaze formula reaching maturity. By understanding the powerful forces that cause melting, you will have a valuable tool to achieve successful clay bodies and glazes at any temperature range. Your knowledge and skill with the materials would be incomplete if the only thing you knew to do was increase the temperature. While higher temperatures will increase melting, it's often not an available or practical method. By experimenting with the methods above, you will have greater flexibility and control over the raw materials in your clay and glaze formulas.

Chapter 8

Mix Your Own Clay or Buy Premixed?

We've all had doubts about how to consistently get a good supply of moist clay for ceramic projects. For every potter who mixes their own clay and has problems, there is a potter who buys premixed clay and has problems. Because moist clay is such a critical part of production, finding the best source can't be left to chance.

Clay Bodies

Combinations of clays, feldspars, talc, grog, and other materials can constitute a clay body. Exactly what combinations and amounts of various raw materials are used will be determined in part by the temperature range, forming method, shrinkage, absorption, fired color, and function of the finished ceramic object. A clay body formula is the final product in the selection process of many possible raw material choices. Some clay body formulas contain only one ingredient, others accommodate many different clays and raw materials. Making good pots or sculpture depends on the suitability, accuracy, and consistency of the clay body formula, whether the clay is mixed in your studio or arrives by truck from the ceramics supply company. The first question to consider is whether your particular clay body produces the results you need. If so, how can you keep getting it?

There are positive and negative aspects of both premixed and self-mixed clay. Every potter will find different areas that are relevant to their studio situation. Knowing the correct questions to ask will result in a clear understanding of your own clay supply needs. After examining each option, the appropriate source for clay will become apparent.

Stock Clay Body Formulas and Custom Formulas

Learning about stock clay bodies and custom clay body formulas can prevent many potential problems later. When purchasing stock premixed clay or developing your own custom clay body formulas, work with formulas that produce good results under a wide range of conditions. The ideal clay body formula can function if mixed slightly differently from the original formula. A few percent more or less of each raw material in the formula shouldn't cause a significant difference in the forming characteristics or fired qualities of the clay body. A good clay body formula will also take slight variations in kiln atmosphere and firing temperatures (a two or three pyrometric cone range is realistic) and still produce acceptable results.

The best situation is to find such a clay body and move toward an aesthetic objective in your work that will allow for slight variations in size, texture, and color. Some potters make the initial mistake of trying to produce an item to exact specifications, only to find that their raw materials and forming methods can't meet an unrealistic ideal. Large commercial dinnerware manufacturers invest millions of dollars to make perfect porcelain plates and even then, 30% of their production has defects.

Whether mixing your own clay or buying from a ceramic supplier, it's always a good idea to mark the pots in some small way for each new batch of clay. The mark can be used as a code to distinguish each batch of mixed clay as it goes through the production process. If a problem develops with the clay, the entire production from the suspect batch can be tested. Without coding, it's difficult to know which batch of clay caused which defects. Don't waste time, effort, and kiln space by using defective clay trying to produce good pots.

Mixing Your Own Clay

Mixing your own clay under specific conditions does offer benefits, but carefully consider if the advantages are worth the labor, effort, and expense. A major benefit is the greater flexibility for changing and adjusting the clay body formula and its moisture content. You can do this much faster when mixing your own clay while controlling quality at the earliest stages of production.

Ask yourself if the clay body depends on a very specific finished characteristic or color. Do the forming qualities of the moist clay require you to closely adhere to the exact clay body formula? If so, consider mixing your own clay. For example, if you use a porcelain clay body that requires clean mixing conditions to prevent contamination and you can't get clean firing porcelain from a ceramics supplier, consider mixing your own clay.

Mixing your own clay insures (if the raw materials are onsite) a steady supply of moist clay for production. You can mix as little or as much clay as required for a specific project or mix several different clay body formulas and store them until needed. You'll have great control over your supply of clay, a crucial factor in any production situation and can mix and test a variety of clay body formulas in a short time.

Clay trimmings can also be reprocessed, greatly reducing wasted materials. However, since clay is, relatively speaking, dirt cheap and your labor is valuable, decide if reprocessing is worth the effort. The time and labor required to store and mix clay trimmings might be better used for more profitable projects. Every pottery business will have to evaluate this factor on an individual basis.

Mixing your own clay offers the intangible benefit of allowing you to be completely involved in the pottery endeavor. Many potters started in pottery or sculpture to realize their artistic goals and mixing clay and making pots are intrinsically tied together. In such situations, the process is just as important as the product.

Mixing your own clay is labor intensive. Under the right conditions, it can offer greater control over the supply and quality of the clay but there is a high price for these benefits. The most expensive part of making ceramic objects is the time and labor involved in producing the work. The cost of clay, glazes, raw materials, and equipment, doesn't even approach the cost of your labor. This central economic fact should be the starting point when deciding whether to purchase premixed moist clay or mix your own. Every hour you spend ordering, stacking, and mixing clay is an hour you won't spend making pots. Think of mixing your own clay as starting a clay-mixing business (with yourself as the customer) to supply your other business (the production of ceramic objects). Once you decide to mix clay, you'll have two businesses to finance, manage, and maintain, with a whole other set of costs and problems. Going back another step in the production cycle would entail mining and transporting the clay to the studio. At some point, it's counterproductive to move backward in the production cycle.

Mixing your own clay is capital intensive. Purchasing clay-mixing machinery is expensive. Maintenance and repairs also cost money. If you intend to do your own maintenance and repairs, add the time that will take to the cost of production. Buying and maintaining a pug mill and clay-mixing machine can use up money that could be spent for other business expenses that might return a greater profit. Purchasing smaller machines than needed will result in slower clay production and possibly higher maintenance cost due to an under-powered, inadequately designed mixer or pug mill. Purchasing larger machines will consume greater amounts of capital and result in unused production capacity. You'll have to devote some serious time and effort to research and find the best machines for your production requirements.

Mixing your own clay means purchasing and storing dry clay materials. Ordering dry clays should be done in a way that insures that a steady supply will always be available so there will be no delays in the clay-mixing operation. The greater the quantity of dry materials you purchase, the lower the cost per pound, but your capacity for storage and the amount of money available must be balanced against the quantity discount. Clay-mixing areas and clay storage areas for dry and wet clay should be as close as possible to production areas to save labor and time when moving the clay. Remember, the more you touch the clay, the more money it costs.

Mixing your own clay will require knowledge of raw materials and the ability to formulate a clay body. Since the formula and clay mixing are under your personal control, you can protect any unique handling or firing characteristics. Raw materials used in the clay body formula can change in chemical composition, particle size, or levels of contamination. Who-

ever develops the clay body formula must know what irregularities will affect the moist clay and how to adjust the clay mix as required by the circumstances.

Buying Premixed Clay

Buying premixed clay lets the professionals do what they should do best – blending clays under accurate quality-control conditions. Ceramics suppliers should be knowledgeable about the current track record of every clay and note any irregular shipments from the mines. Most suppliers want to stay in business and be competitive, which means they try to keep their customers satisfied with a good product. If premixed clay is an option, choose the supplier with the best reputation for quality and customer service.

Buying premixed clay bodies can offer a major advantage over mixing your own clay – the convenience of ready-to-use clay cannot be overstated. Premixed clay allows you to concentrate on producing work for sale or show.

Buying premixed clay saves capital that won't be spent on purchasing and maintaining clay-mixing equipment. This money can be used on the primary business of making ceramic objects, not making the clay to make ceramic objects.

It's always a good idea to buy premixed clay that is coded with the specific batch and mixing date. The code on each box of clay suggests an effort toward quality control and a record for future reference. Mark each of your pots with a code that corresponds to the supplier's code. In this way, you can isolate a bad batch of clay and trace it back to the ceramics supplier's coded batch. If other potters had problems with that particular batch, the supplier will have a record and you'll have a better chance of getting a replacement batch of clay.

Premixed clay is only as good as the clay body formula and the quality-control practices of the ceramics supplier. Suppliers have many different stock clay bodies designed for various temperature ranges, forming methods, fired colors, and kiln firing atmospheres. An advantage of using a stock moist clay body is that many other potters have and use the formula with acceptable results. This doesn't guarantee that the clay body will work in every firing situation. Some clay body formulas generate more customer complaints than others, but if these formulas were extremely unsound, keeping them in production wouldn't be economically feasible. Making a clay body that will fit everyone's needs is impossible. Carefully investigate and test several stock clay bodies to obtain the best clay for your requirements.

Ceramics suppliers list the stock clay body name along with a brief description of the clay's handling and firing characteristics. Clay body shrinkage and absorption figures at various temperatures are also noted. Remember, all this information is gathered from conditions that might not be present in your studio. Kiln size and firing cycles can change both the shrinkage and absorption rates of the fired clay. Use the catalog description only as a guideline. When considering any clay body, test it in your own kiln. Before purchasing a stock clay body, ask the supplier for the names of other potters who use that moist clay. One or two phone calls will produce more information about the handling and firing qualities of the clay than the brief descriptions of the clay in the ceramics supply catalog.

You don't have to mix your own clay to be able to use your own clay body formula. Developing your own clay body can be a creative expression without the labor of mixing the clay. Most suppliers require a minimum order (1000 to 2000 pounds) for private or custom mixed formulas to compensate for the time and effort required to clean the mixing machines and weigh out the clay. A custom mixed formula can be an expensive mistake if you're not completely familiar with clay body formulas and raw materials. The ceramics supplier isn't responsible for the results produced by a private formula and has limited liability for the stock bodies they produce. If a problem is caused by a stock clay, the supplier will replace only the clay and not cover damages caused by the defective clay. It is your responsibility to choose the correct stock clay body or private clay body formula to meet your requirements. Whatever moist clay you choose, do several test pieces in a regular production kiln rather than in a small test kiln that won't give accurate results. Don't commit a whole body of work to a new clay body without thorough testing.

Buying premixed clay can allow you the flexibility to try out several different stock clay bodies from a supplier. Many suppliers give free samples to good customers. Without having to become involved in the clay body formulating and mixing process, you can concentrate on each stock clay body's forming and firing characteristics. By experimenting with moist clays from several different ceramics supply companies, you will have a greatly increased range of choices.

Buying premixed clay can save valuable storage space. You don't need excessive amounts of dry clays or mixing machines. If your ceramics supplier is professionally organized, you should be able to pick up as much moist clay as you need or have it shipped for quick delivery. Choose the ceramics supplier with the best reputation for accuracy and reliability in mixing clay. If the closest supplier isn't the best choice for reliability, choose the most reliable, whatever the distance. The increase in shipping costs and inconvenience of distance doesn't compare with inaccurately mixed clay. Eventually, a raw material problem will show up in the premixed clay. Defects caused by raw materials will happen even when mixing your own formulas. This is just the inevitable result of working with clay. When a problem does occur, a good supplier will do everything possible to help resolve the issue. Don't compound the problem by finding yourself with bad clay from an unresponsive supplier.

Buying premixed clay changes the quality-control aspect to one of monitoring the moist clay as it arrives in the studio. Check each batch of clay for raw color, consistency, and fired results. Most potters don't have time to take a small sample from each 50-pound box of clay and fire it in the kiln. Any amount of testing before committing your labor to a new load of clay is worth the effort. Try to time the next clay delivery while you still have some old clay available, then work the new clay into the firing schedule slowly. While this requires advance planning, it gives some measure of insurance because a whole kiln load of work won't be based on a new batch of clay. Potters often exhaust their moist clay supply and then order a new batch. By the time the new clay arrives, they're behind and start making new pieces without testing. If the new batch of clay is defective, they lose time and money. Plan ahead to avoid this situation.

Buying premixed clay means relinquishing partial control of the ceramics production operation. Since monitoring every aspect of production down to the smallest detail is impossible, carefully choose the areas where control is critical. Most ceramics suppliers regard their stock clay body formulas as proprietary information and won't reveal the exact formula. When problems with forming or firing happen, it can be difficult to track down the cause because you don't know the formula. Reputable suppliers will give you any information on bad shipments of clays from the mine or mixing irregularities that might help in resolving the cause of the defect. In many cases, without the clay body formula it's impossible to re-

solve the problem. You must decide if the occasional mixing irregularities and loss of control are worth the advantages of premixed clay.

Buying premixed clay means you must be an informed consumer. If a raw material is not readily available, the ceramics supplier may make a substitution to the original formula or if a clay is no longer mined, a permanent replacement clay will be used in the formula. Both situations happen more frequently than many potters realize. Notifying every customer about a clay body change every time one occurs is not economically feasible for the ceramics supplier. Always ask about clay body material substitutions before ordering clay. Over the years, many stock clay body formulas change so much that very little is left of the original formula. As mines exhaust their supply of clay or the clay is present but not economically profitable to mine, substitute clays have to be found. It's a challenge to incorporate the correct substitute clay into the formula without changing the working properties, fired color, shrinkage, and absorption qualities of the original formula. Don't assume that because the moist clay body's name stays the same, the actual formula stays the same.

Buying premixed clay forces a reliance on another person or company to supply your studio with a vital raw material. As in any cooperative enterprise, problems will occur and rational compromises have to be worked out to gain the objective – good moist clay when you need it. Some people can't find a reputable ceramics supplier or don't want to compromise their requirements for moist clay. Continuing to use a supplier's premixed or custom mixed clay body in such situations will only cause more problems. In short, there are some potters and ceramics suppliers who, for whatever reason, cannot function together effectively. Recognize this situation and choose another supplier or make your own clay, but don't remain in a problem-prone cycle.

The Economics of Clay

The profit margins on moist clay are very low. If suppliers carefully calculated all their production costs, many would discover that they just break even or make a very small profit from moist clay sales. Suppliers hope to make a profit on the other items sold along with the clay, including raw materials, tools, glazes, books, and equipment. Economic factors dictate the situation many potters face every time they order clay from a supplier – ceramics suppliers (count yourself if you're mixing your own clay) cannot afford to invest in expensive high-tech mixing machines and pug mills. Clay-mixing operations aren't monitored by a staff of highly trained personnel as in larger ceramics industries. Suppliers have no room in their profit margin for these costs of production when they are forced by the marketplace to sell moist clay for pennies per pound. On the other side of the equation, potters can't pay higher prices for moist clay when they don't have large profit margins on their finished ware.

Potters pay literally pennies per pound for moist clay and expect a guaranteed perfect product. These expectations are unrealistic. Would anyone pay $5 a pound for perfect, guaranteed, no-defect, premixed clay? While the clay would be a dream to use, the price would be a nightmare. How much would you have to charge for an object produced from such clay? Could it be sold at that price? The answers to these questions have already been worked out in the marketplace. Potters shouldn't expect a low-tech product (premixed moist clay) to produce a high-tech product (zero-defect pots or sculpture). It just doesn't fit, logically or economically. Whether mixing your own moist clay or buying premixed, the same economic limitations apply.

It makes economic sense to design ceramic pieces that won't be affected by the variable qualities of incoming clay. The objects should also be able to sustain a wide range of forming and firing variables. Inconsistency and diversity are built into the materials and the conditions under which they are formed into finished pots. Allow for as many variables as function and aesthetics will allow while still producing satisfying pots. Don't accept less than perfect work, but broaden your definition of "perfect" to allow for the economic forces.

A thorough and complete understanding of ceramic materials is equally important. Only when you are aware of the positive and negative characteristics of raw materials, can you make an informed decision about which materials to use for a clay body or glaze formula to get the result you want.

The decision to mix your own clay or buy premixed clay from a ceramic supplier should be based on your studio situation, taking into consideration several different sets of criteria. The convenience of having premixed clay arrive at your studio must be weighed against your lack of control in mixing the clay formula. If you have the time and energy and want to control the unique quality of your clay, mixing clay should be an option. The cost of buying premixed clay has to be balanced against the time and labor that could be used to make more pots. One answer doesn't fit all situations, nor should it since every potter has individual requirements. The first step in obtaining the correct clay supply is to understand your own needs.

Chapter 9

The Perfect Clay Body?

Is there a perfect clay body? No. Are some clay bodies better than others? Certainly.

A combination of clays, fluxes, and fillers form a working definition of the term clay body. In the past, one or two elements created a clay body. Clays were dug up from a site and possibly sand or other materials were added to the mix depending on what worked well in past firings. With a scientific understanding of raw materials came increasingly complicated clay body formulas. Just like baking a cake, subtle variations can be introduced that change the characteristics of the whole mix.

One way to think of clay formulas is to break down the total mixture into three basic parts: clays, fluxes, and fillers. Each part serves a function in the formula to determine forming characteristics, drying shrinkage, surface texture, fired absorption, fired shrinkage, and color. Within each part many different individual materials can be used to fulfill the requirement for clay, flux, or filler. For example, if the formula requires flux, there are many frits and feldspars that could fill that part of the formula. However, you must decide which of the available frits or feldspars are appropriate for the clay body. The best clay body formulas have the appropriate raw materials and the correct ratios of clays, fluxes, and fillers to achieve their desired result.

Clays

Clays are grouped by their refractory qualities, particle size, oxide composition, loss on ignition, shrinkage rates, absorption rates, and other defining characteristics. The basic clay groups found in clay body formulas are fire clays, ball clays, kaolins, stoneware clays, bentonites, and earthenware clays. Within each major group are subgroups that further define a particular clay characteristic such as plastic kaolin and nonplastic kaolin. Grolleg is a plastic kaolin, while English China Clay is a nonplastic kaolin. Each group and subgroup encompasses many individual brand names of clay. For example, within the ball clay group are Tennessee ball clay #9, Taylor ball clay, Kentucky ball clay OM#4, Kentucky Special, and Thomas ball clay. Each group of clays, ball clays, stoneware clays, fire clays, and earthenware clays contributes specific attributes to the total clay body formula such as particle size, green strength, fired strength, fired color, shrinkage, plasticity, texture, forming abilities, and low amounts of warping in drying and firing.

When a particular clay isn't available, another clay from the same group or subgroup can be substituted. By choosing a clay from the same group, most of the clay characteristics will remain consistent. In throwing bodies, Thomas ball clay can be substituted for Kentucky ball clay OM#4 ball clay because both are from the same group of clays (ball clay) and have the best chance of matching. Other factors such as plasticity, green strength, particle size distribution, and metallic oxide content should also be considered to get the closest possible match when you need to make a substitution.

Fluxes

Fluxes help lower the melting point of heat-resistant clays and fillers in a clay body. Increasing the amount of flux also increases the glass formation with the clay body. A primary purpose of a flux is to cause the clay body to melt at a predetermined maturing range. In functional pottery, the maturing range occurs when absorption, shrinkage, and fired color are compatible with the glaze, producing a dense vitreous clay body. In high-temperature functional pottery (2232°F and higher), the maturing range of most clay bodies can be two or three cones in length. However, many sculpture pieces are fired just below their maturing range to minimize shrinkage and warping in the clay.

Every temperature range has an appropriate choice of flux materials that will work correctly. Using the wrong flux can have serious consequences. If a low-melting flux is used in a high-temperature clay body, the clay may be over-fired. If a high-temperature flux is used in a low-temperature clay body, it won't melt. In such cases, the flux acts like filler in the clay body formula. The appropriate flux and the correct amount must be used in the clay body. An over-fluxed clay body can bloat, slump, shrink excessively, and fuse to the kiln shelves. Learning about various fluxes will reveal groups of fluxes that work well in each of the temperature ranges. When increasing the flux component of a clay body formula, always make test pieces and place them in a regular production kiln on top of an old kiln shelf. Be aware that firing clay and glazes in small test kilns can produce inaccurate results because small kilns fire and cool faster than large ones. Ceramic materials need endpoint temperatures to melt but also need the time to reach that endpoint temperature for complete melting.

When choosing the flux for a clay body, the minimum and maximum amounts that can be used are fairly flexible. In the fired clay body, 2% to 3% percent variations in the amount of flux won't make a significant difference. An exception is when frits are used in the clay body because they drastically shorten the maturing range of the clay. Frits are a combination of oxides that have already been fired and can be considered as manmade feldspars. They are very fast acting and potent fluxes and form glass when used alone. A low-fire dense clay body with 7% to 10% frit might be under-fired at cone 06 (1830°F) and over-fired and melted at cone 05 (1915°F). When using frits in clay bodies, remember that the maturing range of the clay body can be shortened and some frits are slightly soluble and break down when wet, causing the moist clay body to get extremely hard or rubbery soft, depending on the frit.

Talc (magnesium silicate) is a common insoluble raw material that can be used in low-fire bodies from cone 06 (1830°F) to cone 04 (1940°F). Talc helps reduce dry and fired shrinkage and reduces warping while increasing the chance of a good glaze fit. Many low-fire clay bodies are composed mostly of 50% talc and 50% ball clay. However, when talc is present in high amounts, the clay body won't have much plasticity. When talc and iron are present in high-temperature bodies, a warm brown fired color is possible in reduction atmospheres. When talc is combined with frit or nepheline syenite, the combination can cause the clay body to become very vitreous at low temperature ranges.

In the mid to high temperature ranges, cone 6 (2232°F) to cone 10 (2381°F) feldspars are the best flux choice in a clay body. As an example of their melting characteristics when used alone, they melt at cone 6 and by cone 10 are semiopaque glasses.

The basic groups of feldspar used in ceramics are soda feldspars, which melt at approximately 100°F lower than potash spars, and lithium feldspars, which are the most refractory and can produce semi-opaque matte glazes at stoneware temperatures. Within the groups of feldspars, many individual feldspars can be chosen for a clay body formula. The main reason to use feldspars is their ability to go into a melt easily and slowly over a wide temperature range. Most successful functional stoneware bodies have two- to three-cone limits (maturing range) where they will be dense and vitreous without being over-fired or under-fired. Feldspars are the ideal group of fluxes allowing for this situation to develop in the clay body.

Fillers

Fillers reduce clay body shrinkage and warping in the drying and firing stages. Flint, silica sand, sawdust, mullite, calcined kaolin, calcined alumina, and grogs of various sizes are the most widely used fillers. While flint can be called a glass former, it needs very high temperatures (3200°F) to go into a melt by itself. It is only when flint is combined with a flux that the melting temperature of the flint is decreased.

Flint acts as a filler in that it reduces dry shrinkage and warping in the clay body. If the amount of filler is too high, the clay body's plastic qualities are decreased. Clay bodies designed for slab forming and tile bodies usually have more filler or non-plastic material than throwing bodies. Less warping and shrinkage in tile bodies is a higher priority than plasticity.

A perfect clay body is a subjective term, but the chance of realizing such an ideal goal increases when the correct amount and ratio of clay, flux, and fillers are present. When designing a clay body, take into consideration the forming method, drying shrinkage, firing temperature,

kiln atmosphere, glaze interaction, fired color, fired shrinkage, and fired density.

After testing many formulas and having students try out the most promising results, I developed the Zam Super Body – a good throwing body with a shrinkage rate of 6% in drying (see below). It fires from cone 6 to cone 10 and has a medium brown color in reduction atmospheres. It fires to a light cream color in oxidation and has a total fired shrinkage of 12% at cone 6 and 12.5% at cone 10. The body has an absorption rate of 2.6% at cone 6 and 0.50% at cone 10. As a standard rule, first mix up a small amount of any test clay body or glaze with an old kiln shelf underneath to prevent any possible damage to the kiln. After a good test result, mix up a larger batch and test until the new formula has proven itself over a few kiln firings.

Developing a clay body formula is often a personal choice based on theory, experience, and current knowledge of materials. Listed are the clays, fluxes, and fillers, along with the reasons for choosing each material. A perfect clay body doesn't exist, but it helps to know what considerations are made when a formula is developed.

Zam Super Body

15 parts A.P.G. Missouri fire clay 28-mesh (clay)

Fire clays are the weakest part of any clay body formula when it comes to quality and reliability. In fact, if the clay body contains fire clay, eventually a problem can be traced to this marginal performance clay. The problems in fire clays can range from excessive and small size silica (causing cooling cracks), high organic content, lignites or coal (causing black coring), calcium nodules (causing lime pop), and sand (causing gritty quality in clay). Other impurities that have been found in fire clays are tree branches, metal bolts, paper, rocks, and cigarette butts. Based on its poor quality, many potters choose not to use any fire clay in their clay body formulas.

Overall, the negative aspects of fire clay can be mitigated by spreading the risk and using two different fire clays in the formula. Inspecting the dry clay before mixing will help prevent large and obvious contaminates from entering the clay mix. Some pottery supply companies screen the fire clay, which helps significantly to improve the quality. The screened clay costs more, but if it saves one pot it's worth the extra price. Fire clays will eventually produce a problem in the clay body and using this marginal quality group of clays should be calculated on a risk versus reward basis. You must decide if the good qualities of fire clay in the clay body formula are worth the risk.

Why use fire clay? The coarse or large particle size of the clay makes it ideal for adding tooth or standup ability in throwing and sculpture bodies. Fire clays reduce the dry shrinkage, fired shrinkage, and warping potential of a clay body. Their refractory or heat resistant nature allows for a high-temperature clay body. Why aren't good quality fire clays mined and sold to potters? Simple economics – potters buy less than one tenth of a percent of all the clay mined. The fire clays that are currently being mined meet or exceed the major user industry's requirements. Large industries such as steel manufacturing, casting, and ceramic refractories control the market and the quality of the fire clay. Potters and ceramic supply companies don't have the purchasing power to demand a better grade of fire clay from the mines.

10 parts Hawthorn Bond fire clay 35-mesh (clay)

While it appears that fire clays contribute many potential problems to the clay body formula, they also serve a useful function in their ability to add large particle sizes to the total mix. Some of the best

clay bodies have small, medium, and large clay platelet sizes. The variation in platelet sizes (large platelets in fire clays, medium platelets in stoneware clays, small platelets in ball clays) mechanically interlock when moist, resulting in greater clay surface areas touching which increases plasticity.

Fire clays also contribute iron and manganese particles that in reduction atmospheres can give the random pattern of brown and black specks in the fired clay body. Too little fire clay will lower the maturing range of the clay body and cause the body to become soft with little grit or tooth when being formed on the wheel. Excess fire clay will make the fired clay too porous, nonplastic, and decrease the fired strength of the pots. Clay bodies with no fire clay often feel and throw like cream cheese. How much grit or tooth you want in moist clay is a personal choice.

40 parts Goldart stoneware 200-mesh (clay)

Goldart clay is the backbone of the formula because it's the major material by weight. Stoneware clays are relatively clean, medium platelet size clays and, as their name implies, can be fired to stoneware temperatures cone 6 2232°F to cone 10 2381°F. As a group of clays, they can almost be used as the total clay component in a formula. While Goldart stoneware had high concentrations of sulfur in the past, it has been kept under control for the last 15 years. (Since most clays are mined for industrial use, it's a rare event when a mining company listens and responds to potters' needs and cleans up their clay.)

Stoneware clays have greater plasticity than fire clays, but they aren't as plastic as ball clays. As a group, they make an excellent choice for a clay body formula because of their reliability, particle size, and adaptability with other clays in the formulas. Low amounts of stoneware clay will cause the other clays in the formula to unbalance the mix. The amount and type of other clays will then dictate the direction the formula will follow with less than optimum results. Conversely, too high a stoneware clay percentage in the clay body will detract from the qualities of the other clays in the formula. The correct amount of flux and filler must be included for a balanced clay body formula.

15 parts Old Hickory Thomas ball clay (clay)

Ball clays contribute plasticity to the clay body and increase the rate of shrinkage during the drying and firing stages. A balance of greater plasticity and a minimum amount of shrinkage must be considered before determining the amount of ball clay for the formula. Low amounts of ball clay will produce a formula with little bending ability. Such a clay body will be "short" or crack easily when bent in the forming process. Too much ball clay can produce shrinkage and warping in the drying and firing stages. When a high amount of ball clay is used in a formula, the clay body often feels gummy when moist, leaving loose clay in your hands after pulling up a form on the wheel. The body can also feel rubbery or soft when force is exerted against it during forming operations.

10 parts Flint 200-mesh (filler)

The addition of flint to a clay body decreases warping and shrinkage in the drying stage. High amounts of flint can make the moist clay less plastic. In cone 6 2232°F to cone 10 2381°F throwing bodies, the amount of flint should generally be kept below 14%. However, in porcelain clay body formulas, flint levels can reach 25%. Flint also reacts with feldspar during the firing to augment the development of glass formation within the clay body. While clays and other materials such as feldspars and frits have a silica compo-

nent, the amount of silica isn't usually enough to achieve the optimum effect in the vitrification or melting process in the clay body. Flint 200x-mesh is used primarily in clay bodies. Flint 325x-mesh is frequently used in glaze formulas, but either mesh can be interchanged in a clay body formula. The presence of flint in the clay body promotes a better glaze fit and decreases the chances of glaze crazing defects.

7 parts Custer feldspar (flux)

Feldspar is the major flux or glass former in the clay body, but too much feldspar in the clay body can cause the pot to slump or attach itself to the kiln shelf. Using too much feldspar can also cause the body to shrink excessively and warp during the firing. Over-fluxing caused by excessive amounts of feldspar can darken the fired clay color if any iron is present in the formula. The fired clay can become brittle, weak, or bloated. In extreme overfluxing, the clay body can achieve the "Chernobyl Effect" – a molten mass on the kiln floor.

Too little feldspar in the clay body will lower the amount of glass formation in the fired clay, which can lead to improper glaze fit and moisture seepage through the porous fired clay form. One way to fix a clay body that doesn't hold liquid is to tighten up the body with increased amounts of flux. Once the correct amount of flux is added, the absorption rate of the fired clay will decrease and it will hold liquids. Most stoneware functional pottery should have an absorption rate of 3% or lower. A glaze should never be considered as a sealer or waterproof coating because water will always seep through any small imperfection in the glaze. The only reason to use glazes is for aesthetic considerations and to produce a smooth functional surface for cleaning.

Generally, potash feldspars such as Custer or G-200 are used over soda feldspars F-4 and nepheline syenite because as a group potash feldspars are less soluble. Soda spars can sometimes break down in the body, causing the moist clay to become thixotropic or rubbery in the forming process. The clay can also feel soft and have the consistency of gelatin when being worked on the wheel. As an increasing amount of water is applied to form the pot, it becomes very soft and loses its ability to hold a thrown curve. In time, the clay can't support its own weight and the form usually slumps or can't be pulled higher.

3 parts Sheffield Clay or Redart (both flux & clay)

Sheffield clay is a low-temperature earthenware clay mined by Sheffield Pottery Supply Co. in western Massachusetts. It serves more than one major function in the clay body formula. When a raw material serves more than two or three functions, it should be strongly considered because of the higher degree of integration in the total clay body. Sheffield clay has a high iron content that causes a brown clay body color in reduction and a medium cream color in oxidation atmospheres. Being a low-fire clay, it promotes fluxing action in the clay body. Sheffield clay also contributes different clay platelet sizes to the total clay body. Redart, a low-temperature clay, can be substituted for Sheffield clay. Both high iron clays add color, clay platelet variation, and flux to the clay body.

When a darker color clay body is required, it's always better to incorporate high iron bearing clays than to add straight red iron oxide in the clay body formula. Adding metallic coloring oxides to the clay body for color will make the moist clay take on water very fast during the throwing process, causing the clay to become too soft. Also, metallic oxides can easily over-flux the clay body, especially in reduction atmospheres. If metallic oxides are used in the clay body, they should be limited to 2% or less. A better solution is to find a metallic oxide tied up with clay. Again, having one material cover several purposes produces a greater stability in the overall formula.

Small amounts of earthenware clay can be incorporated into clay body formulas at stoneware temperatures for color, platelet size, and minor fluxing of the clay body. However, earthenware clays or low-temperature clays shouldn't be used in amounts of more than 10% in stoneware bodies because their fluxing action will negatively react with the clay body, causing bloating, warping, and excessive fired shrinkage.

8 parts Maryland Refractories grog 48/f (filler)

Grog is manufactured from virgin deposits of alumina/silica refractory material. It is then calcined or fired to high temperature. Grog can also be manufactured by grinding up fire brick. As a rule, particle size variation is preferred when choosing grog because of the mechanical advantage of interlocking grog sizes and shapes. Different size grog particles touch and combine, causing a cohesive clay body and grog bond in the moist clay body. Grog decreases dry and fired shrinkage in the clay body. High amounts of grog can make the moist clay less plastic. In most stoneware throwing bodies, grog amounts of more than 15% affect the plasticity and handling qualities of the clay.

Since the grog is already fired and has gone through the changes that clay is subject to, it is stable. For every 10% of grog added to a clay body, fired shrinkage is decreased approximately 1%. Little or no grog in the clay body decreases the amount of tooth when the clay is being formed on the wheel. The moist clay has difficulty standing up and will slump during throwing operations. Too much grog in the clay body will cause a gritty moist clay that will be short or nonplastic in forming operations.

Grog is classified by particle size. The lower the number grog, the larger the grog particle size. Grog 8/12-mesh looks like small pebbles while grog 100-mesh is a fine powder. Grog 48/f particle size ranges from 48-mesh (about the size of beach sand) with varying smaller particles, to a powder size. It was chosen because it provides good particle size distribution in the clay body formula.

The Plasticity of Clay

In the past, Japanese potters mixed and stored moist clay for the future generations of potters. In this way, the clay was aged and made plastic. While traditional methods of making clay plastic aren't extensively used today, other methods are available to increase a clay body's plastic qualities. Two important factors determine the moist clay's plasticity – the clay body formula and the amount of time it spends in the moist state. Different clay body additives can be used to accelerate the plasticity process, but the length of time under the right conditions is still a critical factor in the development of good throwing bodies.

The unique characteristics displayed by clay/water structures contribute to the plastic qualities of moist clay. The attraction process operates on many levels. To illustrate one aspect of clay water bonding, consider that under magnification, clay looks like a plate structure, an ideal surface when brought into contact with water. Surrounding the flat platelets of clay is a thin film of water holding the platelets together. A good example of attraction can be shown when paper is torn up into small pieces. The paper represents dry clay, which doesn't bond or stick together at this point. Now add just enough water to soak each piece of paper. Once

the water is absorbed into the paper (clay platelet/water attraction process), the pieces of paper stick together and can be bent or shaped. Dry pieces of paper become plastic when brought in contact with water, which is the same principle that takes place when clay is brought into contact with water.

Increasing the Plasticity of Clay Bodies

The natural plasticity of clay water structures can be enhanced in several ways. In the past, bentonite was added to the clay body. Bentonites are an extremely plastic group of clays, but the ratio of bentonite shouldn't exceed 2% of the clay body formula because it can make the moist clay gummy when throwing on the wheel.

Adding ball clay also increases a clay body's plasticity, but amounts more than 25% can cause excessive dry shrinkage and warping. High amounts of ball clay can make the moist clay take on water at a faster rate during the throwing process, causing the clay to slump and sag during the last stages of forming on the wheel. Excessive amounts of ball clay can also cause handles to crack where they are joined to the main body of the pot. Ball clays take high amounts of water to make them plastic and have correspondingly high shrinkage rates. Any thin area such as an excessively trimmed pot bottom is likely to crack due to the high amount of ball clay in the formula. Such drying cracks occur where a thin piece of clay meets a thicker cross section of clay. The high shrinkage rate of the clay body can't take the stress of thin cross sections of clay next to thick cross sections of clay.

Mold growth in the moist clay can also increase plasticity. Mold in the moist clay increases the binding action or attraction of the clay platelets. Enhancing the film of water that binds each clay platelet with mold will increase the clay-to-clay attraction. When mixing a 100-pound batch of clay formula, add 1/2 cup beer, coffee, apple cider vinegar, or three ounces of yeast to the water. Any one of these agents will start mold growth in the clay water mixture. If kept long enough in warm dark conditions, moist clay will grow mold. Some potters complain that moldy clay smells bad or has green fuzz growing on its surface. While green mold seems to offer the best plastic additions to the moist clay, black mold growth can cause problems because it doesn't blend in with the surrounding clay body. Some types of black mold can cause voids in the moist clay and can produce problems in the forming or firing stages. Stoneware clay bodies seem to successfully accept wider variations of mold growth than porcelain clay bodies. Always mix or wedge the moldy clay before beginning the forming process.

Adding Epsom salts (magnesium sulfate) at a rate of six ounces per 100 pounds of dry clay formula can increase plasticity on another level. Epsom salts increase the attraction of clay platelets in the moist clay state, causing the clay to become flocculated. By adding Epsom salts to the water and then using the mixture in the clay-mixing operation, it disperses efficiently throughout the clay batch. Clay platelets are then drawn together as north and south poles of a magnet are attracted and bind together. The overall effect is a tight, plastic, clay body with good throwing properties.

Additive A is a unique blend of lignosulphonates and other chemicals and is a product of the paper manufacturing process. When used in amounts of 1/16% to 3/4% based on the dry weight of the clay, it can increase the moist clay's plasticity without changing its fired shrinkage, absorption, or clay color. Additive A is pro-duced in several versions, some of which contain barium in a safe nontoxic form. Additive A can eliminate the scumming common on clay bodies where soluble salts are present.[4] When used in a clay body, it has the advantage of increasing the plastic properties of the body without causing excessive shrinkage rates in the drying and firing stages.

Methods of Mixing a Clay Body

Simply mixing the dry clay body formula and adding the correct amount of water is all that's really required to achieve a plastic mass of usable clay. Hand mixing clay will accomplish the goal, but when more moist clay is required, machines are labor and time saving necessities. The moist clay is blended and compacted much better by a machine than could ever be accomplished by mixing the dense, heavy clay by hand. Mixing clay by machine is recommended when consistency and large amounts of clay are required. The goal should be to get each clay platelet surrounded by a film of water. When this is achieved, it will insure the greatest chance for clay body plasticity.

Clay Mixer and Pug Mill

The combination of clay mixer and pug mill is the most efficient and popular method of mixing clay. Ceramics supply companies use both machines in the production of stock clay bodies and private formula clay bodies. Clay mixer and pug mill production of moist clays is the most efficient way to achieve good working qualities in a clay body. The dry clay and water are blended in the clay mixer. Moist clay is then placed into the pug mill and

---

4.   Additive A types 1, 3, and 4 are used in clay bodies with soluble salt problems. Additive A is manufactured by Lignotech USA, P.O. Box 582, Lavonia, GA 30553, PH: (706) 356-1288.

compressed by a mechanical screw. It then goes through a chamber where the air is removed and the clay is extruded out of the pug mill nozzle in usable condition. Clay compacting can also make for a denser fired clay body because pugged milled formulas can run 1/4% to 1/2% less in fired absorption than the same formula not pugged. Compacted clay platelets fuse faster and more completely during the firing than noncompacted platelets.

A further increase in plasticity is achieved by wedging the clay before throwing it on the wheel. Wedging clay by hand is important for several reasons. Ceramics supply companies mix and pug all their moist clay. The tube or block of clay that is extruded from the pug mill can have weak spots or shear lines in the moist clay. A potential problem occurs when fine particles in the moist clay body are rubbed by the pug mill auger blade and separated from coarse particles in the clay, causing two separate clay bodies within the pug mill. When the clay is turned or screwed through the machine, fine particle clays are moved up against coarse particle clays in a concentric ring pattern. When the clay is extruded, the two different clay bodies have a seam line where cracks develop. When the cracks appear, they look very much like the circular pattern of a sliced jelly roll cake. Since the extruded clay is moist and compacted, the cracks might not be visible when the slab of clay is in its plastic shipping bag.

To find out if a pugged milled clay has such a weak area, slice two inches from the extruded face of the moist clay and let the slab sit in water overnight. If the clay shows jelly roll cracking patterns the next day, it must be wedged thoroughly before you attempt to make wide-based forms such as plates. Forms with a wide base are more likely to fail because of their greater horizontal surface area. The sheared lines in the moist clay are spread over a wide surface and upon drying the clay sepa-

rates, causing a crack. Clay should be wedged by hand. This will change the direction of the platelets and remove any internal platelet disruption caused by the pug mill extrusion. Wedging the clay also serves to align the clay platelets for the throwing operation. Potters have different preferences for the hardness or softness of throwing clay. Wedging before throwing helps the potter judge the clay's moisture content. Adjustment can then be made to make the clay harder or softer.

Filter Press

In a filter press operation, dry clay is mixed with water to form a liquid slurry, then pumped into a series of absorbent leaf-shaped bags. As the bags are compressed, excess water is pressed from the liquid clay then the "leaves" of moist clay go on to the pug mill for further mixing and de-airing. In filter pressing, each clay platelet is surrounded by water in the slurry stage. The water soaking period produces clay with greater plasticity than other mixing methods. Filter pressing is expensive, labor intensive, and not frequently used in ceramics supply clay-mixing operations.

Give It a Rest

Whatever the mixing method, the best results are obtained when the moist clay is allowed to rest or age for several days before forming begins on the wheel. After mixing, the moist clay is pliable and plastic and can be bent into shapes, but each clay platelet is not thoroughly wet (filter press clays are the exception), resulting in a lack of plasticity. The same moist clay a few days or weeks later will have most of the clay platelets saturated and surrounded with water, causing a greater increase in the plasticity of the clay body.

The Perfect Formula

Is there a perfect formula body that can accomplish miracles and overcome bad technique or improper firing cycles? No. Can the Zam Super Body do well in salt, soda, wood firing, reduction and oxidation atmospheres? Yes. Does it throw well? I think so. While it's true that one clay body can't do everything, certain combinations of clay, flux, and filler work well under many different conditions. Choosing the correct clay body is a subjective decision and if this formula doesn't meet your needs, I hope it provides a start for your own search to achieve the perfect formula. The Zam Super Body has proven itself over the years with many potters. Hopefully, potters attempting to use it will first begin with a small test batch and try it out before getting out the old mixer and making a ton.

There's no shortcut for making good pots. A super clay body or glaze formula won't lessen the time and effort involved in producing honest pots. Be prepared to test and experiment. Start by reading, experimenting, and learning from other potters to aid in the search for your own clay body formula. The magic formula is in the potter, not the clay. A good potter can go into any studio, anywhere, and scrape the clay off the floor and still make pots.

Chapter 10

Additives for Clay Bodies and Glazes

Most potters are familiar with the problems caused by finding a thick mass of glaze stuck to the bottom of their glaze bucket. The rock-hard cake of glaze seems to settle very quickly, requiring time and labor to mix and keep it in suspension. Other problems can arise when the glaze has dried on the bisque pot and becomes very soft and fragile. Handling the pot at this point significantly damages the dry glaze surface.

Glazes that settle fast in the container and glazes that dry dusty and flaky are some of the most common glaze application problems. Traditionally, Epsom salts and bentonite have been used in glazes to keep them in suspension. Starch, pancake syrup, and other organic gums have been used to bind a dusty soft raw glaze to a bisque surface. Water-soluble organic binders follow the drying characteristics of the glaze and might not cause a binding action throughout the glaze layer cross section because just the upper layer of glaze is tacked down. Alternatively, inorganic binders or glaze hardeners such as sodium silicate and potassium silicate cause the raw glaze to harden throughout the entire glaze layer. A disadvantage of sodium silicate and potassium silicate is their deflocculation quality in the glaze.[5]

To a limited extent, both types of "old technology" organic and inorganic binders work, but more effective and easier to use suspension agents and binders are available and have been used in the ceramics industry for some time. For any clay body or glaze additive to work effectively it must be easy to use and precise in its result without disrupting the glaze surface. The additive should also burn off, leaving a low residue of ash that will not affect the fired result. Many glaze and clay body remedies used in the past didn't meet such standards.

The first step is to decide whether the glaze or clay body needs an additive. Many glaze and clay body formulas work without suspension or binder components. A suspension agent might be needed if the wet glaze sinks to the bottom of the storage or mixing container or if the applied glaze flakes off and is dusty on the bisque surface. In the latter situation, a binder is required to hold the loose soft glaze in place. Binders can also be used in underglaze or overglaze metallic coloring oxide washes. The binder makes the metallic washes brush on smoothly without drying too fast on the clay body surface. If a glaze or wash dries too fast on a surface it can cause "chattering" or grabbing of the brush as the wash is applied. Binders enable a smooth flow and easily applied brush strokes to the bisque surface or a

---

5. Source information on binders *Ceramics Glaze Technology* by J.R. Taylor and A.C. Bull, publisher Pergamon Press.

raw glazed surface as in majolica painting on a raw glaze surface.

All commercial glazes contain binders to prevent the glaze from settling. Binders also aid in a smooth brush flow in the glaze application process. However, if the glaze contains a higher percentage of binder than needed, it can lead to other problems such as longer glaze drying times. The amount of binder in a glaze that causes some glazes to work well for brushing makes them unsuitable for dipping applications. One of the major advantages in mixing your own glaze formulas is the control you have over additives. Each glaze will require a specific additive in an exact amount to produce good application results. Over the past 40 years, many suspension and binder additives have been developed to meet the ceramics industry's needs. Many additives are essentially the same chemically but are produced by different companies. However, some are distinctly different and you must be careful to match the correct suspension or binder with a glaze or clay body formula.[6]

CMC

CMC (sodium carboxymethylcellulose or cellulose gum) has been used by industry for 50 years and is generally considered a nontoxic, biodegradable, water-soluble polymer. In fact, it is used as the primary thickener for a vast array of everyday products including toothpaste, syrup, lotions, and adhesives, to name a few.[7] It is also commonly used to inhibit the formation of ice crystals in ice cream and to impart body and "mouth-feel" to powdered beverages like hot chocolate.

CMC is derived from pure cellulose with wood pulp and/or chemical cotton (from cotton linters) as the raw feedstock. The cellulose is chopped and exposed to sodium monochloroacetate in an alkaline environment under rigidly controlled conditions. Subsequent purification and drying yields the white granular powder known as CMC. Batch sizes are typically 12,000 to 15,000 pounds. Over 100 different grades of CMC are commonly available and differ primarily based on degree of substitution (or DS), viscosity (i.e. molecular weight or chain length), particle size, and regulatory status (technical, food, or pharmaceutical). Common grades of CMC used in ceramic glazes are 7L or 7M. CMC is also commonly used as a binder in ceramics themselves with 7L or 7L1T being typical choices. Several different functions are performed by CMC in glazes – thickener, binder, suspension agent and drying rate inhibitor.[8]

Mixing CMC in Glazes

CMC is soluble in cold or hot water and is not affected by the pH level of the glaze (it disperses more readily in hot water). CMC can be weighed out and mixed into

---

6. Examples of other glaze and clay body additives. Macaloid: A refined hectorite ore (produced by Tam Division NL Industries) is a glaze suspension agent that can be used in clay bodies for greater green strength and plasticity. VeeGum T is basically the same material and can be substituted with the same results. Methocell: A group of water soluble cellulose organic polymers (produced by Dow Chemical U.S.A.) which acts more as a binder than a plasticizer. In some instances, organic binders have an advantage over inorganic binders in that Methocell binders will burn out of the clay body. Some grades of Methocell are used in clay extrusion processes.

7. CMC is manufactured by Hercules Inc., Aqualon Division, 500 Hercules Road, Wilmington, DE 19808-1599, PH: (800) 345-0447. CMC can be purchased through ceramics suppliers.

8. Technical source material for CMC was contributed by R. Scott Dautel of Hercules Inc./Aqualon Division.

water with a blender or mixing spoon. All the CMC/water mixture is then used in the glaze for the correct percentage of CMC to glaze ratios. Adding CMC directly to the dry glaze batch is also an option, but when water is added to the glaze it must be passed through an 80x-mesh sieve three times before the CMC can be thoroughly integrated in the mix. If a glaze is ball milled, CMC can be added before or after the mixing process. Whatever the blending system, the primary goal is to get the correct amount of CMC mixed completely into the wet glaze.

If CMC levels increase above 1%, the wet glaze might look thicker in the glaze bucket than it actually is when applied to the piece. Excess glaze water has to be removed until the correct glaze thickness is built up on the bisque or raw clay surface. Increasing the CMC level also delays the drying time of the applied glaze. Additions of CMC above 1-1/2% might cause the glaze to form rivers on the clay body surface with irregular glaze layers, and the glaze will take an excessively long time to dry. CMC is very potent and most problems with its use are due to using excessively high amounts.

CMC as a Glaze Binder

CMC in glazes contributes several important qualities to the mix of water and raw materials. Its primary function is to increase the mechanical strength of the raw glaze once it has dried on the bisque or nonbisque clay surface. Often glazes with high clay content and/or high amounts of low-density materials such as magnesium carbonate will become soft, fragile, and will form loose powder when drying on the clay body. Handling the work for decoration or stacking in a kiln often dislodges the glaze. Once in the kiln, the glaze has a greater chance of crawling due to the low mechanical bonding action of the glaze to the clay body. A binder added to the glaze will tack down loose glaze particles, allowing for overglaze decoration while creating a harder raw glaze surface. The binder can keep the raw glaze intact and in contact with the underlying clay body until sintering or the first stages of melting take place. The adhesive nature of the binder holds the dry glaze particles to each other and to the underlying clay body. A major cause of crawling occurs when a glaze forms unattached to the clay body and the fired glaze rolls back on itself, leaving dry exposed areas of clay.[9]

When used in a glaze to harden or tack a loose raw glaze in place, CMC can be added in percentages of 1/16% to 2% based on the dry weight of the glaze. The same mixing procedure should be used as when adding CMC to the glaze for its suspension properties. Start with the lowest amount of CMC and then apply the glaze over a wide test area (small glaze application areas produce inconclusive results). After the glaze has dried, note if the dusty, loose, fragile, quality of the glaze has been eliminated. The glaze should have increased durability and remain in place when rubbed. Dried glazed surfaces should be less dusty. If not, increase the CMC in 1/8% increments until the glaze has an intact dry surface.

CMC as a Glaze Suspension

CMC will keep a glaze in suspension. Visualize CMC as a bundle of long strings of rope that, when thrown into a swimming pool (water in a glaze bucket) slowly unwinds, forming a net that entangles and crosses itself in the water. When solid objects are thrown into the water (raw materials such as feldspar, dolomite, whiting, flint, clay, zinc, etc.), the CMC net keeps them from settling to the bottom.

---

9.   See chapter "Glaze Crawling – Causes and Corrections."

The suspension effect not only works in a bucket of glaze, but also when CMC is used in cough syrup. Cough syrup contains insoluble solids just like the active ingredients in a glaze (raw materials). The solids are suspended in the solution rather than dissolved. The same "netting" mechanism allows insoluble materials to be effectively suspended in a liquid. An exception to this principle occurs when soluble materials are used in a glaze (most commonly Gerstley borate, colemanite, soda ash, borax, and pearl ash) because they are dissolved in the water system of the glaze.[10]

For glaze suspension, CMC can be used in 1/8% to 2% amounts based on the dry weight of the glaze. Each glaze requires a different amount of CMC to properly suspend solids due to each formula's inherent suspension properties. Start at 1/8% CMC and if the glaze sinks to the bottom of the glaze bucket, increase the level of CMC in 1/8% increments until the liquid glaze stays in suspension.

CMC to Control Glaze Drying Time

Many glazes dry too fast on the clay body surface (either bisque or once-fired raw glaze surfaces). The greater the percentage of CMC used in a glaze, the longer the glaze will take to dry. CMC also promotes a smooth and uniform brush application of a glaze. The correct amount of CMC is determined by the specific glaze formula and method of glaze application (spraying, brushing, dipping) and the relative absorbency of the clay body surface.

CMC with Underglazes/Overglazes/Engobes

CMC can be used in underglaze/overglaze washes and engobes (3% to 4% based on the dry weight of the underglaze, overglaze or engobe). It contributes a uniform consistency to the wash, allowing for a smooth easy application over raw glazed surfaces or bisque and leather-hard surfaces. Using CMC in the base glaze to develop a nondusty raw glaze surface for overglaze painting is also sometimes necessary. In engobes, CMC enhances the plasticity of the engobe in the wet state, allowing for improved application and adherence on leather-hard clay surfaces.

Stain or Metallic Coloring Oxide Dispersion in Glazes

Thorough dispersion of raw materials is an important factor in mixing any glaze. This is especially true with glaze stains or metallic coloring oxides because an even fired glaze color depends on an even dispersion of coloring pigments. CMC helps stain and metallic coloring oxide elements disperse evenly in the water system of the glaze medium so that even the heavier metallic coloring oxides are suspended throughout the glaze mixture.

CMC in Clay Bodies

CMC increases the plasticity of moist clay bodies. When it's mixed with water, a gel-like substance forms which increases the binding properties of the clay water structure. Clay formulas that are tradi-

---

10. Whenever possible, soluble materials should not be used in glazes because they take on water in storage, causing inconsistent glaze results when the glaze is weighed out. After a glaze is mixed and some water is poured off, the actual glaze formula is changed, which can cause inconsistent glaze results. When a glaze is applied to a piece, the water in the glaze moves toward the center cross section of the form. Upon drying, the water is then carried out or evaporated, leaving greater concentrations of soluble materials on the high edges or ridges of the form. Areas that have greater concentrations of soluble materials can have a dry or bubbled surface texture after the firing. However, in some instances, concentrations of oxides as sodium, potassium, boron, and calcium can only be found in soluble materials such as Gerstley borate, colemanite, borax, pearl ash, soda ash, and wood ash in amounts required by specific glaze formula.

tionally short or nonplastic show the most effect when CMC is present. However, it can also function in any throwing or sculpture clay body with good results.

CMC can decrease the resistance generated by clay in a clay mixer and also acts as a lubricant, which improves extrusion properties when the clay body is processed through a pug mill. The clay extrusions will warp less and have smoother surfaces as they exit the pug mill barrel. Green strength, which is the unfired clay's ability to be moved around the studio or loaded into kilns without being damaged, is aided by the addition of CMC. In large ceramic pieces, the addition of CMC to the clay body can cut down on the amount of ball clay needed for the formula. Lower amounts of ball clay diminish warping and cracking in the drying stage.

To achieve increased plasticity and lower the moist clay's resistance in pug mills and mixers, concentrations of CMC starting at 1/10% up to 2% based on the dry weight of the clay can be used, depending on the particular clay body formula.

VeeGum T, VeeGum Pro, VeeGum CER

The proprietary procedure used by R.T. Vanderbilt Co., Inc. to manufacture VeeGum additives is an aqueous system (wet process), which is designed to produce uniformity and purity in the final product.[11] VeeGum T, VeeGum Pro, and VeeGum CER serve different functions when used in glaze formulas and clay bodies.

VeeGums are mined from several carefully selected veins of smectite ores which are refined and mixed for reliability and consistency. Many different types of smectites can be found in nature. Bentonites are a group of smectite ores which are familiar to potters because of their use in clay body and glaze formulas. However, not all smectites are equal in plasticity and purity. Choosing the appropriate groups of smectites and processing them correctly insures the proper degree of plasticity, purity, and reliability to form the VeeGum series of additives.

VeeGums are inorganic, complex, colloidal, magnesium aluminum silicates that are often used in toothpaste, antiperspirant, paints, pharmaceuticals, and other commercial products. In hand lotions, VeeGum disperses pigments to give maximum color value and improves spreading qualities. VeeGums have been used by potters for more than 25 years.

Each glaze or clay body formula requires a specific type and amount of VeeGum to achieve optimum results. For the most complete dispersion of glaze binders or suspension agents, use hot water when mixing and use all the mixture in the clay body or glaze batch. Any time spent testing and adjusting additives to a formula will be worth the effort in solving the problems of glaze suspension, glaze application, and clay body plasticity.

VeeGum T in Glazes

VeeGum T is primarily used as a suspension agent in glazes due to its extremely high surface area. The small platelet structure of this additive helps float or suspend in water large dense materials that are frequently found in glazes. VeeGum T is more potent than bentonite or Epsom salts that were once the traditional suspension additives used in glaze formulas. Epsom salts are soluble and the suspension effect can change when excess glaze water is poured off or evaporates

---

11.   R.T.Vanderbilt Co., Inc., 30 Winfield Street, PO Box 5150, Norwalk, CT 06856, PH: (203) 853-1400 produces VeeGums.

from the glaze bucket. Epsom salts can also change the wet glaze to an oatmeal-like consistency while imparting a lumpy texture to the wet raw glaze. Lumping and uneven glaze can also cause glaze application problems.

Aside from its superior suspension qualities, VeeGum T won't tint or change the fired color of the glaze as can sometimes happen with bentonites. Being of uniform quality, it can be placed in a glaze or clay body in exact amounts. It suspends powders and metallic coloring oxides more effectively than organic gums and won't migrate to the glaze surface upon drying as with the soluble Epsom salts.

VeeGum T in glazes prevents or retards the wet glaze from settling too fast in the glaze bucket. The actual amount of VeeGum T needed will vary depending on the concentration of dense materials contained in a particular glaze formula. Glazes that have high amounts of frit, feldspar, flint, talc, whiting, dolomite, or any dense material may be more likely to settle in the glaze bucket. A practical first step is to learn how much VeeGum T is required for proper glaze suspension. Start with a 1/4% addition based on the dry weight of the glaze batch. Mix all the dry glaze materials, then mix the glaze water with the VeeGum T separately and add the water to the dry glaze materials. Additions of water can then be added to obtain the proper glaze consistency. Run the wet glaze through an 80x-mesh sieve three times.[12] Let the glaze stand for one hour. If no improvement in glaze suspension occurs, mix a new dry batch of glaze with 1/2% VeeGum T and follow the same mixing and sieving procedures. Adding VeeGum T to an already mixed wet glaze will not fully hydrate the VeeGum T and it will have a delayed effect on glaze suspension properties. A delayed reaction can occur over time and if too much VeeGum is used, the glaze can become as thick as gelatin. Most glaze materials stay in suspension or improve considerably with the addition of between 1/4% and 2% VeeGum T (based on the dry weight of the glaze).

VeeGum T in Clay Bodies

In clay bodies, VeeGum T increases the plasticity in nonflexible (short) bodies such as porcelain, raku, sculpture, and high alumina formulas. It can also be used in throwing, ram press, extrusion, and jiggered clay body formulas. Due to its high surface area (small platelet size), it physically fits into the spaces between larger clay and nonclay particles in the total clay body composition.

Once water is added to the mix containing VeeGum T and clay, long chains of water clay lattices are held together, which forms a plastic pliable mass. The small platelet characteristic of VeeGum T also contributes to a lower vitrification range in a limited number of clay bodies.[13]

VeeGum T in amounts of 1/2% can replace 5% ball clay in body formulas. This attribute is beneficial because sometimes adding any ball clay to a formula changes the fired color, especially with white stoneware and porcelain clay bodies. Also, high concentrations of ball clay contribute to the gummy/rubbery feel of moist clay during the forming operation. Past a certain point, increasing the ball clay component of a clay body formula makes the clay warp and shrink excessively during the drying and firing stages.

Optimum results of VeeGum T can be obtained by adding from 1/2% to 2% based on the dry weight of the clay body. In most clay body formulas, it will not

---

12.   It is always a good practice to place a wet glaze through a 80x sieve three times to insure a uniformly mixed glaze for application. In some instances, a 100x sieve is required.
13.   Several cone 10 porcelain clay body formulas matured at cone 6 with the addition of VeeGum T.

change the fired color, shrinkage rate, or absorption of the clay body. VeeGum T should be thoroughly mixed with (preferably hot) water and all the mixture combined with the dry clay batch. Additional water can then be added to achieve the desired moist clay consistency.

VeeGum Pro

VeeGum Pro has been chemically modified and designed to mix readily with hot or cold water and dissolve into dispersion easily with low-technology mixing equipment. It is not a direct substitute for Vee-Gum T in its suspension properties and should be tested in the glaze batch to arrive at the optimum amount needed to maintain suspension. The most important consideration besides the correct amount is the complete dispersion of the material in the clay or glaze formula.

VeeGum CER

VeeGum CER is a mixture of VeeGum (inorganic, complex, colloidal, magnesium aluminum silicates) and CMC (carboxyethycellulose) that acts as a binder, increasing raw glaze hardness and durability. As a secondary attribute, it keeps glazes in suspension. It also serves as a viscosity stabilizer, controlling the consistency of glaze mixtures. It is nontoxic, odorless, and won't change the fired color of a glaze. VeeGum CER produces a hard, durable, and stable raw glaze structure.

In glazes, VeeGum CER can stop dried glazes from becoming dusty or fragile. It binds the glaze and can prevent it from flaking off the bisque or raw glazed pot.[14] A dusty, cracked, dry glaze is often an indication of future glaze crawling once the glaze has been fired.[15] Glaze crawling is evident when the fired glaze rolls back on itself, exposing bare areas of clay. Frequently, glaze crawling looks like beads of water on a glass tabletop. Glazes containing high percentages of low-density materials such as magnesium carbonate, lithium carbonate, clay, and bentonite can cause crawling problems due to their light, fluffy, fragile drying characteristics. Glazes containing high amounts of Gerstley borate, colemanite, clay, bentonite, borax, pearl ash, soda ash, and zinc oxide can cause crawling due to their high shrinkage rates.

VeeGum CER can tack down and hold a fragile raw glaze in place until the first stages of sintering, at which point the molten glaze is usually stabilized. Glaze crawling can also occur if the bisque surface is dusty, greasy, or has other contamination that will cause a nonadhesive glaze fit. In once-fired raw glazing, the clay body can also have loose dusty clay residues on its surface that act like ball bearings, disrupting the covering glaze and causing a nonbinding mechanical glaze fit. CMC will hold the glaze layer to the clay layer, preventing the glaze from forming off of the clay body.

CER can be added before or after a glaze is ball milled. It can also be added to the dry glaze batch or wet glaze batch, but the glaze must be passed three times through an 80x sieve to thoroughly mix the material. You'll notice a slight decrease in glaze viscosity (glaze applies thinner on the pot) when using CER. To correct thin glaze application, use less water in the initial glaze mixing process. Vee-Gum CER can be added to glazes from 1/8% to 1-1/2% based on the dry weight of the glaze.

VeeGum CER can also be used in underglaze or overglazes washes. It prevents metallic coloring oxides from becoming

---

14.   In some glaze formulas, CMC will be more effective than VeeGum CER.

15.   See chapter "Glaze Crawling – Causes and Corrections."

dusty after drying on the clay body. When used in overglazes washes, it prevents a loose dusty drying condition on the raw glaze surface (underglaze and overglaze washes contain either metallic coloring oxides or stains and water). When added to washes that are painted on bisque or raw ware, the wash flows easily off the brush onto the clay surface without the chattering grabbing action that can sometimes happen when a binder is not present. Overglaze painting with metallic coloring oxides or stains, as in majolica ware, will also benefit from additions of 1% to 3% of VeeGum CER (based on the dry weight of the underglaze or overglaze formula).

Additive A

In the past 40 years, many clay additives or conditioners have been used in ceramics-related industries. Additive A was developed in the 1950s to meet the country's need for increased brick production for housing. At that time, brick production was antiquated – most bricks were fired in periodic kilns that were slow and labor intensive. Due to the increased demand for building bricks, many plants automated their production processing and handling equipment for faster production. Bricks were then made by high speed mechanized processes. Labor and production costs went down, but brick loss rates increased due to the wet unfired bricks being formed and moved around the plant by machines. Many bricks were cracked or damaged by the high speed machines. Due to high loss rates and the relative nonplastic characteristics of brick clay, there was a need for a modifier to increase the green strength and plasticity of the bricks.

During this time of mechanization and expansion, lignosulphates (a byproduct of wood for paper production) was proved to increase the bonding and forming characteristics of moist clay. Archibald R. Gmeiner and Carlton H. Hougue were the two people most responsible for developing and testing this type of new additive.[16] Soon variations of the original additive were tested to meet the needs of local deposits of brick clay found at production plants around the country. In recent years, the additive has found its way into the clay body formulas of production pottery and ceramic sculptures. Clay body color and maturing temperature are not changed because the additive is burned off before dull red heat (approximately 1000°F to 1100°F) is reached in the kiln.

Additive A is a blend of lignosulphonates, organic and inorganic chemicals produced by Lignotech USA.[17] It's used as an addition to brick-making clays and other industrial ceramic products. When used in clay bodies, Additive A increases the plastic characteristics of the clay without the need for additional ball clays or bentonite. Additive A is a calcium lignosulphonate which has the ability to make water wetter, thus reducing the amount of water needed to make a clay body more plastic. Using less water to achieve plasticity in any clay body reduces the risk of clay body defects.

The increase in plasticity is most noticeable in short or nonplastic clay bodies such as raku, sculpture, jigger, and ram press formulas. It can also be used in soda, salt, low-fire and tile clay bodies. The plasticity of a clay body can be increased with additions of ball clays and/or bentonites. However, both types of clay need large amounts of water to make them plastic. When using large amounts of wa-

---

16.   Article "Additive A. . . . from whence it came" by Carlton H. Hougue.
17.   Lignotech U.S.A., P.O. Box 582 Lavonia, GA 30553 technical representative Jerry Wilson (706) 356-1288.

ter in the clay body formula, the potential for shrinkage and warping increases. Excessive amounts of ball clay can also make the body feel gummy and soft when moist, causing problems in the forming stages.

Additive A can replace all or part of the ball clay/bentonite component in clay body formulas. Additive A in the clay body gives you greater flexibility to choose less plastic clays in the clay body formula while also decreasing the amount of total water needed to make the clay body plastic.

Additive A as an Active Lubricant/ Plasticizer

In the clay-mixing process, Additive A acts as a lubricant in the clay mix, which offers less resistance to pug mill and mixer parts. The decreased resistance in mixing lowers energy costs and extends the life of the clay mixer and pug mill. Lowering moist clay resistance and lubrication are critical factors in tile extrusion clay body formulas. Clay will be extruded faster and easier with Additive A. It will also reduce the water of plasticity (the amount of water required to make the clay pliable).[18] With less water used to achieve plasticity, there is less chance of shrinkage, warping, or cracking in the drying and firing stages.

Additive A Increases Clay Body Dry and Green Strength

Additive A substantially increases the green strength (pots that have been formed and are still not dry) and dry strength (pots that have been formed and are already dry) of clay bodies, making for less fragile ware. It will reduce chipping and damage caused by handling the ware. Increasing the durability of unfired ware is crucial for large ceramic forms that are es-

pecially vulnerable to damage when being moved in the studio or loaded in a kiln.

Reprocessing dry clay scraps containing Additive A requires a longer soaking time in water to break the clay down into a plastic mass due to the greater density of the clay.

Types of Additive A

Additive A can be purchased in liquid or dry powder form. Several ratios of Additive A to barium carbonate mixtures can be purchased. Type 1 contains two to four pounds of Additive A per 2,000 pounds equivalent of barium carbonate. Type 3 contains five to seven pounds of Additive A per 2,000 pounds equivalent of barium carbonate. Type 4 contains eight to ten

Soluble salt scumming on a low-fire red clay body.

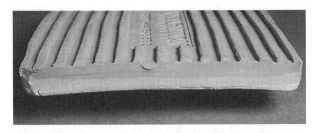

Soluble salt development can occur on tile edges in bone dry or fired ware.

---

18.   Water of plasticity is the amount of water required to surround each clay platelet with a film of water to achieve a plastic mass of clay.

Soluble salt scumming migrates readily to the high edges of the ware.

pounds of Additive A per 2,000 pounds equivalent of barium carbonate.

Types 1, 3, and 4 are only sold in liquid form and Type 2 does not contain any barium carbonate. Types 1, 3, and 4 contain barium that is chemically linked in the polymeric structure of the lignosulphonate. Because of this chemical linkage, the hazards of dry barium powder are largely eliminated. Type 3 reacts with the soluble sulfates in the raw materials and changes into an insoluble barium sulfate. After firing, the ware will be clear burned.

Calcium sulfate and magnesium sulfate can travel to the clay body surface upon drying, causing an insoluble white residue which appears as a white fuzzy material on the dried clay body. Types 1, 3, and 4 can be used in any clay body including low-fire red clay bodies to neutralize soluble salt scumming. In fired ware, the soluble salt scumming appears as a white flake material that can occur after the firing or days or months after the clay is exposed to moisture. The best example of soluble salts in clay bodies is to observe red building bricks after it rains and notice the white residue on their surface.

Besides Additive A contributing plasticity and green strength to clay bodies, the safe application of barium to stop scumming is a considerable inducement to use this additive.

Mixing Additive A

The most effective way to mix the additive is to add water to the dry clay mix until the moist clay starts to ball up, then add Additive A to the mixture. Add more water to get the desired moisture content for the forming operation. Additive A can also be mixed in hot water and thoroughly dispersed. Use all of the water/Additive A mixture in the clay-mixing operation. Complete and thorough mixing of the additive in the clay mixture is critical in any mixing operation.

Every gallon of the liquid form of Additive A contains 5.3 pounds of water and 5.3 pounds of Additive A. When using the liquid form, always base the amount of additive on the dry component weight of the liquid. Additive A can be used in clay bodies from 0.25% to 2%, based on the dry weight of the clay body formula. Additions of more than 5% of Additive A in the clay body will greatly increase green and dry strength, causing the clay to become extremely hard when dry. In some instances, the dry clay can be dropped on the floor without breaking. Start by using 0.25%, then increase the amount of Additive A in 0.25% increments until the desired result is achieved.

The Economic Benefits of Additives

All expenditures for ceramic materials must judged with the knowledge that labor is the largest cost to potters. Any additive to a clay body or glaze must reduce handling cost or cut the defect rate. Apart from a few highly expensive raw materials (cobalt oxide, cobalt carbonate, tin oxide, synthetic red iron oxide, nickel oxide black, nickel oxide green, nickel carbonate, silver nitrate, and stains), most materials that make up formulas are inexpensive. The most expensive factor is your labor and time required to make pots or sculpture.

Clay body and glaze additives can range in price from $2 to $6.50 per pound, depending on the additive. In clay body and glaze formulas, the additive component is usually 1/8% to 2% of the total formula weight. In most clay body formulas, the price per pound of additive will increase the price of the clay by .01 to .02 cent per pound – not a significant cost in the overall expense of the formula. The real savings occur when the defect rate drops due to the use of the additive. If one pot is saved because of the additive, it more than pays for itself.

While the use of clay and glaze additives has increased greatly in the last few years, many potters try to work around problems. They often develop difficult and time-consuming techniques, when just solving the problem would be a better long-term option. Often such "saving" measures are not reliable or are labor intensive. Typically they spend far too much valuable time and labor trying to make do with an ineffective method that doesn't address the problem directly. Solving the problem is always better and less expensive. Set aside some time to find out exactly what kind of glaze or clay body defect you are dealing with and then see if a particular additive will work. Keep in mind that not all defects can be fixed by additives and you may have to explore other methods of correction. An accurate diagnosis is essential for an exact correction. Fixing the problem once is better than struggling with a partial, ineffective fix on a daily basis.

Don't be intimidated by clay and glaze additives. If you are unsure about how and when to use an additive, contact the manufacturer and ask for advice. Describe the problem in simple direct terms. Your accurate description is a critical factor in the recommendation of an additive. However, if you want to experiment on your own and are reasonably sure that an additive is an appropriate fix for the problem, start with the lowest amount. If no change occurs, often increasing the additive to the recommended amounts will bring about a correction to the problem. As with all additives, it's always best to thoroughly test them in each formula. If they don't work, it's usually because you used the wrong one or the incorrect amount of the right one. The current generation of clay and glaze additives are potent, reliable, and consistent. Clay and glaze additives can't make bad pots better or sculpture more beautiful, but they can offer a tool to solve specific production problems.

Acknowledgments

I would like to thank Konrad C. Rieger of the R.T. Vanderbilt Co., Inc. for his time and effort in explaining the various characteristics of VeeGum. His thorough and complete knowledge of ceramics and the ability to transfer the information in a usable condition should be the model for all ceramics teachers.

R. Scott Dautel, of Hercules Inc./Aqualon Division was of considerable help to me in understanding CMC and its application in the field of ceramics. Scott explained the difficult in easy bite-size pieces. I would like to thank Jerry Wilson, of Lignotech U.S.A. for his information and technical help over the years. His concern for accuracy and the time he spent helping me with information about Additive A will always be greatly appreciated.

Two pallets of Redart in 50 lb. bags. Whenever possible, buy clay in quantity to lower the cost per pound. But be careful, in some instances the shipping charges can equal the cost of the clay.

Fire clays as a group are one of the most highly contaminated clays used by potters but they do contribute low shrinkage, low warping, and "tooth" to clay body formulas. Notice the green specks of copper contamination from the fire clay component of the clay body.

A common clay body defect in gas-fired kilns is caused by reducing the kiln too soon and/or too heavily in the glaze firing cycle. Note the over-reduced dark section in the clay body.

Glaze pinholing can be one of the most difficult defects to diagnose correctly because there are over 18 possible causes. A longer glaze firing cycle can correct some types of glaze pinholing.

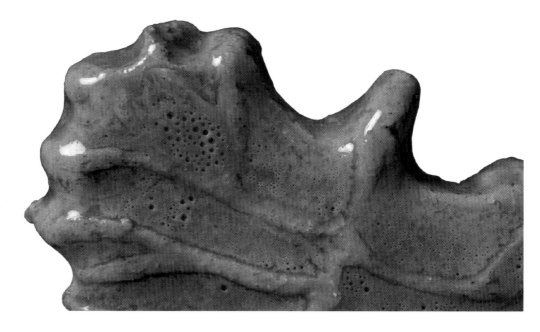

White clay bodies can become gray from too much reduction. Surprisingly, many carbon trapped clay bodies (not bloated clay bodies) can be successfully refired.

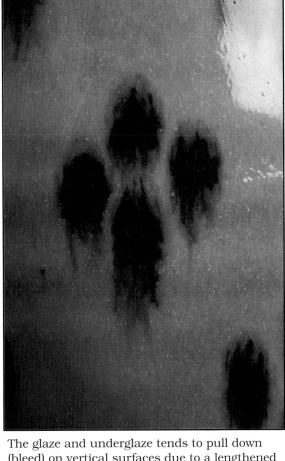

The glaze and underglaze tends to pull down (bleed) on vertical surfaces due to a lengthened kiln firing cycle.

When the crystal field is concentrated, the glaze can become opaque or the glaze color can appear bleached or muted (devitrification).

The rate at which a kiln cools can effect the growth of crystals in glazes. The same glaze in different parts of the kiln can generate different concentrations of crystal growth due to different rates of cooling within the kiln (devitrification).

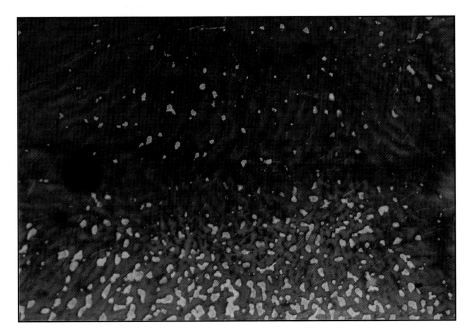

Underside of a pot showing a highly vitreous unglazed clay body which can fuse to kiln shelves. The unglazed area is glossy, indicating excessive glass buildup in the fired clay body.

Firing the glaze kiln too fast can produce jagged dry glazes. Glaze colors can appear pale with rough surface textures.

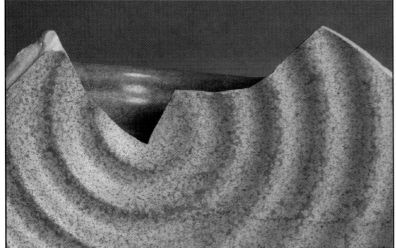
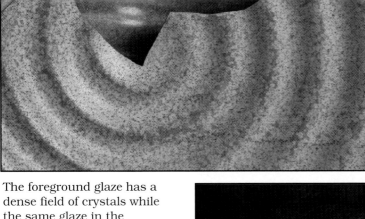

The foreground glaze has a dense field of crystals while the same glaze in the background is a different color and texture. The underside of the enclosed lidded form (foreground glaze) cooled at a slower rate than the exposed top part of the lid shown in the background (devitrification).

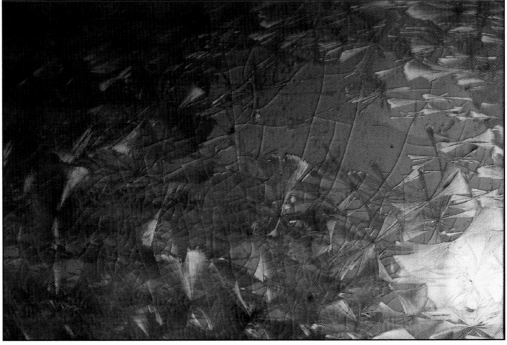

Close up of large (1/2" to 1" diameter) crystal growth in glaze (divitrification).

Glazes with narrow maturing ranges can be rough and under-fired or running, blistered, and over-fired, all within a few degrees of temperature. This glaze surface is dry, dull, and bubbled.

A round edge glaze crack indicates the fracture was present before the pot was glazed. The widest part of the crack points to where it first started on the form (the outer edge of the plate).

A round edge glaze crack can happen in the forming, drying, or bisque firing stages. As a rule, cracks stay the same or get worse. As the clay body and glaze mature, small defects are subjected to greater degrees of failure.

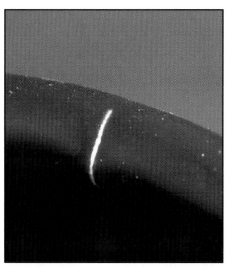

Thin clay cross sections in conjunction with thick clay cross sections will dry and shrink at different rates. Drying and firing stresses cannot be uniformly distributed across the entire form, which results in a crack.

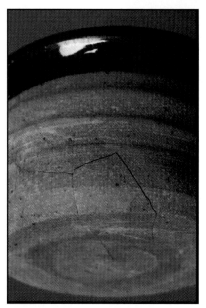

A sharp edge hairline crack caused by cooling the glaze kiln too fast.

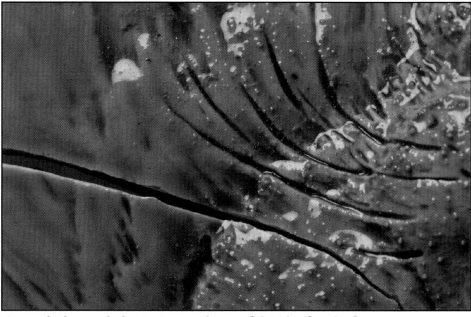

A round edge crack due to uneven drying of the tile after the forming stage.

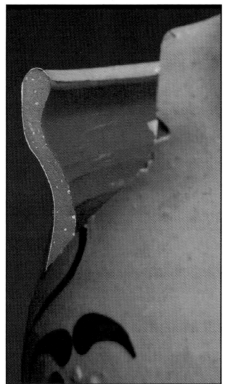

In porous clay bodies, the interface (area where the clay body ends and the glaze begins) is not as well developed as in vitreous clay body/glaze combinations. Notice the glaze layer riding on top of the porous red clay body. Porous clay bodies often cause the glaze to look like it's painted on the clay body.

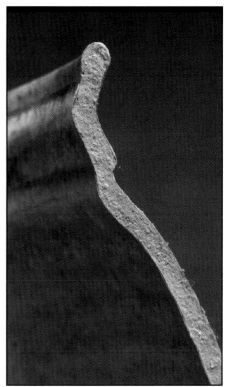

In vitreous clay body/glaze combinations, the interface produces a greater integration between the clay body and the glaze. Notice the bonding between the clay body and the glaze.

Above: As a general rule, the true glaze color is enhanced when the glaze application is thicker as opposed to thinner. A thin glaze application will reveal more of the underlying clay body color. This test tile was fired in a reduction kiln. You can see that the brown clay body influenced the glaze color.

A common clay body defect in gas kilns is bloating due to over-reduction in the kiln atmosphere.

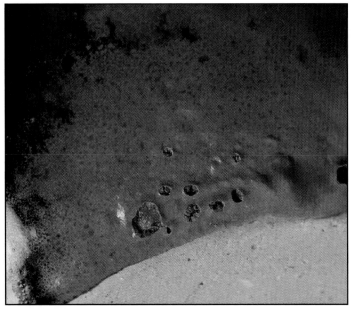

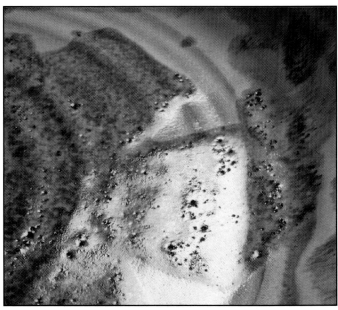

Many glazes appear adequate on horizontal surfaces but always test a glaze on a vertical test tile to determine if it will run or blister when fired to maturity.

When two or more glazes overlap, the combined interaction can cause various glaze defects such as running, shivering, crawling, crazing, or <u>blistering</u>.

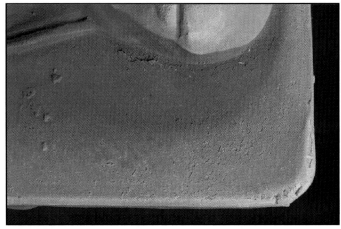

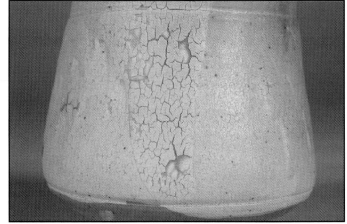

Discolored light areas of soluble salt scumming on a low-fire red tile clay body. During the drying process as water evaporates, soluble salts can migrate to the surface of the clay body.

While direct flame impingement on the ware during the firing can cause interesting "flashing" effects, it can also produce defects due to unequal heating on the clay body and glaze surfaces. Notice the cracked white areas of the pot.

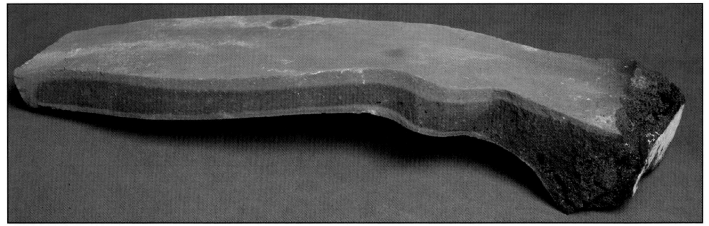

Incorrect bisque kiln atmosphere. The bisque firing introduced carbon into the clay body (the dark gray areas in the red clay body).

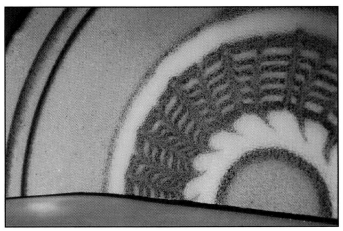

Many small bubbles trapped in the glaze can cause muting or dulling of the underglaze colored slip design. Often a longer glaze firing cycle will allow the bubbles to move through the viscous glaze layer where they will dissipate on the molten glaze surface.

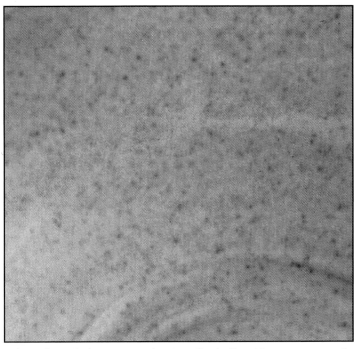

The relatively large particle size of cobalt oxide as compared to the smaller particle cobalt carbonate in a glaze can yield dark blue specks in a blue field.

Soda kiln cone viewing port during a firing. Sodium in the kiln atmosphere can act as a flux on pyrometric cones, causing them to bend at lower temperatures than their calibrated ratings.

Soda (sodium carbonate) glazed platter (16" diameter) from a black clay body fired to cone 9 r.

Top: Traditional gray salt body glaze effects duplicated in a sodium carbonate vapor firing. *Bottom:* Brown salt body glaze effects duplicated in a sodium carbonate vapor firing.

Once-fired cone 04 electric, plate (6-1/4" diameter), clear glaze, yellow slip with brown dendritic design.

Plate close up of brown dendritic design.

Top: Salt (sodium chloride) glazed platter (15" diameter) fired to cone 9 r.
Bottom: Soda (sodium carbonate) glazed platter (14" diameter) fired to cone 9 r.

Chapter 11

Raw Material Substitutions for Clay Bodies

At some point while mixing your own clay body formula or when ordering a private formula mixed by a ceramics supplier, a raw material will not be available. Being prepared for such an eventuality will help you make an accurate raw material substitution when that time comes.

Deciding which material to use as a replacement is an important decision to make sure the clay body formula continues to function as it did in the past. Keep in mind that each raw material found in a clay body formula contributes its own qualities and acts in conjunction with other materials. The combination of materials will develop the fired color, shrinkage, absorption, temperature range, and forming characteristics of the total clay body. Gaining an understanding of possible choices for raw materials in a clay body will offer accuracy and flexibility when the time comes to make such decisions.

Why Substitutions Are Necessary

Economic factors play a significant role in whether raw materials stay in production. Large industrial users of clays, feldspars, talcs, and other raw materials dictate the quality and availability of the materials used in clay body and glaze formulas. Often, when a raw material is no longer available, it simply means that it's not economically viable to continue its production. The actual material might be in abundant supply but the mine or processor has determined it's not worth keeping it in production. Or a large industrial customer no longer needs the material or has found a less expensive replacement. When this happens, the supplier of the raw material has lost a major customer and has determined that current smaller customers aren't worth the investment of time and labor to justify keeping the commodity in production.

Clay mines are not in business to supply potters with clay. As a group, potters comprise less than one tenth of one percent of their market. An example of this economic reality is Burns Brick Co., which mined Ocmulgee clay for brick plants. The company started as a small family-run business, selling clay to potters as a sideline market. At some point, a large corporation purchased the company and decided that processing, bagging, and shipping clay to potters wasn't an economically viable enterprise. The corporate decision was to stop production of Ocmulgee clay to potters and ceramics supply companies. Potters suffer from such variables in the marketplace because they don't represent a significant customer base. Whenever a material has been removed from the ceramics supply company's inventory, a substitute must be found that serves the same function in the clay body.

Because raw materials and clays are mined and processed for industries, each major industry sets the parameters (fired color, plasticity, particle size, level of organic material, dry shrinkage, fired shrinkage, loss on ignition, etc.) for the raw materials used in the production of their particular product, thus almost guaranteeing uniformity of the material. For example, Edgar Plastic Kaolin (EPK), a secondary plastic kaolin, is used in the manufacture of spark plugs. The spark plug company requires an exact chemical composition – white firing, high-temperature clay – and demands consistency with every load delivered to their factory. Potters who use EPK in a clay body formula can expect reliable, dependable clay mined in Putnam County, Florida, since 1892. Whenever possible, take advantage of such stable situations when choosing materials that are "guaranteed" by industry to perform with proven consistency.

Foretelling the future of the larger clay market is impossible but industrial users of clay have an economic benefit in keeping their supplies consistent. You can tag along to some extent and use guaranteed clays whenever you can apply them in your clay body formulas.

When developing a clay body, contact the mines and raw material processors to determine the future stability of the supply. Ceramics suppliers often can't comment accurately on availability because they are only a link in the chain of supply, but they can tell you the names of the mines and their raw material suppliers. It is then up to you to investigate which industries use the material and the prospects for the material remaining in future production. If a large industry consistently uses a material, they have already done the research to insure a consistent, high quality supply from the mine or raw material processor.

Raw material "drift" can also cause the need for a substitution. Over the years a material can change in particle size, organic content, or chemical composition.

Any variation can affect the handling qualities or fired clay color. Many factors can contribute to a reliable clay turning into a different clay. The changes can occur almost imperceptibly, slowly building until the sum of small changes pushes the clay into a problem-producing state. When this happens, you'll need to substitute a new material.

Just because the name on the bag stays the same doesn't mean the clay inside the bag stays the same. An example of this is Kentucky Tennessee Clay Co.'s Old Mine #4 ball clay. In the mid 1970s OM#4 was mined from a single pit of clay. Later the company decided that the overall consistency of the clay would be improved by blending several clays to duplicate the characteristics of the single pit OM#4, thinking the average performance of each clay would make for a consistent total clay mixture. This blending allows one clay to be slightly different or out of specification without throwing off the whole mix. (Blending clays has proven to produce a more reliable product while extending the useful deposits of clay at the mine and most clay mines have adopted this as standard procedure.) While it can be argued that OM#4 has greater uniformity when blended, it can also be stated that the blended OM#4 is different from the original single pit OM#4. Potters who have used the original nonblended OM#4 note a difference in the handling qualities of the clay. In a sense, by using a leveling out process in blending clays, the mine decreased the risk of getting a bad batch of clay. The chances of single pit clay producing a bad batch are greater than with blended clays. Changing their clay mining operation has also eliminated the possibility of a truly outstanding single pit batch of clay. The leveling out process has wrung out the individual character of some single pit clays, resulting in no surprises – good or bad – from the blended clay mixtures. Blending clays is more attuned to mass users of clay than potters who use relatively little of the total clay produced in the United States. All major markets for ball clays demand large quantities of consistent product from the mine. The process of blending clays from different pits at the mine insures a uniform result.

Never substitute a raw material just to save money. This is false economy because the substantial cost in producing any pottery or sculpture is time and labor, not the cost of raw materials. If you are ever tempted to use less expensive clay or feldspar, it can be very costly if they don't function correctly in the clay body formula. Reliable, consistent materials that produce good results should be your goal, not saving an extra penny per pound on the cost of materials. The same principle applies to the use of any clay body additives such as Additive A, Macaloid, nylon fibers, or fiberglass fibers. If any additive results in a better clay body formula with fewer defects, it's worth the extra price. In practical terms, the price per pound of clay can increase if it helps cut down on defects, while using a less expensive clay body can be very expensive in the time and effort required to reproduce a failed piece.

You may have experienced a situation where you need to mix a clay body formula immediately and discover that you don't have the exact material in the studio, forcing you to make an emergency substitution. Try to avoid doing this, it's always better to not be forced to make a substitution. Keep a well-stocked material inventory in your studio and always check with ceramics suppliers and other potters for current availability of the materials used in your clay body. Raw material substitutions should be made only when they are unavoidable.

Some raw material substitutions are made to experiment with an existing clay body formula. When attempting to change a formula, remember to mix up only a small amount of the revised formula. It can be a very expensive experiment if the formula doesn't work and you've mixed hundreds or thousands of pounds of a new clay body formula. If this happens, resist the temptation to make a further revision for a better result. Most times, trying to save a mistake will be confusing and result in even more unusable clay. Compounding revisions of a formula can get complicated fast. It's often better to start again from a formula that works and make a workable adjustment.

Many potters find clay body formulas in pottery books or magazines. Formulas are frequently given out in ceramics classes or handed from one potter to another during craft shows and workshops. Occasionally a specific clay or raw material might be required in the clay body formula that is not currently available or is out of stock. In such instances, a substitute will be required. When substituting more than one raw material in a clay body, the forming characteristics and fired results of the clay body are more likely to change as opposed to making just one material substitution. Limiting the raw material and clay substitutions is always best because it helps insure a close match to the original formula.

Once a small test batch of clay body formula is working well, mix up another small batch and fire it in other kilns or the same kiln. In reduction kilns, the intermediate testing phase is especially important because reduction kiln atmospheres can be inconsistent in themselves. Obviously, the experience gained from using the formula over many kiln firings and with various glazes will be vital in building your confidence with the new clay body. Mixing up several small batches of new clay body formula is better than a single large batch. Note if any minor adjustments to the formula are required. The idea is to build a track record of good results with the revised clay body formula and gain confidence in its reliability over time.

How to Make Clay Body Substitutions: Classifying Raw Materials and Clays

Before making any substitutions, it's important to first understand what constitutes a clay body. A clay body formula consists of several groups of materials such as clay(s), feldspar, flint, talc, grog, silica sand, frit, or any number of other raw materials and additives. Most clay body formulas have between three and eight separate materials and clays. Each component or group contributes to the total purpose of the formula. The number of different clays and materials found in a clay body formula is dependent on the function the clay body must serve. Porcelain clay body formulas usually have kaolin, feldspar, and flint components, while some stoneware clay body formulas can have fire clay, ball clay, stoneware clay, feldspar, flint, and grog components.

When replacing a material in the clay body formula, it's first necessary to determine the specific group of the original material, then choose the material in that group with the closest match in mesh or particle size.

Particle size matching is very important. An unproductive match can occur when using the same chemical composition material with a radically different material size as in flint 325x-mesh which is silica, compared with silica sand 60x-mesh which is also silica. The particle size of silica sand 60x-mesh is too large compared with flint 325x powder. Therefore, it could not be used as a substitute. The larger mesh silica sand wouldn't melt with other clay body raw materials and would change the handling and throwing characteristics of the clay body. The closer the particle sizes match, the less likely it is that a substitute material will change the handling characteristics of the clay body. Particle size can also affect the degree of melting or vitrification that occurs in the clay body. Smaller particle size materials go into a melt faster and more completely than larger size materials because of their greater surface area exposed to heating. In clays, smaller particle or platelet size can make the moist clay body shrink excessively, warp, or crack in the drying or firing stages. Moist clay bodies with large quantities of small particle size materials can also feel gummy or soft during forming operations. Keep in mind the particle size distribution (small structure materials in ball clays and bentonites, medium structure materials in stoneware clays, large structure materials in fire clays, plus grogs and other materials) of the total clay body formula and try not to unbalance the clay body when using substitute materials.

Clays

To make accurate substitutions in clay body formulas, the clay component of the formula can be grouped in classifications. The most common group of clays found in clay body formulas are fire clays, stoneware clays, ball clays, earthenware clays, kaolins, and bentonites. Within each group are many individual clays. A partial list of ball clays contains Thomas, XX Sagger, Kentucky OM#4, and Tennessee #9. Within some groups of clays, subgroups exist such as plastic and nonplastic kaolins as in EPK, a plastic kaolin, and Kaopaque #20, a nonplastic kaolin.

When making a substitution to the clay body part of the formula, try to determine what group or subgroups of clay needs replacement. The most common mistake is choosing a substitute clay from the wrong group of clays. Often, a stoneware clay is confused with a fire clay and the result is a clay body without tooth or standup ability when being formed. In high-temperature bodies, the lack of a true fire clay component makes the clay body less refractory or heat resistant, which can result in warping, shrinking, or bloating during firing.

Once the proper clay group is found, the fired color of the replacement clay must be chosen to match the original clay. Even though one ball clay can be substituted for another, it's also important to choose a ball clay with approximately the same fired color. Both ball clays will be plastic, but a darker firing ball clay can easily change the color or tint of the fired clay body. A color change or tint is most noticeable when substituting any darker firing clay in porcelain or light firing clay body formulas. As the clay body matures, a darker firing ball clay's iron and manganese component becomes more visible due to the fluxing action of the clay body on the two metallic coloring oxides. Dark firing clay bodies can accept a wider range of color variations in substitute clays because the replacement clay color is lost in the dark clay body's fired color.

Clay Processing

Most kaolins, ball clays, and some stoneware clays used for clay bodies are air floated. Air floating begins when the crude clay, ranging in size from lumps a few inches in diameter to powder size, is fed into a dryer. The natural moisture content of the clay (16% to 20% depending on the time of year the clay is mined and the characteristics of the individual clay deposit) is reduced to 1% to 3%. It is then fed into a roller mill (to reduce the particle size of the clay) or hammer mill (to break up large chunks of clay into small pieces). Oversize material is ground again and sand is thrown out. The clay moves by air stream where a precise specific of particle size will sort itself. It is then carried to a spinning blade that only allows a particular particle size to pass through, causing a predetermined mesh size clay. The sorted clay is then swept by air into storage silos, rail cars, or bagged for future shipment.

While making the clay easier to handle, store, and ship, air floating also produces a lower moisture content clay. The air floating and subsequent drying process can result in a longer time for the clay to age or achieve its maximum plasticity when water is finally added during the clay-mixing operation. It has been theorized that air floating decreases the organic content of clay because of excessive drying. Some ceramics suppliers report that a perceived lower organic content adversely affects the moist clay's plasticity. Cedar Heights Clay Co., Old Hickory Clay Co., H.C. Spinks Clay Co., and Kentucky Tennessee Clay Co., assert that the temperature reached during the air floating process does nothing more than drive off free water from the raw clay and the process doesn't lower the organic content of the clay.

Substitute Materials for Clay Bodies

Below are raw materials and clays with an explanation of when to use each substitute material. Not listed are materials that don't have a practical substitute or would involve extensive clay body testing for the purposes of substitution. Acceptable substitutions are listed under their respective categories. For example, Thomas ball clay and Taylor ball clay, both light fired color, low iron content ball clays, can be substituted for each other in a clay body formula.

Ball Clays

Ball clays are the most numerous individual clays in any group of clays. They contribute plasticity to the total clay body formula. Due to their small platelet structures, ball clays act mechanically to bridge the gap or fill spaces between large platelet size clays such as fire clays and medium size platelets found in stoneware clays. The smaller platelets found in ball clays produce greater surface areas for the water film surrounding each clay platelet. More water film structures in the clay body causes increased plasticity in the moist clay.

Each ball clay contains different amounts of naturally occurring metallic coloring oxides (iron and manganese are two oxides that contribute significant fired color) which will affect the fired color of a ball clay. The amounts of iron and manganese in each type of ball clay and the percentage of ball clay used in the total clay body help to promote the fired clay body color. Frequently, a brown fired color clay body using a high iron or manganese content ball clay won't cause a noticeably darker fired clay body. Most ball clays (except a very few high iron ball clays) cause weak color enhancement in a clay body. Old Hickory's F-2 ball clay has an iron content of 4.36% as compared to most ball clays averaging 1.2%. The high iron content of F-2 causes the fired clay body color to become much darker depending on how much ball clay is used in the formula.

In white or light color clay bodies, dark firing ball clays can change the fired clay body to an off-white or cream color. A darker fired color is more likely because the clay body approaches vitrification temperatures due to the fluxing action of iron and manganese in the ball clay or metallic oxides in other clay body materials. It's best to use a light firing ball clay when making a substitution in light firing clay body formulas. Overall, when substituting ball clays, always choose the one with iron and manganese percentages closest to the original ball clay. Hand-building and throwing bodies can accept wider varieties of ball clays with good results than slip casting bodies which are very sensitive to any raw material substitution.

The most widely available *off-white fired color* ball clays are Tennessee #1 = SPG#1, Tennessee #10, Coppen Light, H.C. Spinks C&C, Old Hickory #5, and Old Hickory #1 Glaze Clay, all of which are interchangeable.

The most widely available *cream-colored fired* (a few shades darker than off-white) ball clays are Foundry Hill Cream, #1 Glaze Clay, Jackson, Kentucky OM#4, Kentucky Special, Kentucky Stone, M&D, Thomas, Taylor, XX Sagger, Tennessee #9, Tennessee #5, Spinks HC5, Mississippi M&D, Bell Dark, Gold Label, and Bandy Black. These cream-colored fired clays can be substituted for each other. Bandy Black has a high silica content and produces a good effect in salt or soda kiln firings.

Barium Carbonate

Chinese and German types can be interchanged in a clay body if the particle size is similar. Barium carbonate ties up soluble salt scumming in the fired ware. It can be used in amounts of 1/4% to 2% based on the dry weight of the clay body. By reacting with calcium and magnesium soluble salts, barium carbonate changes the salts into calcium carbonate or barium sulfate which are insoluble and inert. By eliminating soluble salts in the clay body, subsequent firing discoloration is reduced. Some red earthenware clays are more susceptible to soluble salt problems but even so-called clean clays can occasionally have high levels of troublesome salts. Consequently, barium carbonate is found in many different types of clay body formulas.

Barium carbonate added to a clay body formula is considered safe provided a respirator is used when handling the material in the dry state and you wash your hands after clay-mixing operations.

Bentonites

Bentonites can be used in a clay body formula to increase the plastic qualities of the moist clay in forming operations. As a group, they are the most plastic of any of the clays. Usually, 1% to 2% of bentonite is used based on the dry weight of the clay batch. Higher percentages of bentonite can make the moist clay thixotropic (the moist clay body deforms under pressure) and gummy when water is added during hand-building or throwing operations. Bentonites can be classified as to the fired color and degree of plasticity. Due to organic content and other contamination, the darker firing bentonites will have greater plastic qualities than the cleaner light firing bentonites.

Light firing bentonites used in clay bodies are INERT-20 air purified, 325x-mesh Western Bentonite, 200x-mesh Western Bentonite, Bentonite B, and Bentolite White GK129, all interchangeable. Light firing bentonites can be used in porcelain, other white clay bodies, and any dark firing clay body.

Dark firing bentonite, Ibex-200, can be used in dark clay body formulas. When a high iron or manganese content bentonite is used in a white firing clay body formula, it can cause small black specking in the fired clay body. Specking can become increasingly noticeable as the clay body reaches vitrification.

Other clay body additives that can replace bentonite are Epsom salts (magnesium sulfate), Additive A, Macaloid, and VeeGum T all of which contribute greater plasticity to the clay body than any of the bentonites. Frequently, a direct substitution of additive for bentonite can't be used and the appropriate level of additive will require testing.

Feldspars

Feldspars are the major source of flux in clay body formulas at stoneware temperature ranges cone 6 (2232°F) to cone 12 (2419°F). All temperature references to cones are based on large Orton pyrometric cones heated at 270°F per hour. The correct amount of feldspar chosen from the appropriate group will result in a hard, vitreous, fired clay body. Feldspars used in clay body formulas fall into three basic groups: potassium feldspars, sodium feldspars, and lithium feldspars. Within each group are many individual feldspars. When making a feldspar substitution in a clay body, determine if the original feldspar is potassium, sodium, or lithium, then choose the replacement feldspar from the same group. To ascertain if a feldspar is predominately potassium, sodium, or lithium, obtain a chemical analysis sheet from the ceramics supplier or the processor of the feldspar. The analysis sheet will show the percentages of each oxide contained in the feldspar. Disregarding the silica (SiO_2) and the alumina (Al_2O_3) content of the feldspar, find the highest percentage of oxide, which will indicate the feldspar group (see below).

G-200 Feldspar (chemical analysis)

SiO_2	66.78%
Al_2O_3	18.47%
Fe_2O_3	.079%
CaO	.82%
K_2O	**10.61%**
Na_2O	3.05%

The K_2O (potassium) content is the highest oxide in the chemical analysis excluding SiO_2 and Al_2O_3. Therefore, G-200 is a potassium-based feldspar.

Potassium feldspars that can be interchanged are Custer, G-200, K200, and Primas P. Some that are no longer available are Oxford Buckingham/261-F, Yankee, A-3/Elbrock, Maine Spar, Madoc "H", Godfrey, and Clinchfield #202.

Sodium feldspars that can be interchanged are Kona F-4, Nepheline Syenite 270x Minex3, Nepheline Syenite 400x Minex 4, Calspar, Primas S, NC -4, Unispar 50, C-6, and Minnspar 200. No longer available are Eureka, Clinchfield #303, Minpro #4, Bainbridge, #56 Glaze Spar, and #54 Glaze Spar.

Lithium feldspars that can be interchanged are Spodumene Lepidolite, and

Petalite. Lithospare is no longer available. Spodumene (high iron content), mined by Foote Mineral Co., has been discontinued. It produced bubbling when mixed with the clay body water. Spodumene (low iron content) from Gwalia, Australia, is produced by F&S Alloys and Minerals Corp. and mixes well in clay bodies without effervescing in water. Spodumene (low iron content) (LM), Canada is produced by the Tannco Co. Any of the low iron lithium feldspars can be substituted for each other.

Flint

Flint is silica commonly found in clay body formulas as flint. Other materials such as clays, feldspars, talc, pyrophyllite, or wollastonite can also contribute silica to the clay body formula. When added to the clay body, flint reduces dry shrinkage and warping and promotes glaze fit because it forms with fluxes and other materials to create a vitrified, dense, nonabsorbent fired clay body. It can be purchased as Flint 400x, 325x and 200x-mesh, all of which can be used in clay bodies. Flint 200x-mesh can be used whenever an unspecified mesh size flint is required in a clay body formula.

Kaolins

Kaolins can be classified by their plastic and nonplastic qualities when moist. Kaolin contributes a white fired color to the clay body providing other clays in the formula also fire white. Many porcelain clay body formulas contain as much as 50% kaolin with 25% feldspar and 25% flint, so choosing the correct kaolin substitution clay is critical in producing a successful result. Occasionally, some kaolins can't be substituted on a direct one-for-one basis. Grolleg kaolin mined in England is a unique clay that is difficult to substitute due to its handling characteristics and plastic forming qualities. Using a plastic and nonplastic kaolin is often necessary to duplicate the unique qualities of Grolleg kaolin. However, most often making a direct one-for-one substitute from within the same group or subgroup of clays is advisable. Blending different clays to achieve a workable substitution often leads to many hours of trial and error testing with little real gain.

Plastic kaolins are EPK (Florida or Edgar Plastic Kaolin), Putnam, Grolleg, Stockalite, Kaolex D-6, McNamee, #6 Tile, Pioneer, and Laguna #1, Sapphire, Treviscoe, T-7 kaolin, Standard Porcelain (SP), and Super Standard Porcelain (SSP). These can be substituted for each other.

Nonplastic kaolins are Kaopaque 20, Ajax P, Delta, SnoCal 707, Kingsley, English China Clay, Georgia Kaolin, and Velvacast, all of which are interchangeable. Occasionally a raw material or clay like Avery kaolin (Helmer kaolin can be substituted for Avery) can't be readily substituted or there may not be many clays that duplicate its unique properties. Avery kaolin produces a distinctive orange/yellow fired color when used as a slip decoration on wood, salt, or soda fired pots. In such cases, even extensive testing of other clays might not produce an adequate substitute.

Calcined kaolins have already been heated, removing the chemical water and decreasing the clay shrinkage. Calcined kaolins that can be used interchangeably are Glomax LL and Ajax -SC. Calcined kaolin can be produced in the studio by firing any kaolin past dull red heat to approximately 1100°F. Most clay body formulas don't require a calcined clay component.

Fire Clays

Fire clays are highly refractory, nonplastic, large platelet size, coarse clays that contribute tooth to the moist clay body so that it will stand up during handbuilding or throwing operations. Adding fire clay to the clay body decreases clay body shrinkage and warping as the moist clay dries. Increasing the fire clay component also adds heat resistance to the clay body. As a group of clays, fire clays are potentially the weakest part of any clay body formula because of their variability in chemical composition and/or particle size. At any time, fire clays can include coal, twigs, sand, or excessive amounts of silica, all of which can cause problems in the forming or firing stages of the clay body. Fire clays can be subgrouped primarily by their relative plasticity to other fire clays and fired color.

Plastic fire clays are light tan fired color. Acceptable substitutions are Imco-400 fire clay (Lincoln 60 fire clay ground finer), Imco-800 fire clay (different than Imco-400), Sutter 200 fire clay and Pine Lake fire clay (no longer mined).

Medium plastic fire clays are light tan fired color. Acceptable substitutions include A.P.G. Missouri fire clay 28x-mesh, A.P.G. Missouri fire clay 20x-mesh, A.P.G. Missouri fire clay screened, Hawthorne Bond fire clay 20x-mesh, Hawthorne Bond fire clay 35x-mesh, Lincoln 60 fire clay 20x-mesh, and Greenstripe fire clay (high shrinkage rate and finer grind than A.P.G Missouri fire clay 28x-mesh). Sheffield Pottery, Inc., Sheffield, Mass., is one of the few ceramics suppliers offering screened A.P.G. Missouri fire clay, which greatly reduces the impurities in the clay.

Nonplastic fire clay North American Fire clay 20x-mesh is a light tan firing fire clay.

Talcs

Talcs contribute silica and magnesium to the clay body. In low-fire clay bodies cone 06 to cone 04 (1830°F to 1940°F), talc promotes glaze fit and can represent 50% of the clay body. In high-temperature clay bodies cone 6 (2232°F) to cone 10 (2381°F), talc acts to bring the total formula into a dense, vitreous fired clay body. Talc can also affect iron in the clay body,

causing a light brown or red tone in high-temperature reduction fired clay bodies.

Not all talc is the same. On the East Coast, Nytal HR100 Talc is available, with Pioneer-2882 being a good substitute talc on the West Coast. Westex talc is a plate-like nonfibrous talc that can be used in clay bodies but might produce a slight off-white color as compared with Nytal HR 100 and Pioneer-2882. Some other substitute talcs are Sierralite (high alumina content), Soapstone 78SS (dirty for use in glazes), TDM 92 (high organic matter), and Talc 80/20 (partly calcined which can be used in dry press clay bodies). Each talc has its own distinctive characteristics which can influence clay body plasticity, maturing temperature, fired clay color, and eventual glaze fit.

Stoneware Clays

Stoneware clays mature from cone 6 (2232°F) to cone 10 (2381°F) temperature ranges. As a group of clays they are medium platelet size and fairly plastic when moist. In many high-temperature clay bodies, stoneware clay is the majority of the clay used in the formula.

Light tan firing stoneware clays are Goldart stoneware (air floated, 200x-mesh, consistently low sulfur content), Goldart Ceramic Grade fire clay (50x-mesh Goldart stoneware clay but not air floated), and Roseville stoneware (air floated, no sulfur content, slightly lower maturing range than Goldart stoneware clay). These three make suitable substitutions for each other. Due to its excellent deflocculation properties, Roseville stoneware clay is a better choice for a stoneware clay in a slip-casting formula than most other stoneware clays. Although Yellow Banks 40 (air floated) stoneware matures at a lower temperature than Goldart, Yellow Banks 401 fired at cone 8 has a 1% absorption versus Goldart's 4.17% approximate absorption. Yellow Banks 401 is still a good substitute for clay bodies in the cone 6 (2232°F) to cone 8 (2305°F) temperature range. Jordan stoneware clay (very plastic and fired to light orange color) is no longer produced.

Brown firing high iron content stoneware clays that can be successfully substituted for each other are Newman Red/Neuman Red, C-Red/Carbonadale Red (similar in fired color to Newman Red but more plastic), and Lizella stoneware (lower iron content and lighter firing than Newman Red). Sheffield Pottery offers screened Lizella stoneware. Ochmulgee stoneware (high iron content) clay that was acceptable if screened to remove dirt, cigarettes, and rocks, is no longer produced.

Earthenware Clays

Earthenware clays are a group of low-temperature clays. The most common commercially mined earthenware clay is Redart, a high iron content, red to brown firing clay. Sheffield Slip Clay is a low-temperature clay that fires a lighter red to brown color than Redart because of its lower iron content. In some clay body formulas, it can substitute for Redart provided it is not the only iron-bearing clay in the clay body formula. Ranger Red Clay/Ranger Shale produced by Trinity Ceramics Supply in Dallas is another high iron content red firing clay that can be substituted for Redart. It is frequently used as brick clay. Ranger Red Clay/Ranger Shale is not air floated as is Redart. Ranger Red Clay has a slightly lower iron content. Yellow Banks 101, air floated and mined by United Clays, Huntingburg, Ind., also has a lower iron content than Redart but can used as a direct substitute.

Grogs

Grogs are added to clay bodies when more tooth or standup ability is needed in forming operations. Grogs decrease a clay body's warping and shrinkage during the drying and firing stages. Compared with clay, grog has a large particle size and is nonplastic. Grog is inert, having been calcined or fired during its manufacturing process. Grogs have an irregular particle shape with sharp edges as compared with some silica sands which are oblong and have rounded smooth edges. The sharp edges makes it ideal for locking itself into the clay body during throwing operations. A grog's fired color can also be an important factor in choosing an accurate match when the clay body color might reveal a darker or lighter grog substitutions. Dark firing grog will show as brown or black specks in a light or white firing clay body. This effect is especially noticeable when the clay is subject to reducing atmospheres in a kiln. *When making a grog substitution in a clay body, always try for a close match in particle size and fired color.*

For every 10% of grog added to a clay body, the fired shrinkage of the body is decreased by approximately 3/4%. However, with additions of grog, a clay body's plasticity is also decreased. Several factors are important in choosing a suitable grog substitute. Grogs are produced in various mesh sizes ranging from powders to large pebble sizes. The mesh size of the grog refers to the particle size of the material. Higher mesh numbers indicate a smaller particle size. For example, a 20x-mesh grog is pebble size while a 100x-mesh grog is a fine powder. Grogs with more than one set of numbers followed by a slash with another set of numbers indicate the particle size ranges in the grog. Grog 20/48x-mesh has particle size ranging from coarse 20x-mesh to finer 48x-mesh. Maryland Refractory 48/f is a 48x-mesh grog decreasing in size down to a fine powder.

Some grogs are processed from used industrial firebrick that has been ground up. The brick is occasionally contaminated with metallic oxides or other impurities. The amount of contamination and the defect it can produce in the fired clay body is dependent on the original use of the firebrick. Virgin grog such as Harbison-Walker Refractories Calamo grogs and Ione grogs are mined from flint clays that have a low alkali/iron content, high chemical purity, and are consistent in chemistry. When substituting grogs, note if the clay body can accept slight imperfections caused by grog manufactured from used firebricks. When in doubt, use a virgin grog. Your ceramics supplier should be able to furnish information on the different grogs.

Grog mesh sizes frequently used by potters are Calamo 80, Ione 406 65x which can be substituted for each other. Other grog mesh sizes that can be used interchangeably are Calamo 60, Ione 412 40x, HCR H1 48/f, Maryland Refractories 48/f, and Muddox 28x (fires slightly darker than other grogs listed). Calamo 35, Ione 420 20x, Maryland Refractories 48M, Maryland Refractories 20/48, and HCR H1 20/48 can be substituted for each other, as can NCR H1 12/20, Calamo 22, Maryland Refractories 12/20, and Muddox Coarse (fires slightly darker than other grogs listed).

Molochite

Molochite is a white firing porcelain grog produced in several mesh sizes. It is frequently used in porcelain and other white clay bodies because of its ability to blend into a white clay body color. Molochite 30M can be substituted for Molochite 50-80M. Finer powder grinds are Molochite 120M and Molochite 200M, which can be substituted for each other.

Mullite

Mullite (35x, 48x, 100x, 200x), Cordierite 40x, and Kyanite (35x, 48x, 100x, 200x) are all nonplastic raw materials that are available in various mesh sizes ranging from powder to large pebble sizes. They can be added to the clay body to cut

shrinkage and warping. However, increasing the amount of a nonplastic material in a clay body will correspondingly decrease the clay body's plasticity. When using any inert material, particle size and fired color should determine the criteria for substitution.

Silica Sands

Silica sands are silica in a large particle form. They are produced in several mesh sizes. The shape of the silica sand can be a factor in the tooth or feel of a moist clay body in throwing or handbuilding operations. Round or smooth shaped silica sand rolls past each other and doesn't produce as much interlocking action in the moist clay body as irregular sharp sand or grog. You can find out the shape by asking the ceramics supplier or by looking at it under magnification. High silica sand numbers indicate finer grinds and lower numbers indicate coarser or larger sizes of the material. Silica sand 30-mesh compatible types are F-65 Silica Sand round, F-70 Mystic, and F-95 Silica Sand round by U.S. Silica Co.

Clay Additives

Clay additives that are used primarily to increase plasticity in the moist clay body are CMC, VeeGum T, Macaloid, Epsom salts, Additive A, and yeast, all of which can be substituted for each other. Clay additives used to increase the green strength of the moist clay in forming operations are nylon fibers Dupont P105, fiberglass fibers, and Additive A. Most additives are used in amounts of 1/16% to 2% based on the dry weight of the clay body. The particular additive and the amount needed will be determined by the clay body formula and the intended use of the clay body.

Metallic Coloring Oxides and Body Stains

Metallic coloring oxides and body stains are used to enhance or change the fired color of a clay body. Metallic coloring oxides or their carbonate forms can be variable in the color shades they produce from one batch to the next. Body stains, which contain metallic coloring oxides and other stabilizing color enhancing properties, are carefully blended, fired, and ground to a powder. They are more expensive than metallic coloring oxides but produce consistent colors and color variations not obtainable with metallic oxides or metallic carbonates. A high percentage of metallic coloring oxide or stain can yield intense color in a clay body but due to their nonplastic nature, they can decrease the moist clay body's handling qualities. In reduction kiln atmospheres, higher amounts of metallic coloring oxides and/or stains can cause over-fluxing and brittleness in the clay body. The clay body formula, its forming method, and the kiln atmosphere conditions where it's fired will determine the limits for additions of metallic coloring oxides and stains.

Before making a substitution of metallic coloring oxides or stains, consider the original fired color of the clay body. With the correct amount of coloring additive, a white firing clay body can produce blue, green, tan, orange, or pastel shades of these colors. However, a tan or brown fired clay body (already having natural metallic coloring oxides from the clays in the formula) will only produce a darker fired color when additional metallic oxides or stains are added to the clay body. Each metallic coloring oxide or body stain contributes a unique color to a clay body that can limit the options available for a possible one-for-one body color substitution. The kiln atmosphere and the particular formula of the clay body can also further complicate a simple direct coloring oxide or body stain substitution. Testing a substitute metallic oxide or stain is

worth the effort and will prevent costly mistakes.

Metallic Coloring Oxides/Carbonates

When making substitutions, allow for the oxide form to be approximately one-half times stronger than its carbonate form. For example, cobalt oxide/cobalt carbonate, copper oxide/copper carbonate, manganese dioxide/manganese carbonate, nickel oxide/nickel carbonate. Copper oxide red and copper oxide black can be substituted for each other as well as nickel oxide black and nickel oxide green.

Iron oxide is the most commonly used clay body metallic coloring oxide. It can produce light to dark brown colors in clay bodies (1/4% to 2% red iron oxide based on the dry weight of the clay body). The fired color of the clay body is also affected by the kiln atmosphere, the original clay body fired color, the maturity of the clay body, and percentage of iron oxide added. Red iron oxide (90% approx. Fe_2O_3), and Spanish red iron oxide (81% approx. Fe_2O_3 ore) are almost identical in their effect on clay body color. Iron oxide red is also produced in refined grades such as red NR 4284, red iron oxide #2199 and both iron oxides are more than 90% Fe_2O_3. They cause the clay body to fire darker in color than the natural red iron oxide ore. Black iron oxide isn't the best choice for a direct substitute for any of the red iron oxides because it can easily over-flux the clay body.

Due to its expense and the subsequent amount needed to color a clay body, cobalt oxide isn't usually considered as a body coloring agent. Cobalt can develop a wide range of blues when added to a white clay body and when used in high percentages in brown clay bodies can produce a black clay body. Cobalt carbonate can be substituted for cobalt oxide but remember to allow for cobalt oxide being one-half times stronger than cobalt carbonate.

Frits

Frits contain oxides predetermined as to quantity and chemical composition which are then melted, fast cooled, and ground into a powder. In a sense, frits are manmade feldspars. They enable a consistent blend of oxides to be melted in a specific batch rather than gambling on inconsistent oxides found in nature. Frits can contain soluble oxides in an insoluble form while also tying up toxic oxides in safe glassy matrixes.

Frits are generally not used as a clay body flux because of their strong and fast melting action even in low-temperature clay bodies. In clay bodies fired above cone 02 (2048°F), frits are not recommended because they are an inappropriate flux for higher temperature ranges. However, small amounts of frit can be used to create low-temperature vitreous clay bodies which will have certain limitations. The most severe drawback is the short maturing range found in fritted clay bodies. Sometimes the clay body can easily be under-fired or over-fired within a one-cone range. Using the correct amount of frit for the individual clay body formula is critical as is using the appropriate type of frit.

Some frits are slightly soluble and when used in a clay body can break down, leaching into the water system of the moist clay body. The clay can then become rock hard or soft, like putty (thixotropic) when pressure is applied to the clay mass. The most common reason potters don't use frits is their expense, but such an assessment isn't economically sound if the clay body performs as required.

When substituting any frit in a clay body, test it thoroughly before mixing a large quantity of clay body. Listed are the most commonly used frits and their equivalents.

Ferro	Glostex	Pemco	Hommel	Fusion
3110	GF134	P-IV05		F-75
3124	GF113	P-311	90	F-19
3134	GF111	P-54	14	F-12
3195		P-67	399	F-2
5301		P-1084		FZ-24
3819		P-25	259	FZ-25
3269	GF114	P-25	259	FZ-25

Summary

Every potter who mixes their own clay or has their clay mixed will eventually need to make a raw material substitution, but it should always be the last resort. Any time you make a change, it endangers the success of the end product, no matter how closely the substitution matches. Thoroughly understanding raw materials and the clays available is your best insurance when the time comes to make a change in the clay body formula. This understanding must be obtained from several sources. No one source – past experience, ceramics teachers, fellow potters, magazines, books, or ceramics experts – will offer a comprehensive understanding of a raw material. You must gather and evaluate many sources of information.

In addition to empirical information, at some point you must reach into the raw material bag and learn about it on a practical nuts and bolts level. Sometimes the material acts differently in the studio than it does on the written page. The material can even behave differently from one bag to the next bag. It is only through experience and repeated kiln firings that a commonsense workable knowledge of ceramic material begins to fall in place. Building upon small pieces of information can lead to a greater understanding of the materials used in clay body and glaze formulas.

When deciding which feldspar to use in a clay body, it's important to know if the feldspar is potassium, sodium, or lithium and how it reacts with different clays, flint, talc, or any other clay body component. How the combination of these materials and feldspar melted at cone 06 1830°F, cone 6 2232°F, and cone 9 2336°F would be very useful information, as would knowing how the clay body would look in different kiln atmospheres – wood, soda, salt, reduction, oxidation, electric, or raku. The combinations of materials and potential kiln atmospheres can become very complex very fast. Try starting with a few basic materials and build on your experiential and empirical knowledge. Read, listen, do, and try again.

Acknowledgments

Ms. Dorna Isaacs, Hammil & Gillespie, Inc. has given her valuable time in helping me with information about the raw materials her company offers to the ceramics industry.

Mr. Joe Koons, Technical Services, Laguna Clay Co., was most informative in his explanations of West Coast raw materials.

Mr. Ken Bougher, Technical Services Director, Old Hickory Clay Co., was very helpful in his advice on ball clays. His 30 years of experience in the industry and plain talk explanations of ball clay classification greatly added to the subject of clay body substitutions.

Mr. Bill Lisonbee, Lab Technician, Laguna Clay Co., has been a consistent source of reliable information on West Coast clays and their individual characteristics. Thank you for your help with the article.

Mr. John Williams, President of Trinity Ceramic Supply, has offered his time and expert advice in supplying technical characteristics on many clays used in clay body formulas.

Mr. Bill Leach, Kentucky Tennessee Ball Clay Co., thank you for the information you have given me over these many years. Your extensive knowledge of clays has been most appreciated.

Mr. Tom Landon, Ceramic Engineer, H.C. Spinks Clay Co., offered information and advice on ball clay air floating procedures.

Mr. William Edwards, Quality Control Manager, Cedar Heights Clay Co., supplied technical information on stoneware clays.

Mr. Eric Nederberg, President of United Clays, P.O. Box 194, Huntingburg, Ind., was very informative on supplying information on Yellow Banks 101 and Yellow Banks 401 clays.

Mr. Bill Rogers, Vice President of Sales & Marketing, Ceramics, Zemex Industries & Minerals, Atlanta, Ga., thank you for the technical information about EPK.

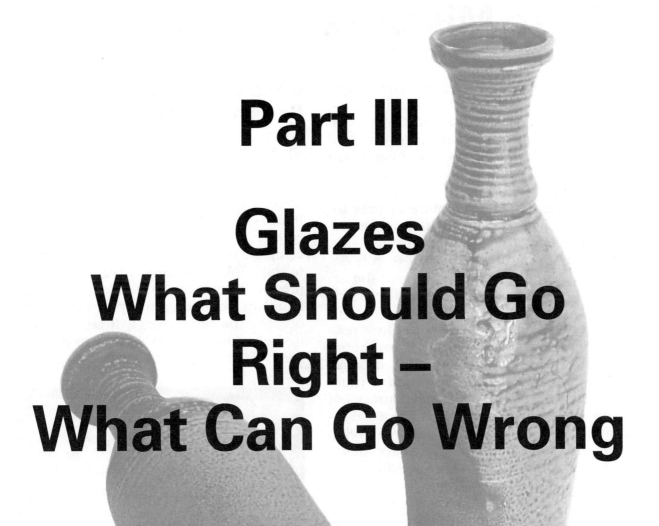

Part III

Glazes
What Should Go Right –
What Can Go Wrong

Chapter 12

Glaze Mistakes to Avoid

After the pots are formed and bisque fired successfully, a potter's greatest frustration often develops in glaze application or firing mistakes. Sometimes excellent pots are lost because of insufficient knowledge of glaze preparation and firing techniques.

Making ceramic sculpture or pots involves many procedures that must be precisely mastered to produce a good result. It's human nature for potters to concentrate their energies and efforts on the areas they enjoy or do well and overlook other areas that aren't as much fun or gratifying. Some potters love to throw pots and correspondingly spend many hours on this enjoyable activity. But because they don't take the time to learn and practice glazing skills, their well-thrown pot can be poorly glazed. Although it's difficult, it's critical that new potters develop the discipline to learn and practice all aspects of ceramics, even the ones they don't like.

Applying the glaze and firing the kiln often gives potters the most problems. The further along the ceramic piece is in the production process, the greater the investment of time and energy that's at stake. How often have you heard or thought, "This is a good piece. I hope it's not ruined by my glazing," or, "I worked all month making those pots and when I unloaded the kiln, the glazes ran on the kiln shelves."? At some point, all potters face inferior glazes and unproductive kiln results. It takes effort and the ability to master the proper techniques to turn such situations into positive results.

Good Glazing Starts with Correctly Firing the Bisque Kiln

Bisque firing irreversibly changes the raw clay so it can accept glazing without being deformed by the water in the glaze. It also causes organic materials to be driven out of the clay body. In order for the complete combustion of organic materials to take place, excess oxygen must be present during the kiln firing. In electric kilns, an oxidation atmosphere is present because the kiln is fired with a greater air-to-fuel ratio, creating excess oxygen for combustion of organic materials in the

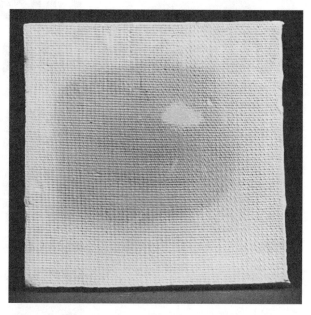

Carbon trap in bisque tile. Not enough oxygen is present in the bisque kiln firing to combust organic materials in the clay body (gray center area of the tile).

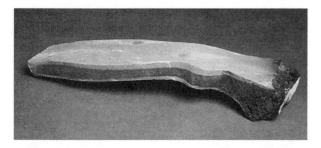

A low fire, high iron content clay body exposed to a reduction atmosphere in a gas fired bisque kiln. Note the carbon trap black areas and bloating on the right side.

The cross section of a bloating clay body fired in a reduction kiln.

clay body. However, bisque firing in a gas kiln can create neutral or reducing conditions which can cause organic materials to be trapped in the clay body.

Most potters use an electric kiln for bisque firing, but many fire their pots in gas kilns. Either way, knowing how to correctly fire the kiln is critically important. The pots should be bone dry when placed in the kiln. If they are damp, keep the temperature below 212°F until the excess water evaporates from the ware. For the average size functional pottery forms (1/4" to 1/2" thick and 2" to 14" tall) a ten-hour total bisque firing time is normal. Most low-fire and high-temperature clay bodies can be bisque fired from cone 010 (1641°F)

Glaze blistering. A lack of excess oxygen in bisque firing leaves unvolatized organic material in the clay body which forms a gas. It then passes through the molten glaze surface, causing glaze blisters.

Organic materials trapped in a bisque clay body cause bloating and black coring at higher temperatures.

Bloating in the clay body (small raised bumps in the clay) caused by organic material in clays not being completely burnt out in the bisque firing. When the ware is glaze fired at a higher temperature, unburned organics try to escape as gases that are trapped by the vitreous clay body.

to cone 06 (1830°F). For larger or thicker ceramic pieces, increase the firing time.

Heating the kiln too slowly won't cause problems, but a fast temperature increase can cause the pots to crack or blow up from escaping steam in the clay. After the bisque firing, when the pots are cool to the touch, they can be taken out of the kiln and glazed. If glazing is delayed, cover the pots with a lightweight plastic sheet (dry cleaner plastic bags are lightweight) to prevent dust, hand oils, and dirt from contaminating the bisque surface. Any foreign material that lands on the pots now can cause glaze defects later.

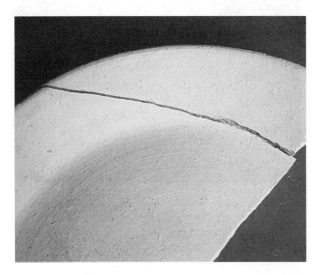

A bisque plate crack caused by a fast heating and/or cooling cycle. Plates, wide based forms, or tiles can also crack on their outer edges when placed too close to the kiln heat source.

Raw Materials in the Studio

The overall layout of the studio should be designed so that ceramic pieces follow a logical progression to their completion. Try to eliminate wasted steps by arranging the equipment, tools, work tables, kilns, and raw materials so they are accessible and functional. For example, a wedging table should be placed next to the potter's wheel so the clay can be wedged and placed on the potter's wheel without wast-

ed motion. Ware racks for storing glazed pots should be arranged near the kiln to ease loading and unloading. Storage areas for kiln shelves, posts, pyrometric cones, and other kiln supplies should be within easy reach of the kiln.

When ordering raw materials, be very specific as to the trade name, mesh size, and manufacturer or processor of the material. It's common to reorder the correct glaze material without specifying the mesh size. For example, whiting is the generic name of a material commonly used in glazes. It's produced in various mesh sizes that all look like white powder, but using a coarser grind of whiting can cause a clear glaze to become opaque. To insure consistent glazing results, state the raw material trade name, manufacturer or processor, and the mesh size.

Be sure to have the appropriate materials in your studio before you need them. Before starting a production cycle, look through your studio and make a list of any supplies you need, then call your ceramics supplier and order them. This way, you can focus your energy on actually creating the ceramic object(s), not on the risky situation of trying to use a substitute material. A well-stocked studio saves time and prevents costly mistakes. There is nothing more frustrating than having a ceramic

Most ceramic raw materials are white or off-white. Glaze materials should be stored in lidded containers with the material name on the container.

project delayed because of the absence of a needed raw material or tool.

All raw materials should be stored in leak-proof containers with the label of the material securely on the container. Often a label falls off or is not readable, causing a mystery material that is impossible to identify and therefore, impossible to use correctly. Liquid glazes should also be clearly marked and stored in covered containers near the glazing area.

Commercial Glazes Versus Making Your Own

A planned approach to buying commercial glazes or making your own glaze will help promote a system that produces the glazes you want rather than ones you have to accept. Most liquid commercial glazes are formulated for brush application with a high amount of binder, which makes it difficult to use them for dipping and spraying. Test any glaze before committing it to a whole kiln load of pots. Many beginning potters start with commercial glazes and eventually develop their own glazes that more accurately reflect their personal statement in clay.

Some glaze colors such as reds, yellows, and oranges are easier to obtain with commercial glazes. While more expensive, commercial glazes do offer reliable results in many colors and textures. The average cost of materials to make your own clear glaze is $6 per gallon compared with a commercial clear glaze that can cost more than $26 per gallon.

When using any glaze formula, stay with glazes from the same temperature range. It's not a good idea to use low-temperature glazes and high-temperature glazes in the studio unless they are carefully separated and labeled. The danger of a low-temperature glaze being fired in a high-temperature kiln is too great. Choose one temperature range for all your glaze formulas and clay bodies. The most popu-

lar cones and temperature ranges are cone 06 (1830°F), cone 6 (2232°F), and cone 9 (2336°F).

Testing the Glaze

One of the most costly and frequent mistakes made in the studio is glazing a kiln load of pots with an untested glaze. Glaze testing takes time, but not testing can waste much more time if you have to replace a kiln load of damaged pots. Try to include a few new glaze test pieces in every kiln load of production pots. Commercial glazes should also be tested on your clay body with the firing characteristics of your kiln. The test tiles should be at least 3" to 4" high and have a smooth side and a rough or scored surface side. Various surface areas on the clay can show how the glaze will flow when molten. Some glazes work well on smooth clay surfaces, but can be razor sharp on rough areas after fired and cooled. A vertical test tile will better indicate if a glaze is likely to run or drip. The basic idea is to obtain as much information from the test tile as the surface area will allow. Test the same glaze at various thicknesses on a tile and then make up several tiles with the same glaze to be placed in different locations in the kiln.

Glazing the Pots

The proper glaze thickness, regardless of the glaze application method (dipping, spraying, brushing), is most important to a successful glaze. If the glaze is applied too thin, the true glaze color is less likely to cover the clay body color. The fired glaze can have a rough, pebble-like surface texture if the clay body irregularities are not filled by a thicker glaze layer. A thicker glaze layer will reveal the true color and/or opacity of the glaze, but a too-thick application can cause the glaze to run and drip off vertical ceramic surfaces. Glazes differ as to how thick or thin they can be applied. Nevertheless, most will fire with good results if the glaze layer is between 1/2mm to 1mm thick (stack three cardboard match book covers to approximate the correct glaze thickness).

Glazing Hints

*   Remove any dust or dirt from the bisque pots before glazing.

*   Mix wet glaze thoroughly, bringing up any glaze at the bottom of the container, then pour the wet glaze through an 80x-mesh sieve three times to remove any coarse particles.

*   Stir the wet glaze in the container every five to ten minutes during the glazing operation to prevent the glaze from settling.

*   Dip several test pieces in the glaze to judge the glaze thickness.

*   Whether the glaze is sprayed, dipped, or brushed, the end result should be a smooth, coating of glaze with no cracks or pinholes in the dried glaze surface.
*   When firing electric kilns, don't place pots near the kiln elements. When firing gas kilns, don't place pots near the burner ports. Direct flame or heat impingement can cause glaze and clay body defects.
*   Glazed pots should be completely dry before loading them in the kiln.

Glaze Firing Hints

*   Test fire any glaze before using it on a kiln load of pots.

*   Keep a kiln log or record of each firing. Note details of the firing so a good kiln result can be duplicated.

Direct flame impingement on the ware causes flashing brown areas of clay body and glaze cracking.

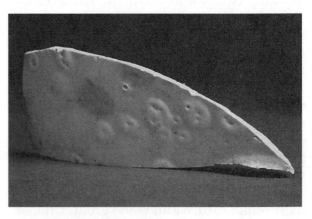

Glaze blisters caused by fast firing.

* The best firings happen when every space in the kiln is completely filled with pots. If there aren't enough pots to fill the kiln, use posts and shelves. Increasing the thermal mass inside the kiln increases the radiant heat and promotes even heat distribution throughout the kiln. Increased thermal mass also slows the heating and cooling cycle, resulting in increased clay body strength and glaze maturation.

* Always wear the proper safety goggles (protection from infrared and ultraviolet light emitted from the kiln) when looking in a firing kiln.

* Consider the endpoint temperature (the highest temperature reached during the firing) and just as importantly, the time it takes to reach that temperature. Materials in clay bodies and glazes need time to melt.

* Always be present when the kiln shuts off. Sometimes an automatic kiln shut-off device fails and the kiln will keep firing.

* Unload the kiln only when it's cool enough to touch the pots with your bare hands.

Excessive glaze drips on the vertical surface (over-fired glaze kiln).

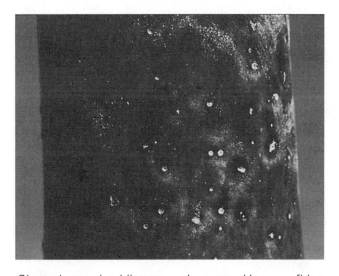

Glaze sharp edge blisters can be caused by over-firing the glaze.

Thick glaze application can cause glaze to run during firing.

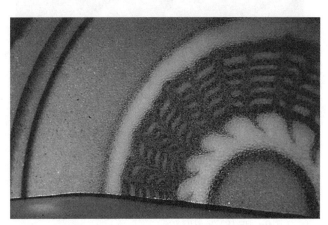

Small trapped bubbles in the fired glaze can cause opacity.

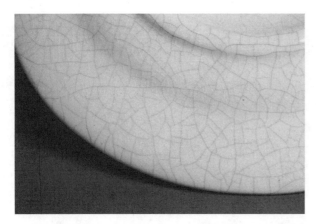

Glaze crazing – a fine network of lines in the fired glaze.

Glaze specking caused by glaze raw material contamination.

Glaze crawling – glaze rolls up on its edges, exposing the clay body surface.

Common Glaze Defects and Corrections

* **Fired glaze drips and runs off the pots**. Apply a thinner glaze coat and/or fire the kiln at a lower temperature.
* **Matte surface texture glazes fire glossy**. Fire the kiln to a lower temperature.
* **Fired pots stick to the kiln shelf, warp, have glaze drips, or shrink excessively**. Fire the kiln to a lower temperature.
* **Clay body texture shows through rough fired glaze surfaces**. Apply thicker glaze coat.
* **Sharp-edged blisters or craters in the fired glaze**. Fire the kiln to a lower temperature and/or fire the kiln slower.
* **Dry rough fired surfaces with dull glaze colors**. Fire the kiln to a higher temperature and/or increase the firing time.
* **Opacity in fired clear glazes**. Fire the kiln to a higher temperature and/or increase the firing time.
* **Pinholes in fired glaze**. Increase the glaze firing time and densely pack the kiln with pots, shelves, or posts to increase the thermal mass.
* **Fired glaze has a network of cracks (crazing)**. Try a thinner glaze coat. Don't fast cool glaze kilns. Adjust the glaze formula by adding 5, 10, and 15 parts more flint to the glaze.
* **Unfired glaze cracks after the pot dries**. Try a thinner glaze coat. Add binder to the glaze such as CMC in 1/8% to 2% amounts based on the dry weight of the glaze to stabilize and hold the raw glaze as it is drying.

* **Black specks in the fired glaze surface**. Indicates contamination on the ware before glazing or glaze contamination.
* **Fired glaze pulls or beads away from clay surfaces (crawling)**. Dust, grease, or other contaminating material on the bisque pots and/or glaze application too thick. Also some glazes have high amounts of material that shrink excessively in the firing. Additions of a binder such as CMC in 1/8% to 2% amounts based on the dry weight of the glaze will hold the raw glaze together until the first stages of melting.
* **Fired glaze has an orange peel-like surface texture**. Apply thinner glaze coat and/or a longer glaze firing time.

Keep it Simple and Record Your Results

Producing pots or ceramic sculpture can be very exciting but you may reach a point in the forming, glazing, or firing stages where there are too many variables and too many inconclusive results. It seems like a good glaze leads to variations which can lead to many test pieces scattered around the studio, eventually leading to clutter and confusion. Raw material inconsistencies, kiln firing cycles, glaze application thickness, overlapping glaze effects, and other unplanned ceramic events can also result in countless variations of glaze colors and textures. Work with just a few glazes formulas at any one time until you feel confident of their consistent fired results, then slowly expand on that base of knowledge. If the formulas are within the same temperature or cone range, it's less confusing with less potential for error.

Working with many ceramic raw materials requires attention to clay body and glaze formulas, raw material inventories, glaze firing results, and many other details. Choose a record-keeping system that works based on your own needs. Many potters use separate blank notebooks for kiln firing results, pottery forming technique notes, and glaze/clay body formulas. The main objective should be to keep the little bits of information organized and easy to find when needed. Over time, many favorite glaze formulas can get lost in the studio. The few minutes it takes to organize now saves hours later. Keeping accurate notes on your results increases the chance of duplicating a desired glaze or clay body color or texture. It is also a useful tool in gaining an understanding of how to solve problems with clays and glazes.

Chapter 13

Gerstley Borate and Colemanite

Raw materials used in clay body and glaze formulas can change slightly in chemical composition and/or particle size over time. Under normal circumstances, such minor variations don't influence the outcome of a clay body or glaze. For example most feldspars used by potters fluctuate in their sodium, potassium, lithium, alumina, and silica contents. However, the feldspar mining companies monitor and adjust the given amounts of each oxide contained in the feldspar to close tolerance. The economic incentive for such high quality control is determined by the large industrial users and their need for a consistent product. Feldspars as a group are mined in large quantities and used in many products throughout the United States. The economic incentive for the mines is to keep feldspars consistent to insure a market share for their product.

Gerstley borate does not enjoy such economic clout since it only serves small markets of potters and the roofing tile industries. On an economic level, potters are at a distinct disadvantage because of the limited amounts of Gerstley borate they purchase. A similar situation applies to colemanite, another ceramic material used by potters. Potters represent a marginal market for these materials so there's no financial reason for the mines to improve the product for pottery use. Yet in the small market of pottery, Gerstley borate and colemanite are two of the most widely used raw materials found in glaze formulas.

The History and Use of Gerstley Borate and Colemanite in Glazes

The lack of information surrounding the use of Gerstley borate and colemanite in glazes has contributed to frequent glaze defects. Both glaze materials can and often do change drastically, sometimes from one bag to the next, and when a variation happens it alters the glaze.

Gerstley borate and colemanite are naturally occurring ores that found their way into low-, medium-, and high-temperature glaze formulas. They have been regularly utilized in glazes for many years. In the past, Turkish colemanite could only be purchased in minimum quantities of 500 tons. In the 1970s, the supply of colemanite from Turkey was delayed long enough for ceramics industries to look for a substitute and many formulas were recalculated to accept Gerstley borate. Both minerals supply the fluxing action that brings other glaze materials to a complete melt and both contain high amounts of B_2O_3 (boric oxide) which can enhance colors and promote mottled semiopacity in glazes.

Why are Gerstley borate and colemanite used in formulas if they cause glaze defects? Many Gerstley borate and colemanite glazes now used in the United States were developed in the 1950s and '60s and the formulas were passed from teacher to student then to other potters without a critical evaluation of the raw materials. These two materials do work well for long periods in glazes, but eventually they will cause a glaze defect. Obviously, if the glaze formulas failed all the time or most of the time, they wouldn't be passed along to other potters. The time delay between a glaze failure was so long that many potters didn't realize these variable raw materials were causing glaze defects. Compounding the problem was the fact that the types of glaze defects – pinholes (small round-edged holes in the fired glaze), blisters (sharp-edged craters in the fired glaze surface), crawling (bare spots on the clay body where the fired glaze rolled back on itself), peeling (bare spots on the clay body where unfired dry glaze lifted off the pot's surface in sheets), and dry glaze (sandpaper texture) – produced by Gerstley borate and colemanite can be caused by many other factors. While potters were discovering the problems associated with Gerstley borate and colemanite, many potters were left without this knowledge. Many glaze formulas were then passed from one potter to the next. Both materials have found good use in raku formulas where variability of a glaze result is a desired goal.

Gerstley Borate

Gerstley borate is mined domestically by U.S. Borax Inc., which produces more than one million tons of borate minerals per year. However, the amount of Gerstley borate mined is less than 1,000 tons per year, almost all of which finds its way into pottery glazes. Potters represent the major market for this product, but their demand is marginal compared with U.S. Borax's other minerals. The mine is located near the small town of Shoshone, Calif., near the Nevada state line. The Death Valley region is about 50 miles away from the Gerstley borate mine. James Mack Gerstley found the original deposit of calcium borate in 1923, which local townspeople called Gerstley's borate. Once the ore is extracted from the mine on the side of a hill, small rail cars take the fist-size pieces to be crushed and screened to 1/4" lumps. Bulk trucks then take the ore for shipment to customers.

Gerstley borate is formed from lake bed sediment. It was originally clay on the edge of a lake into which a borate spring flowed, depositing ulexite (a sodium calcium borate) seven million years ago. The soft lake bed sediment with the borate enclosed eventually turned into the mineral now mined. A distinctive characteristic of Gerstley borate is the volcanic glass mixed into the clay during its formation period. The resulting clay contains high amounts of calcium and silica. It's the only borate deposit in that region with a glassy volcanic component. The predominant borate mineral found in Gerstley borate is ulexite (Na_2O $2CaO$ $5B_2O_3$ $16H_2O$) with small amounts of colemanite ($2CaO$ $3B_2O_3$ $5H_2O$), probertite (Na_2O $2CaO$ $5B_2O_3$ $10H_2O$) and gangue (pronounced gang). Gangue is composed of bentonitic clay which is mud and other insoluble or "tramp" materials found with the minerals. This bentonitic clay gangue contains mostly calcium and silica; in addition there are small amounts of imbedded sandstone and basalt which often reveals itself as brown/black pepper-like specks in the off-white Gerstley borate powder.

Gerstley borate is considered a raw unprocessed ore and gangue is a natural rock component found with the material. Gangue isn't economically desirable but can't be avoided in the mining process. The bentonitic clay gangue associated with Gerstley borate makes it unique. Thus, Gerstley borate has no single chemical notation due to its variable mineral consistency and gangue components.

Solubility, low-temperature fluxing, chemical inconsistency, high amounts of carbonates, and contamination all characterize the potential causes of problems related to this popular glaze material. When introduced in water, Gerstley borate will dissociate into sodium or calcium borates and can be classified as "sparingly soluble." As the glaze solution sits, the borates continue to dissolve and form a water-soluble compound. Pouring off some excess water in a Gerstley borate glaze or water evaporation in glaze storage can change the fired glaze result. Often a batch of glaze is fine initially but after storage, the same batch can produce pinholes and blisters in the fired glaze.

Since the partially dissolved Gerstley borate travels in the water system of a glaze, it can collect in greater concentrations on the lips and higher edges of pottery as the glaze water evaporates off the pot. The effected areas can result in pinholes, blisters, and dry surfaces in the fired glaze. Gerstley borate could be made into a frit (a material fired to a molten state, quenched to form a glass, and ground into a powder) which would decrease its solubility but the major frit manufacturers find it too costly and time-consuming to produce a Gerstley borate-based frit for the small pottery market.

The exact melting point of Gerstley borate is difficult to define. The two minerals in Gerstley borate don't melt at the same temperature (ulexite melts at 1535°F and colemanite melts at around 1652°F). Since the borates in Gerstley borate melt at various temperatures, the result can be a semiopaque mottled glaze surface. A common defect associated with Gerstley borate is its low melting point and its subsequent use in glazes fired above cone 6 (2232°F). Gerstley borate in high-temperature glazes can partially volatilize, causing an over-fluxed pinhole or blistered glaze surface. The same set of defects can also occur due to the high amount of carbonates in Gerstley borate which release carbon dioxide gas. As the gas bubbles travel through the glaze layer, some become trapped in the layer and others break open on the fired glaze surface. Over-fluxed glazes can also run or drip off vertical ceramic surfaces on the pot or a pool of glaze can collect in horizontal areas.

Colemanite

Colemanite ($Ca_2 B_6O_{11} 5H_2O$) is a mineral with a set formula as opposed to Gerstley borate. However, it is still an unprocessed ore and the gangue component can change with geologic conditions. It also contains some clays, marl, limestone, sandstone, and volcanic stuff but in much lower concentrations than Gerstley borate. Colemanite is used primarily in the fiberglass and metallurgy flux industries. Deposits exist in the United States, Argentine Republic, and Turkey. In the past, Turkish colemanite was the only one imported to the United States. Turkish colemanite comes from mines located in several different basins with different geologic conditions, resulting in colemanite of slightly different chemical compositions. Because of this, it has a slightly variable chemical composition but much less so than Gerstley borate.

Production is from open pit and underground mines. The mineral colemanite is thought to form from the alteration or leaching of ulexite. Sodium contained in the borate is very soluble and is slowly dissolved in water, leaving the calcium borate behind. Once the water leaves the lake, the remaining layers of relatively pure calcium borate (colemanite) can be mined.

While colemanite is available to large industries, potters might not see it regu-

A typical Gerstley borate blister/pinhole pattern in a glaze surface.

larly stocked on their ceramics supplier's shelves. Importers of the mineral will only sell it in container loads (44,000 pounds) and most ceramics supply companies can't tie up the capital it would take to purchase such a large quantity of a raw material to sell a few pounds at a time. If you do find colemanite, always note the source since there can be variations in the material due to the country of origin.

When melting in a glaze, colemanite doesn't produce as much gas as Gerstley borate does, but it can still cause pinholes or blistering of glaze surfaces because it's a low-temperature flux. Using too much colemanite in high-temperature glaze formulas will result in "boiling off" or over-fluxing the glaze. Colemanite can produce opacity in low cone 06 (1830°F) temperature glazes and is a strong flux in high-temperature glazes above cone 6 (2232°F). Boric oxide and calcia in colemanite don't melt at the same temperatures and the delay in complete amalgamation can cause the glaze surface to appear mottled. While it is stated that colemanite is insoluble, it does appear to partially dissolve in the water system of glazes in storage much the same as Gerstley borate. Colemanite can cause glaze crawling (a glaze defect that looks like water on a glass table top) due to the large amount of water contained in its crystal structure and its subsequent high shrinkage rate when heated.

Gerstley Borate Versus Colemanite

In most glazes, the materials can be used interchangeably on a one-for-one basis. However, there are several important characteristics of each material that could affect a glaze. Colemanite contains approximately 40% boron compared to approximately 28% boron in Gerstley borate. In glazes that rely on a specific level of B_2O_3 for a multi-hued surface appearance or color development, a direct substitution might not produce an exact match in color or surface mottling. Gerstley borate causes a slightly lighter color in glazes but, due to its higher level of carbonates, it can cause more pinholes and blisters in the fired glaze surface. Gerstley borate glazes are more likely to have mottled irregular surface textures.

Both Gerstley borate and colemanite contain calcium, which can cause flocculation in the liquid glaze. Particles in the glaze are attracted to each other and aggregate into larger clumps. The glaze often appears thick and lumpy and looks like oatmeal. It doesn't flow or pour well, which makes it exceedingly difficult to use for spraying, dipping, or painting glaze applications. Increasing the amount of water in the glaze only causes excessive shrinkage and cracking as the glaze dries. Adding any one of the most common deflocculents (soda ash 1/20 to 1/10 of 1%, Darvan #7 1/4 to 1/2 of 1%, or sodium silicate 1/4 to 1/2 of 1% based on the dry weight of the glaze) will repel particles suspended in liquid and correct the thick consistency of the glaze.

Both Gerstley borate and colemanite have small amounts of free water or pore water which is driven off by heating to approximately 248°F. However, both minerals have large amounts of bound water, which is classified as the water of crystallization. This type of water is contained in the crystal structure and is not driven off until 1112°F or approximately dull red heat in the kiln is reached. Due to the large quantity of bound water in each mineral, it can cause high shrinkage rates as the water is driven off during the firing. If the kiln is heated too fast from the start up to dull red heat, Gerstley borate and colemanite glazes can crawl, peel, crack, or jump off the pot, landing on the kiln shelves. All these glaze defects are due to excessive shrinkage or steam created by the bound water being driven off too fast.

Since both glaze materials are essentially low-temperature fluxes, using a glaze with large amounts of either Gerstley borate or colemanite can cause part of the glaze to vaporize in the kiln. This effect is most noticeable when a metallic oxide or stain is coloring the Gerstley borate or colemanite glaze. Often a colored glaze sprays small particles on a light or white glaze nearby during the firing or the colored vapor lands on the kiln shelf under the pot. When Gerstley borate or colemanite are used in overglaze washes (a mixture of coloring oxide or stain with Gerstley borate or colemanite painted over a dry raw glaze) volatilization can spit little dots of color on adjoining light or white glaze areas. Glaze or overglaze wash volatilization can occur at low temperatures but is most frequent at high temperature ranges above cone 6 (2232°F).

The Economics of Gerstley Borate and Colemanite

The law of supply and demand impacts hardest on potters when they try to purchase high quality consistent raw materials. Since potters represent less than one tenth of one percent of the raw material markets in the United States, the choice and availability of materials are limited by that economic reality. As one importer told me, "You can't make any money from people who buy colemanite by the pound. We only deal with people who want truck loads." The majority of materials on the market today are there because large industries need a specific ball clay, kaolin, talc, flint, dolomite, feldspar, etc. Consistency in chemical composition and particle size are required by the large industries that order the materials. Potters can take advantage of these guaranteed raw materials but clay body and glaze formulas often require other materials that are not used by large industries.

In the past, Gerstley borate had a higher level of contaminates which have since been decreased by screening the ore to a 3x-mesh size at the mine. Currently, Hammill & Gillespie on the East Coast and Laguna Clay Co. on the West Coast perform a critical service for potters. They are the only ceramics supply companies who invest the money for a minimum truckload purchase of Gerstley borate from U.S. Borax, Inc. and then pay to have it ground to a 200x-mesh powder and packaged in 50-pound bags. Each shipment of Gerstley borate processed (approximately 25 tons) is assigned a batch number.

How to Work With, Around, or Without Gerstley Borate and Colemanite

If the glaze formula requires Gerstley borate or colemanite for a specific color response or a mottled surface texture, try to purchase the material in large quantities. Since Gerstley borate and colemanite can change in chemical composition from one batch to the next, buying a whole bag at one time is best. At least it will eliminate a possible inconsistency caused by a different batch of material. Each 50-pound bag is marked with a batch number and if possible you should request the same batch number when reordering. When mixing the glaze, don't pour off excess glaze water as this might change the actual glaze formula. Always store Gerstley borate and colemanite in airtight containers and mix up only enough glaze for one glazing session. Gerstley borate and colemanite do not store well in a liquid glaze.

The actual amount of Gerstley borate or colemanite in a specific glaze can determine if it can be removed totally from the formula without noticeably affecting the fired glaze. If the amount of Gerstley borate or colemanite is below 5% in the glaze, it can often be eliminated. In such instances, another flux material in the glaze formula contributes to the melting process and the Gerstley borate or colemanite won't be missed. However, as little as 5% of Gerstley borate or colemanite in any glaze is less likely to cause a defect than greater amounts.

In glaze formulas that don't require the color and surface mottling effects produced by Gerstley borate and colemanite, a substitute glaze material should be considered. Whenever possible, choose materials that are nonsoluble and chemically consistent for glaze formulas. In low-fire glazes cone 06 (1830°F), a possible substitute for Gerstley borate or colemanite would be Ferro frit #3195 or Ferro frit #3134. In medium- to high-temperature glazes above cone 6 (2232°F), use Ferro frit #3195 or a sodium-based feldspar (nepheline syenite, F-4 feldspar) or a potassium-based feldspar (Custer feldspar, G-200 feldspar) depending on the specific glaze requirements such as exact firing temperature, glaze texture, and glaze color.

Start by making a one-for-one replacement with the substitute material. Mix up a small amount of adjusted glaze and apply it to a vertical test tile. Place the test piece in a regular production kiln. Use an old kiln shelf under the test piece when first trying adjusted glaze formulas. If the fired glaze is too dry and looks under-fired, add five parts additional substitute material to the glaze. The glaze should first be calculated to a 100% batch weight so additions of five parts of substitute material will yield 105 batch weights. If the fired glaze runs off the tile, it has too much flux so take out five parts of the substitute glaze material. If the fired glaze color is not satisfactory, choose another substitute material.

Safety

Any material used in clay and glaze formulas must be handled with common sense and care. Keeping a clean studio with materials stored in properly labeled containers is an important first step in developing a safe studio environment. Your ceramics supplier should be able to furnish a Material Safety Data Sheet (MSDS) for each raw material they sell. The sheet lists the chemical product, company identification, composition information on ingredients, hazard identification, first aid measures, toxicological information, and other safety considerations when handling the material. Read this information carefully as it will give guidelines for handling and storage.

Gerstley borate and colemanite present little or no hazard to humans and have low oral and dermal toxicities. Neither mineral is irritating and they cannot be absorbed through the skin. Inhalation treatment is not necessary since they are not likely to be hazardous but prolonged exposure to dust levels should be avoided. As with any dry material used in the studio, store Gerstley borate and colemanite in sealed containers and always wear a dust mask when handling the dry powder. Gerstley borate and colemanite have not proven harmful if the fired glaze is slightly soluble.

While Gerstley borate and colemanite can be used as a substitute for each other in many glaze formulas, they are different minerals. Since both function the same in glaze formulas, as fluxes of almost equal strength, it is not surprising that many potters thought they were the same material. What makes Gerstley borate unique is its high level of gangue minerals that have not been processed out of the ore. The variable quality of the mineral can cause wide alterations in the fired glaze and offers subtle differences in the fired glaze when compared with colemanite. Many, but not all potters are looking for raw materials that are uniform and consistent in chemical composition. Gerstley borate and colemanite should not be considered if you are looking for long-term consistent glaze results. However, they are ideal materials for raku glazes where inconsistency and variability of glaze results are considered desirable.

No matter where it's mined, colemanite is a cleaner ore than Gerstley borate. It also is a slightly stronger flux in glaze formulas. However, economic considerations will keep this material in limited and sporadic supply to potters. The minimum tonnage required for its purchase from the importers is beyond the reach of ceramics suppliers. Both colemanite and Gerstley borate will cause the wet glaze to flocculate or become thick and lumpy. The mineral content of the glaze water can marginally aggravate or decrease glaze flocculation but the general rule is that if the water is fit to drink, it's probably not affecting the glaze by either flocculation or deflocculation.

When incorporated into glaze formulas, Gerstley borate and to a lesser degree colemanite will eventually produce a glaze defect. Many potters use one or both glaze materials without problems, but the history of both materials suggests that they will eventually cause glaze defects. It is amazing that Gerstley borate and colemanite are interchangeable in many glaze formulas considering their different chemical compositions. It is equally impressive that they function well for long periods in glaze formulas considering their chemical variables. Both raw materials still have a place in glaze formulas. The trick to using them is knowing what they can and cannot do at any given time.

Acknowledgments

I would like to thank Mr. Tom Wilhelm, Senior Technical Representative for U.S. Borax, Inc. for his help in reviewing the article and his advise on technical information.

Mr. Robert B. Kistler, Exploration Manager, for U. S. Borax, Inc. supplied information on the geology and formation of Gerstley borate. His descriptions of how the mineral was formed greatly helped in my understanding of Gerstley borate.

Mr. Jacob Mu, of U.S. Borax, Inc. supplied information on the chemical compositions of Gerstley borate and colemanite.

Chapter 14

Eight Steps to Stop Crazing

Understanding glaze theory is important if you want to solve any glaze problem. Unfortunately there are no short cuts to knowledge in ceramics. However, what is often not available to potters is a step-by-step guide for solving the most common glaze problem – crazing. This guide is designed for the potter alone in their studio faced with a crazed glaze. I hope it's simple, short, and effective. When you're lost, you need to know the correct path to your destination. Are you lost?

Crazing presents itself as a series of lines or cracks in the fired glazed surface. The craze pattern can develop upon removal from the kiln or years later. Crazing happens when a glaze is under tension. Even the most stable glazes are under slight compression. While crazing is classified as a glaze defect, it can also be corrected by adjusting the clay body. The goal is to adjust the glaze and clay body to cool at a compatible rate with the glaze coming under slight compression. Listed are some important considerations before starting a correction.

* If craze lines are tightly packed and close together (spaced less than 1/8" apart), the chances of eliminating the lines are decreased. This is a significant indication of the degree of difficulty in fixing the problem. The closer the lines, the harder the fix.

* If the clay body has a high absorption rate (more than 4%) after firing, the chances for correcting the crazing are low.

* If several corrections have been tried with no success and the glaze is common (i.e. gloss transparent, satin matte, matte, gloss blue, black, brown, etc.), try another glaze formula with the idea of arriving at a better glaze fit on the clay body.

* If the glaze is unique and can't be changed, try another clay body.[19]

After considering the above points, try a correction or combination of corrections to solve glaze crazing.

1. Crazing can often be eliminated by a thinner glaze application. With some glazes, a thinner coat is not an option but often a slight decrease in glaze thickness will stop crazing.

2. Add increasing amounts of flint to the glaze formula, the finer the mesh the better. Most flint used in glazes comes in 200-, 325-, and 400-mesh. Finer grind sizes might be available on special order from a ceramics supplier. Also try fused silica, a calcined silica with a very

---

19.   A common low-fire white cone 06 to cone 04 clay body formula is ball clay 50, talc 50, whiting 3. The whiting in the clay body prevents crazing in many glazes.

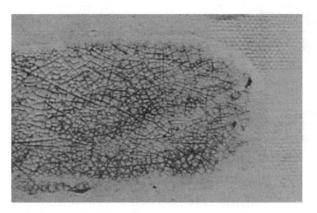

The original glaze craze pattern.

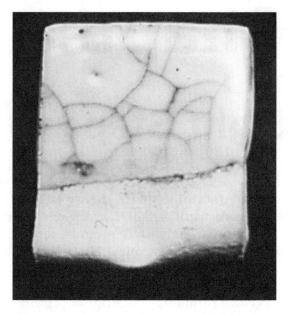

After adding ten more parts of flint to the glaze, the craze lines move further apart.

low shrinkage rate.[20] The low shrinkage rate helps stop crazing. Most glaze formulas have some room for increasing the flint without the glaze becoming opaque or dry when fired. Try additions of 10, 20, and 25 units of measure (the glaze has 50 grams) of flint, increase flint to 60 grams, 70 grams, and 75 grams. Don't change the other glaze materials.

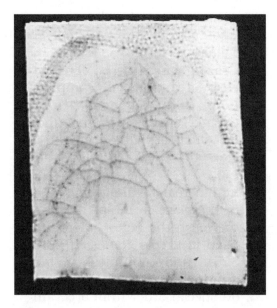

After the addition of ten parts of flint to the glaze, the craze lines move further apart.

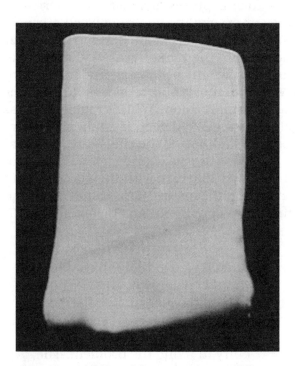

After the addition of five more parts of flint to the glaze, there are no craze lines in the glaze.

20. Siltex 44 is the trade name of fused silica produced by Kaopolite Inc., 244 Morris Ave., Union, NJ 07083, PH: (908) 789-0609. Call the company and ask if they have a distributor in your area.

3. Fire the glaze kiln to the correct cone over a longer time. During the last quarter of the glaze firing cycle, try stretching out the firing by two or three hours. This will give the clay body the best chance to tighten up or reach its maturity, which will help in achieving a good glaze fit.

4. Fire the glaze kiln one or two cones higher only if the glaze will not be adversely affected. By firing higher and/or longer, the glaze and clay body might be adjusted to a better fit. Remember, what has to change is the rate of shrinkage in the clay body, glaze, or both, which results in the glaze being under slight compression. However, if the clay body is already over-fired or on the edge of its maturity range, firing higher will cause increased crazing in the glaze.

5. Add flint 200-mesh to the clay body. Increase flint by 5, 10, and 15 units. Flint found in clay bodies remains a crystalline solid that has different characteristics than flint in a glaze, but it will still work to stop crazing in a glaze.

6. Slowly cool the glaze kiln. Don't open the kiln door until the temperature is below 200°F. The kiln should be cool enough to unload without gloves. Waiting for the kiln to cool will cause no problems, but fast cooling increases the chance of crazing. If the pots ping when the kiln door is open, the glaze is under stress and is more likely to craze.

7. If you're using a low-fire body and the glaze crazes, try bisque firing one or two cones higher than the glaze firing temperature. This might bring the clay body/glaze to a better fit.

8. If the glaze contains frit and it crazes, try using a frit with a lower coefficient of expansion. Your ceramics supplier or the manufacturer of the frit will have the coefficient of expansion rates for each frit. Materials with low coefficients of expansion (flint) are less likely to cause crazing. Other high coefficient of expansion materials can also cause crazing in the glaze and these can be substituted with lower coefficient of expansion materials but this process is best accomplished through a glaze calculation method.

Frequently a combination of the above methods will work, depending on the severity of the craze problem. Be flexible in your thinking while evaluating the test results. If the test results show the craze lines moving further apart, continue with the corrections. If the craze lines are closer together or staying the same, try something else. While the eight steps listed aren't the only corrections for glaze crazing, they have consistently shown results.

Chapter 15

Five Steps to Stop Shivering

Statistically not as common as other defects, shivering can cause a severe glaze problem when it does happen. Shivering occurs when a glaze is under too great a compressive load. The fired glaze defect looks like a paint chip peeling off the underlying clay body. Shivering can develop when the glazed pot cools or sometimes years later! Essentially, when the glaze is under extreme compression the glaze might buckle anytime. While shivering is classified as a glaze defect, it can be corrected either through adjusting the glaze, clay body formula, or a combination of both.

Shivering and crazing are at opposite ends of the same basic problem. The glaze and clay body do not fit when cool. Crazing happens when the glaze is under extreme tension. Interestingly, ceramic materials fail ten times faster under tension than compression. Correspondingly, crazing (glaze under tension) is ten times more prevalent than shivering.

Glaze shivering on the edges of a bowl.

Recognizing and understanding a problem is the first step in solving any glaze defect. Shivering can happen at any temperature range and can occur in oxidation or reduction kiln firings. Frequently when a glaze shivers or peels off the fired clay surface, it is likely to start on the edges or raised areas of the clay. The chip-size pieces of shivered glaze can range

Glaze shivering on the edges of a pitcher lip and handle.

Glaze shivering on the edge of a bowl, exposing the clay surface.

from 1/16" to more than 2" in size. When tapped slightly with a hard object, many seemingly stable clay/glaze surfaces will flake off, sometimes removing part of the supporting clay body. When attempting any correction your goal should be to get the clay body and glaze to cool at a compatible rate, with the glaze coming under slight compression. Several points must be considered before attempting to fix a glaze shivering defect.

 * Clay body formulas containing too much free silica can cause shivering. Fire clays are known to have randomly high levels of free silica. Fine grind grog, also high in silica, can also cause shivering especially if burnished or rubbed to the clay surface in the forming process.

 * Too much and/or too early reduction in a clay body causes an unstable carbon bond between the clay and glaze layer that can result in shivering.

 * Thicker glaze applications are more likely to aggravate shivering if any or all of the above conditions are present.

To correct shivering, add high expansion materials to the clay body and/or glaze (feldspars or other alkali bearing materials). Decreasing low expansion materials in clay bodies and glazes such as flint, petalite, lepidolite, spodumene, and high amounts of lithium carbonate in glazes will also stop shivering. Sometimes a combination of both methods will be necessary. Keep in mind that this process can be carried out to a greater extent through a glaze calculation method.

 1. If only one glaze shivers on the clay body, adding five, ten, or 15 units of feldspar to the glaze will correct shivering, or add-ing other alkali bearing materials[21] (i.e. if the glaze has 10 grams of feldspar, increase feldspar to 15, 20, and 25 grams). Don't change the amounts of other materials in the glaze formula. Adding any flux or glass former will increase the chance of the glaze becoming glossy or running off vertical surfaces. The ideal fix is to get just enough feldspar or frit into the glaze to correct shivering and not overload the glaze with more flux than needed.

 2. Decreasing the flint in a glaze by five or ten units of measure will also adjust the clay body/glaze fit.

 3. Occasionally, a combination of adding feldspar/frit to a glaze and taking out flint will be necessary to stop shivering. In rare instances, the same correction must also be carried out in the clay body.

 4. If many different types of glazes shiver on the same clay body, start the correction by adding five, ten, and 15 units of feldspar (or other alkali-bearing materials) to the clay body.

 5. Decrease the amount of flint in the clay body by five or ten units to correct shivering in a glaze.

Other less practical methods for correcting shivering include lowering the maximum firing temperature or firing faster to maximum temperature. Both will reduce the expansion coefficient of the clay body. Reducing the amount of lime or iron in the clay body also im-

---

21. Materials containing high amounts of sodium or potassium such as frits can be used to correct shivering in a glaze but keep in mind that frits can lower the melting point of a glaze if used in high amounts.

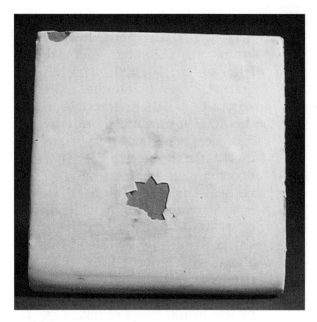

Glaze shivering causing white slip to peel off the red clay body.

very severe (glaze under extreme compression), it can tear or break the underlying clay body, causing the whole piece to crack apart upon cooling. Shivering can also cause underglaze colors or underglaze slips to flake off the fired clay body surface. A slip or engobe that doesn't fit a clay body can sometimes flake off, which can look similar to a glaze shivering defect. Keep in mind that shivering is most likely encountered as a peeling away or chipping of the fired glaze often found on ridges or lips of pieces. While glaze shivering can ruin pieces, it can be corrected by following the steps outlined. In rare instances, if the corrections don't work, changing to another clay body formula with a different shrinkage rate will solve a shivering glaze problem.

proves the glaze/clay body fit. Another glaze correction involves substituting a soda feldspar for a potash spar because soda spars have a higher coefficient of expansion (high shrinkage). Some glazes will change color as a result of this substitution. However effective the corrections might be, they will often produce complications in the color, surface texture, or firing range of the glaze and clay body.

In most instances, shivering can be corrected by adding feldspar, frit, or other high expansion materials to the existing glaze. Shivering can also be corrected by substituting high expansion materials for low expansion materials in the formula by glaze calculation. When shivering is

A defect that looks similar to shivering. The yellow engobe (yellow clay) not fitting the red clay body causes the engobe and covering clear glaze to peel off the clay body.

Chapter 16

Glaze Crawling – Causes and Corrections

If a fired glaze looks like beads of water on a glass tabletop, you're looking at crawling. The same forces of surface tension acting on beading water can also affect fluid molten glaze. Glaze crawling has many possible causes. In some cases, a few solutions can be tried simultaneously to fix this common glaze problem. First, make sure the problem is crawling and not a similar glaze defect. The glaze should appear beaded up or have rounded edges where it draws away from the exposed clay body. The bare patch of clay body can be quite dry or have a slight shine to its surface. In extreme cases of crawling, beads of glaze drop off the pot onto the kiln shelf. If the glaze has the potential to crawl, thicker glaze applications will exacerbate it.

Crawling occurs when the unfired glaze and the underlying clay body don't build and hold a uniform continuous bond. Often the simplest correction is a thinner glaze application, but there are other solutions too. The most common causes of crawling are listed in their general order of occurrence, along with the appropriate corrections.

Glaze Crawling Causes and Corrections

* Greasy or dusty bisque pots. Grease or dust on the bisque causes a disruption of the clay body and glaze surface. In once-firing, a dusty clay surface will cause the glaze to form without being attached to the underlying clay surface. To prevent dust, place a cover over the pots after unloading a bisque kiln, blow any dry clay off once-fired ware before glazing, and wash your hands before touching pots to insure a clean absorbent surface for glaze application.
* High clay content glaze formulas also have high shrinkage rates that can sometimes be observed as cracks in the glaze as it dries on the pot. Shrinkage continues during the fir-

Glaze crawling occurs when the glaze rolls back on itself, exposing the red clay body surface.

ing, causing a flawed bond with the underlying clay body. To correct this, use calcined clay for half the clay component in the glaze formula. Calcined clay has already been fired and shrinks less than unfired clay when used in the glaze formula. Another alternative is to use a clay that shrinks less than the original clay component of the glaze formula. If the original formula calls for ball clay in the glaze, a high shrinkage clay such as kaolin with less shrinkage might be substituted. Less glaze shrinkage at this stage can eliminate crawling as the fired glaze begins to mature. Both VeeGum CER and CMC act as binders, so adding either to the glaze will help keep the high shrinkage and light density glaze materials together long enough for the sintering or melting process to take hold.[22] The best situation is a uniform continuous bonded glaze layer over the clay body surface.

* Low density and high shrinkage rate materials in the glaze formula can cause crawling. Magnesium carbonate, a light soft fluffy material, has a very low density. Bentonite and other types of clays shrink excessively. Both characteristics contribute to crawling. Low density materials don't compact well on the clay body when the water leaves the glaze and a soft powder-like surface forms. Often the glazes are difficult to handle and load into a kiln without damaging the dried raw glaze surface. Once the water evaporates, it can leave light density materials unpacked and loose, causing an insufficient bond with the clay body underneath the glaze.

Materials with excessive shrinkage rates such as Gerstley borate, colemanite, soda ash, and borax can hold massive amounts of mechanical or chemical water. Zinc in a glaze can also cause crawling due to its shrinkage rate at high temperatures. A glaze material that is too heavily ball milled can also cause crawling due to the increased amount of surface area that must be wetted for glaze application. To correct, substitute a coarser grind of the light density material and/or use VeeGum CER or CMC in the glaze as a binder.[23] Often frits can be used (less shrinkage due to the calcining process) in place of Gerstley borate or colemanite. Shrinkage rates can be reduced by using the same material in a coarser grind. In some situations, lesser amounts of the high shrinkage material can be used in the glaze.

* Bisque firing faults that can cause crawling occur when the firing temperature of the bisque kiln is not high enough for correct glaze absorption. The ware is too absorbent, causing a thick buildup of glaze. Thick glaze applications are more likely to crack on drying, which can cause crawling. Too high a bisque temperature or uneven hot spots on the bisque ware can cause the glaze to adhere in-

---

22. & 23. VeeGum CER and CMC are both glaze binder additives. Either can be used from 1/8% to 2% based on the dry weight of the glaze. They can be purchased through a local ceramics supplier. Some testing will be required to learn the correct amount of glaze binder for a glaze. All glazes should be mixed wet through an 80x-mesh sieve to insure complete blending of raw materials and binders.

completely, which can cause crawling at the firing stage. To correct, fire the bisque kiln evenly throughout and choose a bisque temperature that will allow the glaze to build up uniformly and to the proper thickness. Most stoneware clay bodies can be bisque fired at cone 06 (1830°F). Porcelain bodies usually require a cone 04 (1940°F) bisque firing due to their high refractory clay composition.

* Wet glazed pots in a fast firing kiln will eventually increase the chances of a problem. Some potters start the kiln firing before the water has fully evaporated from the glazed pots. Fast heating can cause the water in the glaze to turn into steam, which blows off parts of the glaze as it expands. To correct, place glazed pots in the kiln when they are dry to the touch. Increase the kiln temperature slowly (from 212°F to 1100°F) to drive off mechanical and chemical water in the glaze at a safe rate.

In a once-firing cycle or raw glazing (no bisque firing), steam in the clay body and glaze can increase the crawling potential of any glaze. Many once-fire glaze formulas contain high amounts of clay that can shrink excessively upon drying, causing crawling in the glaze. To correct, try adding VeeGum CER or CMC. Many once-fire glazes adhere well with the addition of either glaze binder.[24] Spraying the glaze on the pot decreases the amount of water needed in a glaze and reduces the chances of the raw glaze shrinking and eventually crawling off the pot. Again, slow heating in the 212°F to 1100°F ranges allows any water present in the clay body and glaze to be released safely.

* Overlapping glaze applications can cause crawling due to the base glaze or the overlapping glaze drying to a dusty condition. The dusty glaze is frequently soft and fragile to the touch, showing a noncompacted dry surface texture. When this happens, the mechanical bond between the two overlapping glazes is compromised. The glaze in such a condition might crawl even if no overlapping glaze is applied. The dusty glaze or overlapping glazes act like ball bearings, causing a nongripping condition. To correct, try adding VeeGum CER or CMC. If the materials that are causing the soft or dusty glaze surfaces cannot be re-

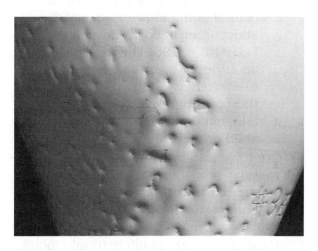

Glaze crawling – overlapping glaze application.

---

24. VeeGum CER and CMC are both glaze binder additives. Either can be used from 1/8% to 2% based on the dry weight of the glaze. They can be purchased through a local ceramics supplier. Some testing will be required to learn the correct amount of glaze binder for a glaze. All glazes should be mixed wet through an 80x-mesh sieve to insure complete blending of raw materials and binders.

placed, add VeeGum CER or CMC in the base glaze or the overlapping glaze or both. [25]

* Refractory and dusty underglaze stains or metallic coloring oxides are often applied to raw ware or bisque. Frequently, different color metallic oxides or stains are used with a clear or semitransparent glaze covering the color wash. Some stain and metallic oxide colors are more refractory than others and don't readily go into a melt. Metallic oxides or stains containing manganese, chrome, cobalt, and nickel are very difficult to melt. Often underglaze washes are refractory and will cause the covering glaze area to crawl or bead up during the firing. To correct, Ferro frit #3195 can be used to flux or melt refractory colors. Try a mix of 60% stain or metallic oxide to 40% Ferro frit #3195 for a cone 06 (1830°F) firing. For cone 6 (2232°F), use 70% stain or metallic oxide to 30% Ferro frit #3195. For a cone 9 (2336°F) firing, mix 80% stain or metallic oxide to 20% Ferro frit #3195. The frit acts as an adhesive agent tacking down the refractory stain that allows the covering glaze to take hold and bond with the underlying stain or metallic coloring oxide.

Once the underglaze wash has dried on the raw clay or bisque pot, it should develop a smooth hard surface that will insure a stable bond with the covering glaze. If the underglaze wash is dusty and flakes off, crawling of the glaze is likely to take place. To correct, add 1/2% to 2% VeeGum CER or CMC (based on the dry weight of the underglaze wash binders) to tack down dusty underglazes (for 100 grams of blue stain, add two grams of CMC). Add water until the mixture is the consistency of watercolor paint, then screen the wet mix through an 80-mesh sieve. The binder also enables the underglaze to flow off the brush in a smooth motion, preventing the brush stroke from skipping across the clay or bisque surface. In situations where an underglaze wash is both refractory and dusty, frit and binders can be used together.

* Excessive glaze water penetration in the bisque body happens when thin-walled pots are first glazed on one side. The water in the glaze penetrates through the pot wall, causing a damp or wet clay surface on the opposite unglazed side of the pot. If a glaze is applied to the wet surface, crawling can occur because the glaze doesn't bond properly with the underlying clay body. To correct, when glazing thin-walled pots, wait for the opposite clay body surface to dry completely before applying the glaze coating.

* Spray glaze application glazes are likely to crawl if the spraying continues after the first glaze layers are still wet. Excess water in the glaze as it evaporates leaves dry glaze particles loosely compacted. Any interruption of the glaze bonding surface can promote an unstable platform for the forming glaze. To correct, spray glaze until the surface becomes moist, then stop. The glaze should pack or compress

---

25.   VeeGum CER and CMC are both glaze binder additives. Either can be used from 1/8% to 2% based on the dry weight of the glaze. They can be purchased through a local ceramics supplier. Some testing will be required to learn the correct amount of glaze binder for a glaze. All glazes should be mixed wet through an 80x-mesh sieve to insure complete blending of raw materials and binders.

itself on the clay body surface, resulting in a stable bond.

If the glaze is sprayed from too far a distance, a dry, dusty, lightly packed glaze layer can develop, which may promote glaze crawling. To correct, after the sprayed glaze is dry, touch or lightly rub the glaze surface. It shouldn't dust off excessively on your fingers. The glaze must remain fixed and in place on the clay or bisque surface. Practice spraying with different concentrations of water to glaze and at varying distances from the clay surface to obtain the best results. The raw material makeup of a glaze formula determines the amount of water required for successful spraying. In short, some glazes need more water for good spraying results than others. Test the dry material to water ratios and the spraying distances that work best to arrive at good results.

* Soluble salts in the clay body can cause crawling. Soluble materials can be found in high iron content earthenware clays and fire clays. Often soluble salts will leach out to the surface when the clay dries. At that point, the clay frequently develops a layer of material that looks like white fuzz. Bisque firing won't completely remove the salts that form a loose surface the moist glaze needs to grab. The glaze layer will then make insufficient contact with the clay body, causing the glaze to mature in midair. Over ball milling or grinding of the glaze batch can release soluble material that can also cause crawling. To correct, don't waste time trying to wash or scrape the salt

deposits off the bone dry or bisque clay. Mix barium carbonate into the clay body (1/4% to 2% based on the dry weight of the clay body) to prevent the formation of soluble salts. Additive A Type 1, Type 3, or Type 4 used as a clay body additive (1/16% to 1/4% based on the dry weight of the clay body) will also neutralize soluble salts.[26] The barium carbonate component in Additive A is tied up safely with a ligneous polymer.

* Chemical changes in a glaze can occur due to soluble glaze materials leaching into the glaze water. An increase or decrease in the water pH levels can also develop due to the breakdown of raw materials or from the original water source.[27] Glazes stored in the liquid state for long periods can develop bacteria or mold growth. Any changes in pH or organic conditions can alter the glaze bonding capacity to the clay or bisque pot. To correct, try to use insoluble glaze materials whenever possible or add acid-based or alkaline material to adjust the glaze water pH level. One or two drops of bleach per gallon of glaze can counteract mold or bacteria growth in the glaze.

* High surface tension glazes contain large amounts of alumina, tin, zircopax, superpax, or any of the other zirconium silicates that can cause the fired glaze to become stiff when molten. Often glazes containing such materi-

---

26. Additive A Type 1, Type 3, and Type 4 also improve plastic and green strength properties of moist clay without changing shrinkage, fired color, or fired clay absorption. Produced by Lignotech U.S.A., Box 582, Lavonia, GA 30553, PH: (706) 356-1288.

27. pH is calculated from 0 to 14, 7 is neutral. Less than 7 is increasing acidity, more than 7 is increasing alkalinity.

als are opaque when fired and some glazes have matte surface textures, all factors that contribute to a high surface tension glaze in the molten state. Frequently, the glaze won't run or pull down on vertical surfaces and won't fill itself into voids or crevices in the clay body. Pinholes can often be seen in the fired glaze surface. A glaze with a high surface tension will condense or pull into itself, exposing areas of bare clay. Conversely, a glaze with a low surface tension flows out, filling surface cracks and voids in the underlying clay body. To correct, reduce the percentages of alumina, tin, or other high surface tension producing glaze materials. In some cases, substituting a lower surface tension raw material will be necessary, but most glaze crawling isn't due to high surface tension but to other factors such as glaze adhesion, glaze thickness, and glaze raw material shrinkage rates.

While not as common as other types of glaze defects, crawling does happen. Two primary areas will cause crawling to develop. Glaze application stage crawling occurs when high shrinkage and low density glaze materials dry on the surface being glazed, or whenever the clay body and glaze surface is disrupted and a mechanical glaze/clay surface bonding doesn't take place. The glaze forms away from the clay body surface. At some point in the firing stage, molten material is left in midair, dropping away to form crawling and a beaded pattern of glaze. In severe cases, beads of glaze can come off the pots and be found on the kiln shelves. If the dried raw glaze is very dusty, thickly applied, fragile to the touch, or shows any cracking, it has a high probability of crawling.

Glaze surface tension crawling, while not a common a cause of crawling, can develop when the molten glaze develops a high surface tension. The fluid glaze then rolls back on itself or beads up, leaving exposed clay. It's difficult to find an adequate substitution for a glaze material to lower the surface tension of the glaze. Cutting down on the actual amounts of problem materials is the only solution that will stop crawling and still maintain the desired color, surface texture, and opacity of the glaze. Glazes with low surface tension when firing will expand rather than contract. Low surface tension glazes will go on into clay body cracks, sealing or covering such clay body irregularities.

While the causes of glaze crawling can be broken down into several areas, the fired results are the same. If a glaze shows signs of crawling, discover the specific cause of crawling then decide on a method of correction. When faced with crawling, ask these questions. Was the bisque surface dusty or greasy before glazing? Was the glaze loose, dusty, or cracked when it dried on the pot? Does the glaze have high surface tension, producing raw materials in its formula? All are conditions that can suggest a potential glaze crawling problem. Knowing where the problem started will produce a faster fix.

Information about ceramics is widely scattered. A realistic and practical work goal should be to identify a problem, find information and techniques to solve the problem, and enact a solution. The one thing that will always be consistent is the inconsistency of raw materials and techniques. Problems should be expected in ceramics and the ability for solving problems should be developed. Variability is an aspect of ceramics. It is simply a reality, so plan for it.

Chapter 17

Color and Opacity for Base Glaze Formulas

Base glaze formulas can consist of feldspars, frits, clays, dolomite, flint, talc, Gerstley borate, whiting, magnesium carbonate, barium carbonate, zinc oxide, strontium carbonate, and other ceramic raw materials. They do not contain any metallic coloring oxides, stains, or opacifiers. Ordinarily, base glaze formulas will produce three classifications of glaze: gloss, satin, and matte. While some glazes don't fall exactly into a specific group, the important characteristic of base glaze formulas is the absence of any coloring ingredient. Base glaze formulas can be found in any temperature range for any type of firing such as oxidation, reduction, soda, salt, raku, or wood kiln atmospheres. Base glazes are a good starting point for obtaining different colors, textures, and opacities in future glazes.

As a standardized notation method, base glazes are calculated to 100% batch weights. Coloring oxides, stains, opacifiers, gums, suspension agents, dyes, and other additives are always listed after the 100% batch weight of the glaze. Many glaze formulas list bentonite 1% or 2% as a glaze suspension agent. Bentonite should also be noted after the 100% batch weight. It then makes it possible to compare the ingredients of one glaze with another, using the same standard system. Using the 100% batch method of listing glazes also allows you to compare your glazes with those made by others who use the same system.

For this series of adjusting color and opacity, cone 6 glaze formulas have been chosen. However, the same procedures of adding coloring oxides, stains, and opacifiers can be applied to cone 06 or cone 9 base glaze formulas listed in the glaze formulas section of this book (Part V Clay Body and Glaze Formulas).

Example of Base Glaze (100% Batch Weight)		Example of Base Glaze w/Metallic Oxide and Bentonite	
Cone 6 Satin Glaze		**Cone 6 Satin Blue Glaze**	
Whiting	15	Whiting	15
Nepheline syenite 270x	40	Nepheline syenite 270x	40
Flint 325x	38	Flint 325x	38
EPK	7	EPK	7
Total	**100%**	**Total**	**100%**
		Cobalt oxide	5%
		Bentonite	2%

One of the most common situations potters encounter involves using several different glaze formulas to achieve various effects on their pots. Using many different formulas can offer numerous results that can make glazing too complicated. You may not be in the best position to learn how each raw material, coloring oxide, or opacifier functions to produce a specific glaze result. Often the desired multiple-fired glaze effects aren't worth the effort of stocking raw materials, weighing out formulas, mixing formulas, and the added stress of handling many materials. There is also the possibility of glaze incompatibility when applying overlapping glazes with different formulas on the same pot. The combination of many glaze formulas sometimes produces too many raw material combinations to track in a logical cause and effect manner. Looking at a whole table full of glaze tests, it's possible to become frustrated by the overwhelming number of tests, some of which look like they might be good glazes while other results are impossible to interpret.

It's quite natural to acquire different glaze formulas from many sources such as fellow potters, teachers, books, magazine articles, workshops, and your own glaze testing. There is nothing wrong with this method of increasing your glaze palette, but there are other ways to develop new glazes that can also lead to a greater understanding of ceramic raw materials. If you don't have a basic knowledge of how coloring oxides, stains, and opacifiers can change a glaze, experimenting can be a time-consuming and frustrating undertaking. A simpler approach is to use only a few base glaze formulas (glaze formulas that are either clear, satin matte, or matte) adding various metallic coloring oxides, stains, and opacifiers to achieve varied fired results. In this way, additions to a few reliable base glazes will likely produce dependable colors and/or opacity in the new glaze variations.

The base glaze formulas are designed to work at the specified temperature range in oxidation or reduction kiln atmospheres. Some base formulas might produce slight variations in opacity and texture, depending on your kiln firing cycle, kiln size, glaze application thickness, method of glaze application (brushing, dipping, pouring, spraying), clay body formula, and kiln atmosphere. Glaze results can also be altered by raw material inconsistencies, kiln firing variables, application methods, and common errors in weighing out raw materials.

Coloring oxides, stains, and/or opacifying materials can then be added to the base glaze formulas that work best on your clay body. When test firing the glaze, keep in mind that a small test kiln will heat and cool faster than a larger production kiln. High-volume production kilns have greater thermal mass due to their size which will accommodate a greater number of bricks, shelves, posts, and pots. Their thermal mass takes longer to heat and cool, which produces a more thorough melt in clay bodies and glazes. While small test kilns can give an approximation of a fired glaze (greater accuracy in predicting glazes occurs with gloss glazes than with satin or matte glazes), the most accurate results are obtained by testing the glaze in the kiln where it will eventually be used.

The actual glaze formulas aren't as important as your ability to manipulate the formula based on how it fires in your own kiln and on your clay body. Using this simple method of adding coloring oxides, stains, or opacifiers, any temperature range of base glaze formulas can be adjusted. Hopefully, it will offer you a greater understand of how raw materials function in coloring and opacifying glazes. The knowledge gained from understanding what a specific coloring oxide, stain, or opacifier will produce in a glaze is valuable information. It will offer greater control in glaze development.

Base Glaze Formulas

Your goal is to find a successful clear satin and matte glaze. Start by choosing two or three base glaze formulas in the same category (clear glazes, for example). Apply them to vertical test tiles (vertical testing of glazes will determine if they run or drip) using an old kiln shelf underneath. This should be the standard procedure until you become familiar with the glaze characteristics in your kiln. Because different clay bodies can alter the fired glaze, make the test tiles from the same clay body that will be used in your finished pieces. It is also a good practice to place several test tiles of the same glaze in different positions in the kiln. Not all kilns heat equally and especially in reduction kilns, the atmosphere is sometimes not distributed evenly throughout the kiln. Several test tiles will better indicate how the glaze reacts at different temperatures and atmosphere conditions in the kiln. To broaden the types of base glaze formulas, follow the same procedures for testing satin glazes and matte glazes. At the end of testing, the objective should be gloss, satin, and matte base glazes that work well on your clay body. Once reliable base glaze formulas have been developed, it's easier to formulate variations.

Example: Cone 6 Clear Gloss Base Glazes

Zam #4 Clear, Gloss		Zam #5 Clear, Gloss		Zam #6 Clear, Gloss	
Nepheline syenite 270x	20	Ferro frit #3195	60	Nepheline syenite 270x	41
Whiting	20	Flint 325x	22	Zinc oxide	6
EPK	20	EPK	12	Whiting	16
Flint 325x	20	Whiting	6	Barium carbonate	7
Ferro frit #3124	20	Bentonite	2%	Flint 325x	30

Example: Cone 6 Satin Base Glazes

Zam #8 Satin		Zam #11 Satin		Zam #12 Satin	
Whiting	15	Nepheline syenite 270x	29	Custer feldspar	25
Nepheline syenite 270x	40	Magnesium carbonate	11	Dolomite	16
Flint 325x	38	Zinc oxide	3	Whiting	3
EPK	7	Gerstley borate	14	Zinc oxide	3
		Flint 325x	35	EPK	18
		EPK	8	Flint 325x	35

Example: Cone 6 Matte Base Glazes					
Zam #13 Matte		**Zam #14 Matte**		**Zam #15 Matte**	
Nepheline syenite 270x	60	Nepheline syenite 270x	60	Nepheline syenite 270x	45
Whiting	15	Dolomite	15	Whiting	18
EPK	10	Kentucky ball OM#4	10	EPK	20
Flint 325x	15	Flint 325x	15	Flint 325x	5
				Zinc oxide	12

Adding Color to Base Glazes
(Metallic Coloring Oxides/Carbonates)

Adding color to base glazes depends on many factors. The total amount of metallic coloring oxide/carbonate or stain deposited in the base glaze, the maturation point of the glaze, the kiln atmosphere, the firing cycle of the kiln, the underlying clay body, the glaze application thickness, and the base glaze composition all influence the actual fired glaze color. Generally, 1% to 2% of metallic coloring oxide/carbonate yields a slight tint in a base glaze, 5% will produce a medium color response, and 10% to 12% will yield a darker full color response. For this example, I've used cobalt oxide but any number of coloring oxides/carbonates or stains can be used alone or in combination. The possibilities include cobalt carbonate, cobalt sulfate, chrome oxide, copper oxide black, copper oxide red, copper carbonate, copper sulfate, crocus martis, illmenite powdered, iron chromate, iron oxide red, iron oxide black, iron oxide yellow, iron sulfate, manganese dioxide powdered, manganese carbonate, nickel oxide black, nickel oxide green, nickel carbonate, potassium bichromate, yellow ochre, raw sienna, rutile dark, rutile light, burnt umber, and vanadium pentoxide.

Using 5% cobalt oxide in each type of base glaze will produce gloss blue, satin blue, and matte blue glazes. However, the intensity and shade of blue will be different depending on the particular base glaze.

Example: Cone 6 Base Glazes Gloss, Satin, and Matte with the Same Metallic Coloring Oxide					
Zam #4 Clear, Gloss Blue		**Zam #8 Satin Blue**		**Zam #13 Matte Blue**	
Nepheline syenite 270x	20	Whiting	15	Nepheline syenite 270x	60
Whiting	20	Nepheline syenite 270x	40	Dolomite	15
EPK	20	Flint 325x	38	EPK	10
Flint 325x	20	EPK	7	Flint 325x	15
Ferro frit #3124	20	Cobalt oxide	5%	Cobalt oxide	5%
Cobalt oxide	5%				

Adding Color to Base Glazes (Stains)

A stain is a combination of metallic coloring oxide(s), stabilizers, and opacifiers calcined or fired to high temperature, then pulverized into fine powder. The advantage of stains over metallic coloring oxides is their reliable color reproduction and their ability to produce specific shades of color not readily accessible through raw metallic coloring oxides. There are many colors and shades of stains. The two largest stain producing companies are Mason and Drakenfield. Each produces a color stain chart and a listing of their available stain colors. As with metallic coloring oxides, 1% to 2% stain will yield a slight tint to a base glaze, 5% will produce a medium color response, and 10% to 12% will yield a darker full color response.

The stain color can be greatly affected by the base glaze, kiln atmosphere, firing temperature, glaze application thickness, clay body formula, and kiln firing cycle. It's critical to test any stain color in a glaze to insure the desired result.

Opaque Base Glazes

Making a base glaze opaque can be accomplished in several ways. The examples given use materials suspended in the glaze to form a semiopaque or opaque white glaze with metallic coloring oxides, stains, and opacifiers added after the 100% batch weight of the base glaze formula. Depending on the opacity of the clear base glaze formula, adding 1% to 3% opacifier will produce a slightly opaque glaze, 5% to 8% will produce semi-opacity, and 10% to 20% will produce complete opacity. In semiopaque and opaque base glaze formulas, the same percentages will produce even greater levels of opacity since the base glaze is somewhat opaque before the addition of an opacifier. The level and quality of the opacity produced in the base glaze will be affected by the base glaze formula, (some base glazes are already semiopaque due to the choice of glaze fluxes and/or the alumina silica ratio in the glaze), the amount of opacifier added to the base glaze (higher amounts of opacifier decrease glaze transparency), and the particular opacifying agent (superpax will produce a flat uniform white as compared to titanium dioxide which tends toward a frosty irregular surface white).

One of the most widely used opacifier in glazes was zircopax, a zirconium silicate. It is produced in several types which are listed in their order of particle size. The smaller the particle size, the lower amount of opacifier required in the glaze formula. The smallest particle size starts with excelopax, superpax A, superpax plus, zircopax plus, superpax, and zircopax A. For the best match, choose the closest particle size. Opax, ultrox, and treopax are also opacity-producing materials that can work as direct substitutes in the majority of glaze formulas. Zirocopax plus and superpax plus have slightly higher zirconium contents than the other opacifiers and it takes less to get the same level of opacity when replacing nonplus opacifiers. Zircopax is no longer being produced, but zircopax plus is an appropriate substitute. Zirconium silicate-RZM can be substituted for zircopax, while zircon G milled and zirconium spinel are coarser and tend not to be a close match for zircopax. Zinc zirconium silicate will opacify and harden fired glazes. Another opacifying agent, tin oxide, will produce a soft or "butterfat" white in glazes. Tin produces a softer white than the "refrigerator whites" produced with the zirconium silicates. Titanium dioxide and zirconium oxide can also produce different qualities of opacity in glazes.

Example: Cone 6 Gloss Base Glazes
with Metallic Oxides, Stains, and Opacifiers

Zam #4 Gloss, Blue		Zam #4 Gloss, Black		Zam # 4 Gloss, White	
Nepheline syenite 270x	20	Nepheline syenite 270x	20	Nepheline syenite 270x	20
Whiting	20	Whiting	20	Whiting	20
EPK	20	EPK	20	EPK	20
Flint 325x	20	Flint 325x	20	Flint 325x	20
Ferro frit #3124	20	Ferro frit #3124	20	Ferro frit #3124	20
Cobalt oxide	10%	Black Mason Stain #6600	10%	Superpax	10%

Adding metallic coloring oxides, stains, or opacifiers to a single type of base glaze can further increase the range of colors or opacity possibilities.

Stains, metallic oxides, and opacifiers can also be added to different base glaze formulas.

Staying with one base glaze for each variation will yield a known quantity to compare the effects of different coloring oxides or stains in the glaze. From just three different base glaze formulas it is possible to obtain many glaze colors and textures by incorporating coloring oxides, stains, and opacifiers.

Example: Cone 6 Gloss, Satin, Matte Base Glazes
with Stains, Opacifiers and Metallic Oxides

Zam #4 Gloss Black		Zam # 8 Satin White		Zam #13 Matte Blue	
Nepheline syenite 270x	20	Whiting	15	Nepheline syenite 270x	60
Whiting	20	Nepheline syenite 270x	40	Dolomite	15
EPK	20	Flint 325x	38	EPK	10
Flint 325x	20	EPK	7	Flint 325x	15
Ferro frit #3124	20	Superpax	5%	Cobalt carbonate	5%
Mason Stain Black #6600	10%				

When Mixing the Glaze

If the glaze sinks to the bottom of the glaze bucket, it may need a suspension agent (see below). If a glaze is brittle, dusty, or fragile when drying on the bisque pot, VeeGum CER, or CMC will tack down and stabilize a raw glaze (see "Additives for Clay Bodies and Glazes"). All base glazes take a wide range of coloring oxides and stains.

Glaze suspension agents such as Vee-Gum T (Macaloid), bentonite, or gums VeeGum CER, or CMC can be added to any glaze. Follow the directions below.

If using VeeGum T or VeeGum CER, measure it, place it in hot water, and mix. Use all this mixture in the glaze batch. VeeGum T can be used to keep any glaze in suspension (1/8% to 2% based on the dry weight of the glaze).VeeGum CER can be used to prevent a dusty raw glaze surface (1/8% to 2% based on the dry weight of glaze).

Bentonite, a very plastic clay, can keep a glaze in suspension (1/8% to 2% based on the dry weight of the glaze).

With the addition of any glaze suspension agents or gums, the liquid glaze should be placed through an 80-mesh sieve three times to insure all materials are mixed.

Chapter 18

Raw Material Substitutions for Glazes

At some point when mixing glazes it will become necessary to use a substitute raw material. We have all been in our studios ready to mix a glaze and found ourselves without a critical material. An event like this usually happens when we are getting ready for an upcoming big show or sale. In ceramics, a little information at the right time can go a long way in resolving many common glaze material substitution problems. In an ideal world, we would plan months ahead for the time when a glaze material would have to be replaced. However, we often face such situations without preparation. When they occur, we have two choices – grab a handful of any white powder and use it in the glaze batch, (risking a bad result) or learn what materials can be substituted for a favorite feldspar or metallic coloring oxide.

Why Are Substitutions Necessary?

In the long term, the most common reason for glaze material substitutions is one of economics. We know that potters comprise a tiny segment of the raw material market, so when your favorite feldspar is no longer available, it doesn't necessarily mean it has been mined out of existence. There may very well be enough feldspar at the mine to keep potters supplied for hundreds of years. What is means is that mining the spar for large in-dustrial customers is no longer profitable. Large buyers of materials dictate market decisions, not potters. Over time, many of your favorite glaze materials will become extinct because the industrial demand has dried up.

Many potters find the need to substitute a raw material when trying to use glaze formulas from a magazine or book. Often a particular feldspar or frit can no longer be obtained and a replacement is required to test the new glaze. Many unforeseen variables exist in ceramics such as different interactions of glaze and clay bodies or various kiln heating and cooling rates. Other changes involve the variability in raw materials, glaze application thickness, glaze kiln atmospheres, or individual glazing techniques. Any change can alter the substitution glaze enough to produce an unacceptable result. When more than one material is substituted, the odds of throwing off the glaze go up. The general rule in such situations is that the more replacement materials are required in a formula, the further removed from the original the fired glaze result will be.

An insidious and sometimes subtle shift can occur due to a change at the mine. The transformation can happen from one bag to the next or more likely, slowly over a period of years. The old bag of Kentucky Ball Clay OM#4 in your studio might not yield the same results as a new batch of the same named ball clay. Many ball clays are blended from different pits at the mine. The mines do an excellent job of maintaining quality control, but changes in materials for any number of reasons can and do happen. Always be prepared to make a substitution due to a slow or sudden shift in a raw material's composition. Just because the name on the bag is the same doesn't mean that what's inside the bag is the same every time.

Good studio organization and planning involves ordering and stocking raw materials before beginning a glazing cycle. When it's time to reorder materials, always be exact as to the chemical name, common name, mesh size, and the mine or processor of the specific material. The ceramics supplier should have this information available for every raw material. Be aware that the ceramics supplier orders the material from a processor and sometimes several different processors sell their own versions of a raw material. Each company can produce a product with a slightly different chemical composition or particle size but still refer to it by the same generic name. The slight difference may be distinct enough to affect the glaze. Try to order whole bags of glaze materials (the company name will often be on the bag). Ordering by the bag insures continuity and consistency of materials and as an added advantage, costs less per pound.

In most instances, substituting a raw material to save money isn't an effective cost cutting strategy. The most expensive part of any glaze formula is the time and effort required to put the glaze on the pot. Using a less expensive glaze material will not be a true savings if it causes a higher defect rate or if the substitute material doesn't produce acceptable results. The most economic way to judge raw materials is by assessing their reliability and ease of use, not their initial cost to purchase. Substituting one feldspar for another to save one or two cents per pound will result in a loss if the substitute feldspar doesn't function properly in the glaze. Many "savings" have a hidden cost, such as an errat-

ic supply of the material that could cost a delayed production.

Another example of false economy is not using CMC, VeeGum CER, VeeGum T, or any other seemingly expensive glaze additive in the glaze mix. The amount needed of any binder or suspension agent in a glaze is a small percentage of the total glaze formula. If an additive saves one pot from a glaze application or firing defect, or makes the glazing operation more efficient, it more than pays for itself. In looking at the cost of making pots or sculpture, your effort and time are where any improvements will yield the most productive results. All else is just a marginal increment of gain. Don't waste time chasing pennies, chase dollars.

Substituting a Raw Material

Before mixing any glaze from materials in your studio, check to make sure the materials are still available and are in current production. Keep informed on which materials have changed or are no longer being produced. Ask yourself if it is worth the time and effort to mix a glaze with a material that can no longer be obtained from a supplier. We all know potters who hold onto their last pound of Albany Slip or Oxford feldspar, two extinct materials. At some point, they must find an adequate substitution for these once-popular materials. Question your supplier and other potters as to a material's availability and consistency before committing yourself to a glaze formula.

Some potters replace a material, mix a 30-gallon batch of the glaze, and use it on all their pots. After the glaze is fired, if it doesn't meet their expectations they wonder what went wrong. Never use an untested material extensively on a whole kiln load of pots. The potential for losing time and labor on such experiments are not worth the risk. Mix up a small test sample, placing the glaze on several vertical test tiles throughout the kiln. Use an old kiln shelf under the glaze test pieces to prevent damaged shelving if the glaze runs. Fire the test pieces in the same kiln you'll use for regular production pots to achieve consistent results.

Achieving a perfect substitute all the time for every possible glaze is impossible. Many alternative materials, while almost identical, have trace elements that might slightly change the color or texture of the original glaze. Several factors can hinder the substitute material from giving an exact match – differences in particle size, chemical composition, or processing methods. A precise equivalent material isn't possible in all situations because of the substitute material's potential incompatibility as to firing temperature, time to temperature, glaze thickness, reaction with the clay body formula, or response to the kiln atmosphere. The raw material substitution guide is designed to help the potter make an informed choice when substituting materials. The substitutions listed will work in a high percentage of glazes.

Raw materials used in glazes can be classified in many different ways. Chemical composition and particle size are just two useful indicators in choosing a replacement material. Always look for similarities in chemical composition and particle size when trying to substitute one material for another. It's a good practice to keep an analysis sheet on the raw materials used in your clay body and glaze formulas. Your supplier can send a chemical analysis sheet with every raw material ordered that will list the mesh size and the chemical composition of the material. The analysis sheets can offer a basis for comparison with any of the raw materials used in glaze formulas. Remember, at some point a raw material used in a glaze formula may need to be replaced with a suitable substitution.

Frequently clay is a component of glaze formulas. It contributes silica and alumina to the glaze and helps keep the liquid glaze in suspension. Clay is commonly classified as earthenware, stoneware, kaolin, fire clay, ball clay, and bentonite. Some groups can be divided into subgroups (for example, kaolin can be plastic or nonplastic). The best procedure when substituting one clay for another in a glaze formula is to choose a replacement clay from the same group or subgroup of clays. This will insure the optimum glaze match.

Listed are raw material substitutions and an explanation on how and when to use each substitute material. Raw materials and clays not on the list either don't have a practical substitution or involve glaze calculation to arrive at a close material match.

Glaze Materials

Albany Slip, a dark brown firing, earthenware type, high iron content clay, is no longer being mined. The land in Albany, New York, is more valuable as real estate than for its clay deposits. Many ceramics supply companies have developed Albany-like substitutes – Alberta Slip, Seattle Slip, Sheffield Slip Clay Formula, A.R.T. Albany Slip Synthetic by Laguna Clay Co., Albany Slip Substitute, Jasper Slip Clay, United Clays – with different degrees of success in producing an exact match. How successfully they match true Albany Slip depends on the amount of Albany Slip required in the original formula, the firing temperature of the glaze, and kiln atmosphere.

Alumina hydrate is used in formulas to promote hardness and opacity in fired glazes. Alumina oxide can be substituted for alumina hydrate on a one-for-one basis in most glaze formulas. Calcined alumina, which has already been fired, can also be used as a substitute for alumina hydrate and alumina oxide, but it might cause raw glaze fit problems due to the calcining process. Alumina hydrate, calcined alumina, and alumina oxide are not frequently used in glaze formulas and are better suited for kiln shelf washes.

Ball clay contributes silica and alumina to the glaze formula. Due to its small platelet structure, ball clay also suspends the liquid glaze in the glaze bucket. Higher amounts of iron and manganese in each type of ball clay contribute to a darker fired ball clay color. However, it might not affect the fired color of the glaze that contains the ball clay as part of its formula. In most glaze formulas, the percentage of ball clay in the formula is low compared to the total of other glaze materials. Therefore, the effect of a dark versus light firing ball clay isn't significant in the fired glaze result. In clear or white glazes, dark firing ball clay can tint or shade the fired glaze. In glazes with any color, a dark or light firing ball clay might not affect the fired result.

It is always best to replace a light firing ball clay with another light firing ball clay. Cream color ball clays should be replaced with another cream color ball clay. Some light firing ball clays are Tennessee #1 (SPG#1), Tennessee #10, Coppen Light, H.C. Spinks C&C, Old Hickory #5, and Old Hickory #1 Glaze Clay. Off-white or cream fired color ball clays are Foundry Hill Cream, #1 Glaze Clay, Jackson, Kentucky OM#4, Kentucky Special, Kentucky Stone, M&D, Thomas, Taylor, XX Sagger, Tennessee #9, Spinks HC5, and Gold Label.

Barium carbonate. Chinese and German types can be interchanged in a glaze. Both types act as secondary fluxes, helping to bring primary fluxes to a melt. High amounts of barium carbonate can cause opacity in glazes and can modify the color and/or texture of glazes containing metallic coloring oxides or stains. When less than 6% barium carbonate is used in glazes that don't contain metallic coloring oxides or stains, there is often no noticeable change in the glaze when all or part of the barium is removed. Frequently strontium carbonate added to 3/4 the amount of barium carbonate will make an adequate substitute when color or texture are not required in the glaze.

Bentonite can be used in a glaze formula to keep the liquid glaze in suspension in the glaze bucket. Usually, 1% to 2% bentonite is used (based on the dry weight of the glaze batch). Higher percentages are used in once-fire glaze formulas to insure a better raw glaze fit with the unglazed clay body. One way bentonites can be classified is by their light or dark fired color. Some light firing bentonites used in glazes are HPM-20 air purified, 325x-mesh Western Bentonite, 200x-mesh Western Bentonite, Bentonite B, and Bentolite White GK129. Ibex-200 is a dark firing bentonite that can be used in darker color glaze formulas.

Other more effective suspension agents can be substituted for bentonite. Epsom salts (magnesium sulfate), Macaloid, Vee-Gum T, and VeeGum CER can also be used as glaze suspension agents. CMC can be used as a glaze suspension aid but its primary function is as a glaze binder.

Bone ash. Natural calcined animal bones (calcium phosphate) or synthetic bone ash (tri calcium phosphate) produced from other calcium phosphate materials can be used interchangeably in most glazes. They contribute opalescence and opacity to glazes. However, in some glaze formulas requiring natural bone ash, synthetic bone ash cannot be substituted because it will modify the glaze color.

Borax is a soluble flux infrequently used in glazes. When utilized in amounts of more than 10%, it has all the inherent application and firing problems associated with any soluble material. An insoluble form known as fused borax or calcined borax can also be substituted using half the total amount of borax.

Dolomite is a raw material often used in glaze formulas. It contains approximately one part calcium and one part magnesium. Frequently equal parts of whiting (calcium carbonate) and magnesium carbonate can substitute for dolomite. For example, if the glaze formula requires ten parts of dolomite, five parts of whiting and five parts of magnesium carbonate can be substituted for dolomite. This will not be an exact substitution, but a close match. Materials formed in nature combine their oxides better than adding equivalent amounts of a separate oxide. Trace elements in natural materials also prevent an exact match. Camadil dolomite is one of many different brands of dolomite sold by ceramics suppliers.

Feldspar is one of the most common materials found in stoneware glazes. Feldspars can be classified into three groups: potash feldspars (Custer, G-200, K200, Primas P, no longer available are Oxford, Buckingham, Yankee, Clinchfield #202, Keystone, Maine, Madoc H, A-3, Elbrook); sodium feldspars (Kona F-4, Nepheline Syenite 270x, Nepheline Syenite 400x, Calspar, Primas S, NC-4, Unispar 50, C-6, Minnspar 200, no longer available are Eureka, Bainbridge, #56 Glaze, Lu-Spar #4, Minpro #4, Clinchfield #303); and lithium feldspars (Spodumene,[28] Lithospar, Petalite). No longer available is Lepidolite. Choose a feldspar from its own group when making a substitution.

Flint or silica is one of the most common raw materials found in glazes. It is sold as Flint 400x-, 325x-, and 200x-mesh, all of which can be used in glaze formulas. Siltex 44[29] and Silica IMSIL A-25 are fused amorphous silica. Because of their low expansion rates, their use in some glazes can correct glaze crazing defects. Both low shrinkage brand name types of silica can be used in place of Flint 400x, 325x, or 200x.

If a glaze formula calls for Flint 200x-mesh and only Flint 400x-mesh is available, Flint 400x-mesh would be a good substitution. A closer match of Flint 325x-mesh would be the best option. Some glazes are more sensitive to finer grind materials. The smaller mesh materials can increase glaze melts (increased surface area produces more of a reaction with other glaze materials and increased reaction to heat), which might cause a glossier glaze surface. Another possible result of using finer mesh flint is removing craze lines from a glaze or preventing glaze pinholes.

An unproductive match occurs when using the same chemical composition material with a radically different material size, as in Flint 325x-mesh (which is silica) compared to silica sand 60x-mesh (also silica). The particle size of silica sand 60x-mesh is too large compared to Flint 325x so it can't be used as a substitute. The larger mesh silica sand won't melt in the glaze.

When substituting glaze materials, use the same chemical composition material in the nearest mesh size to the original material. The closer the particle sizes match, the less likely it is that a substitute material will change the glaze.

Frit contains oxides predetermined as to quantity and type which are then melted, fast cooled, and ground into a powder. In a sense, frits are manmade feldspars. Frits enable a consistent blend of oxides to be melted rather than having to deal with the inconsistent oxides found in nature. Frits can contain soluble oxides in an insoluble form and can contain toxic materials in safe nontoxic glassy matrixes. When substituting any frit, do some testing before mixing a large quantity of glaze.

---

28.   Spodumene (high iron content) produced by Foote Mineral Co. is no longer being mined. It had produced bubbling when mixed with glaze water. It also caused bubbles when used as part of the clay body formula during the mixing process. Spodumene from Gwalia, Australia (low iron content) is produced by F&S Alloys and Minerals Corp. It seems to mix well in glazes and clay bodies without effervescing in water. Always test any substitute glaze material before mixing large quantities of glaze.

29.   Siltex 44 is the trade name of fused silica produced by Kaopolitle Inc., 244 Morris Ave., Union, NJ 07083, PH: (908) 789-0609.

Ferro frit		Pemco		Hommel		Fusion
3110	=	P-IV05			=	F-75
3124	=	P-311	=	90	=	F-19
3134	=	P-54	=	14	=	F-12
3195	=			399	=	F-2
3819	=	P-25	=	259	=	FZ-25

Listed are the most commonly used frits in glaze formulas and their equivalents.

Gerstley borate is a calcium borate ore frequently used in glaze formulas. It contributes a strong fluxing action and can create opalescent opacity in the fired glaze. The borate content of this common glaze material can be inconsistent from one batch to the next. In many glaze formulas, Colemanite can be substituted without a noticeable difference in the fired glaze result. Both Colemanite and Gerstley borate are variable and cannot be depended on for consistent results in glaze formulas.

Kaolin can be classified as to plastic and nonplastic. Since its primary purpose is to contribute silica and alumina to a glaze, any of the kaolins can be substituted in a glaze formula. However, it's always best to substitute from the same group. Plastic kaolins are EPK, Putnam, Grolleg, Kaolex D-6, McNamee, #6 Tile, Pioneer, Laguna #1, Sapphire, Treviscoe, and T-7 kaolin. Nonplastic kaolins include Kaopaque 20, Ajax P, Delta, SnoCal 707, Kingsley, English China Clay, Georgia Kaolin, and Velvacast.

Avery kaolin cannot be readily substituted due to its unique properties. It was a major component in slips and engobes used in salt, soda, and wood firing kilns. Helmer kaolin is now used as a direct substitute and has successfully produced browns, oranges, and light yellow flashing effects when used in engobes.

Calcined kaolin has been fired, which reduces its shrinkage due to chemical water being removed. Any calcined kaolin can be used interchangeably (such as Glomax LL or Ajax-SC). Calcined kaolin can be produced by firing any kaolin past dull red heat (approximately 1100°F). Calcined and regular kaolin can be used interchangeably but the reduced shrinkage of the calcined kaolin can change the raw glaze fit as it dries on the pot.

Soda ash (sodium carbonate) is highly soluble and not usually found in glaze formulas. Baking soda (sodium bicarbonate) can be used as a substitute since it changes to the carbonate form when heated to 850°C.

Talc contributes silica and magnesium to a glaze. Moderate amounts of talc in a glaze cause opacity. Not all talc is the same. On the East Coast, Nytal HR100 talc is available with Pioneer-2882 being a good West Coast substitute talc. There are many other talcs such as Sierralite (high alumina content), Soapstone 78SS (dirty for use in glazes), TDM 92 (high organic matter), or Talc 80/20 (partly calcined) which can be used in dry press clay bodies.

Whiting (calcium carbonate) is a high-temperature source of calcium that can make a fired glaze harder. It can also develop a chemically resistant glaze surface. It is produced under different trade names by many companies in various mesh sizes. Several kinds of whiting that can be interchanged successfully are Snowcal 40, Vicron 2511, York White, Whiting 55C, Whiting 3C Calcium carbonate, and Goldbond Whiting #10 White. Always choose a replacement calcium carbonate with approximately the same mesh size as the original.

Atomite, a trade name for a particular whiting with a very fine particle size, might produce a transparent, gloss, clear, glaze as opposed to a coarser grade of whiting that does not thoroughly dissolve in the molten glaze. A larger particle size whiting can produce a white, opaque clouded condition in the fired glaze. Furthermore it can cause the liquid glaze to settle to the bottom of the glaze bucket due to its density. Remember, most raw glaze materials look like white or off-white powder and feel like similar powders. Telling the difference in the mesh sizes of powders is almost impossible so rely on the chemical analysis sheet for this critical information.

Metallic Coloring Oxides, Carbonates, and Opacifiers

Cobalt oxide is one of the most potent metallic coloring oxides when used in glaze formulas. The smallest amount of cobalt will create a blue tint in almost any glaze. Cobalt oxide is 1-1/2 times stronger than cobalt carbonate so allow for the difference in any substitution. For example, if the glaze formula requires one part cobalt oxide and you're substituting cobalt carbonate, use 1-1/2 parts of the cobalt carbonate. When cobalt oxide is substitut-

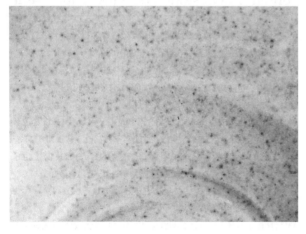

Cobalt oxide in satin matte glaze causes a blue field with blue specks.

ed in glazes requiring cobalt carbonate it can sometimes produce a speckled blue field of color instead of just a blue glaze field. Cobalt oxide is coarser and has a larger particle size than cobalt carbonate. The blue specking is more likely to occur in satin matte or matte glazes where the larger particles of cobalt oxide aren't fully incorporated into the molten glaze. Cobalt oxide blue specking is less likely to occur in gloss or transparent glazes.

Copper oxide. Copper oxide black (cupric oxide) and copper oxide red (cuprous oxide) are two of the most reactive metallic glaze coloring oxides. The range of glaze colors they can produce depends in part on the kiln atmosphere and the composition of the base glaze formulas. Copper oxide and copper carbonate can produce green, brown, black, turquoise, and red in glazes. Red copper oxide and black copper oxide can be used interchangeably but the red tends to not go into a complete suspension in the liquid glaze. Some red copper oxide always floats on the liquid glaze surface but does not affect the color or texture of the fired glaze. Both red and black copper oxides can cause a speckled color in some glazes. Copper carbonate can be substituted for copper oxides by using 1-1/2 times more than the amount of copper oxide required in the glaze formula. Copper carbonate, because of its smaller particle size, disperses readily into the fired glaze.

Manganese dioxide is a metallic coloring oxide that can produce purple or brown in glazes. Manganese carbonate can be substituted for manganese dioxide powder in a glaze by using 1-1/2 more manganese carbonate than the amount of manganese dioxide in the formula. Manganese dioxide granular isn't suitable for glazes because it doesn't disperse into a glaze melt due to its large particle size.

Nickel oxide. Nickel oxide black, nickel oxide green, and nickel carbonate are strong coloring agents for glazes. They can produce browns, grays, and under some conditions yellows and violets in glazes. Nickel oxide black and green can be used interchangeably, while nickel carbonate should be substituted at 1-1/2 the amount to replace one part green or one part black nickel oxide. Black nickel oxide changes to green nickel oxide above 1112°F.

Red iron oxide (ferric oxide) can produce browns, grays, greens, yellows, and many other variations of earth tones in glazes. Spanish red, an ore, is one of the most common types of iron oxide available for potters. Synthetic iron oxides are numerous, with differing strengths of iron content and purity. Iron oxide red #2199, iron oxide #84, and iron oxide #98 can be substituted for Spanish red iron oxide but the exact ratio of substitution should be tested. Keep in mind that the synthetic brands of iron oxide can be stronger than natural iron oxide ores and a one-to-one substitution won't always produce an exact match. Other types of iron oxide derivatives such as red NR #4686 and red NR #4284 also have to be tested to match Spanish red iron oxide glaze colors. Black iron oxide (ferric) is a slightly coarser grind than red iron oxide and produces more greens and browns in glazes than the red iron oxides.

Rutile is titanium and iron combined in nature. It will produce pale tan, light brown, or blue in glazes. The color variations produced by rutile depend in part on kiln atmosphere, base glaze formula, glaze thickness, firing temperature, and the time it takes to reach that temperature. Ceramic light rutile or fine rutile is a light brown fine powder. Milled Ruflux 61 or dark Rutile is coarser in particle size and a darker brown color in the raw state. A one-to-one replacement of ceramic light rutile to ruflux 61 dark rutile is possible with the understanding that dark ruflux 61 colors will be darker in the fired glaze.

Zircopax is a zirconium silicate used to increase opacity in glazes. It is pro-duced in several types which are listed in their order of particle size. The smaller the particle size, the less opacifier is required in the glaze formula. The smallest particle size starts with excelopax, superpax A, superpax plus, zircopax plus, superpax, and zircopax A. The best match will occur when choosing the closest particle size. Opax and ultrox are also opacity producing materials that can work as direct substitutes in the majority of glaze formulas. Zircopax plus and superpax plus have slightly higher zirconium contents than the other opacifiers so less can be used to get the same level of opacity when replacing nonplus opacifiers. Zircopax is no longer being produced but zircopax plus is an appropriate substitute. Zirconium silicate-RZM can be substituted for zircopax while zircon G milled and zirconium spinel are coarser and tend not to be a close match for zircopax. Another opacifying agent, tin oxide, will produce a soft white in glazes. Tin produces a softer white than zirconium silicates.

Substitution Risks and Rewards

The best position to be in when mixing glazes is not to need any substitute materials. When using a substitute material, keep in mind the potential for many uncharted variables to change the fired glaze. Using a material other than the one called for in the glaze formula adds an element of risk, but some glaze material substitutions are less risky than others. The main philosophy in ceramics is that nothing is perfect and nothing stays the same. The best results when making substitutions come about when planned in advance. Glaze testing should be carried out over a series of separate kiln firings to achieve accuracy in the formula and confidence in the results.

Learning how each material works in a glaze and its basic composition gives you a greater flexibility and freedom to continue working on the original glaze project. It also offers the chance to experiment with various materials in the exploration of new glaze textures and colors. Knowledge of raw materials allows the flexibility to make the correct choices for assembling glaze formulas. There is a wide assortment of glaze raw materials and clays to choose from in building a glaze formula and often more than one possible substitute material is available. The correct choices are dependent not on chance but on a thorough knowledge of the materials.

Acknowledgments

Mr. John Cowen, President of Sheffield Pottery, Inc. was most informative and helpful in his knowledge of current ceramic glaze materials. The best ceramics supply companies know the products and materials they stock and Sheffield Pottery has set a high standard in product service and supply.

Mr. Bill Lisonbee, Lab Technician, Laguna Clay Co., supplied many useful insights into West Coast glaze materials and their current availability for use in glaze formulas. Bill's extensive practical guide to materials was of considerable help in compiling information for this article.

Mr. Paul Pustulka of Tam Ceramics was most helpful in supplying information on zirconium silicate-based opacifiers and their uses in glazes. Tam Ceramics produces many of the opacifiers used in ceramic glazes.

Doug Gilliam, owner of Piedmont Pottery Supply Co., was most generous with his time and knowledge in explaining the unique challenges of ordering ceramic raw materials from large suppliers and mines. He supplied friendly, accurate raw material information to his customers and myself over the years.

Mr. Eric Nederberg, President of United Clays, offered information on an Albany Slip substitute clay, Jasper Slip.

Chapter 19

Soda Vapor Firing

In 1972, the New York State College of Ceramics at Alfred University was one of the first art departments to commit itself to the testing and development of a substitute salt firing system. In evaluating approximately 240 different sodium compounds, two materials met the required conditions of duplicating salt glazed effects on exposed clay surfaces while also offering an environmentally cleaner alternative to salt firing. After initial testing, sodium carbonate and sodium bicarbonate showed the most promise as salt substitutes. At that time, not much was known about sodium carbonate and its influence on clay bodies and glazes. However, salt glaze clay bodies and glaze formulas proved to function equally as well in soda firing.

Soda firing, as in traditional salt firing, is accomplished by the introduction of sodium carbonate (a white powder) into the firing kiln as the ceramic ware reaches maturity. When sodium carbonate is dropped into the kiln firebox it vaporizes, leaving carbon dioxide and water as byproducts. The remaining sodium vapor travels throughout the interior of the kiln, reacting with the exposed ceramic surfaces. In preparation, the ware in the kiln is partially glazed, leaving bare clay areas to take advantage of the effects of vapor glazing. The exposed clay surface contains alumina and silica which, when in contact with sodi-

A 43-cubic-foot soda kiln.

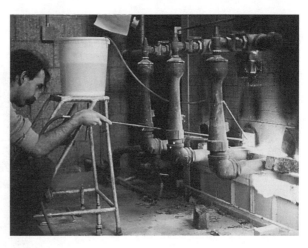

Spraying a sodium carbonate/water mixture in the kiln.

A salt glazed (sodium chloride) covered jar, cone 9 r.

Salt glazed (sodium chloride) jugs, cone 9 r.

A salt glazed (sodium chloride) platter, 15" diameter, cone 9 r.

A soda fired (sodium carbonate) platter, 15" diameter, cone 9 r.

um vapor, forms into a sodium, alumina, silicate glaze. Soda fired glazed surfaces can range from smooth glossy to the orange peel-like texture found in conventional salt glazed pottery.

The primary objective of the soda firing research was to exactly duplicate salt fired effects on clay and glazed surfaces. During the first year of tests, new soda kilns were built and somewhat complicated methods of introducing the sodium carbonate were tried and eventually discarded. The vapor coverage on the pots was almost complete when the sodium carbonate was mixed with water, forming a soup-like consistency and then sprayed into the kiln. Such a system proved to be too cumbersome and time-consuming for practical application in a working pottery.

During 1973, it was decided to place a dry powder sodium carbonate on an angle iron and insert it in the kiln as high as possible over the firebox. About one pound of sodium carbonate fit on the angle iron and it was inserted in the kiln. The angle iron was then slowly turned over to dump its contents into the firebox, producing a sodium vapor. This simple and effective method was also used in past salt firings. However, a complete orange peel coverage of the ware was not achieved until smaller kilns (20 to 40 cubic feet) were built in other locations after 1974.

Since the following article (Alternatives to Salt Glazing) was published in *Craft Horizons*, June 1973, some modifications to soda firing techniques have occurred (see Soda Kiln Firing Update). In the past 25 years, several important characteristics of soda firing have become apparent. The design and size of the kiln plays a large part in the ability of sodium carbonate (soda ash) or sodium bicarbonate (baking soda) to duplicate uniform orange-peel effects similar to traditional salt kiln results. Also, the method of introducing sodium carbonate into the firing kiln determines to a greater extent than salt (sodium chloride) how evenly the sodium vapor forms on unglazed clay surfaces. If the size of the kiln and the method of introducing sodium carbonate aren't carefully considered, the clay and glazed surfaces will closely resemble a wood/salt firing. Flashing patterns of glazed and unglazed soda orange-peel areas can be randomly deposited on the ware. Whether the potter wants a traditional complete orange-peel coverage of the pots or an irregular pattern of soda vapor glazing, the objective in both processes is to deposit only the sodium vapor on the ware and not the unvolatilized sodium carbonate.

Alternative to Salt Glazing

by Jeff Zamek (originally published by *Craft Horizons*, June 1973 Vol. XXXIII No. 3)

Anyone who has observed a salt firing has seen the "deadly" white cloud that covers the immediate area with sodium chloride and hydrochloric acid. These pollutants directly and quite dramatically affect the refractories and metals associated with the salt kiln in an adverse way, and in a more subtle fashion, also affect the ecology of the locale. For these reasons, many salt kilns have been shut down in urban areas or in areas with stringent pollution laws. Expensive antipollution devices can be installed but they are generally not practical for the studio potter.

As a graduate student at the College of Ceramics at Alfred University, New York, I became involved in research concerning a workable alternative for the standard sodium chloride or salt-glazing procedure. This research was initiated specifically to meet the pollution control restriction for the new art division facilities at Alfred. I wanted to maintain the integrity of salt glazing effects and surfaces without the polluting characteristics of salt glazing. Sodium carbonate (soda ash) and sodium bicarbonate (baking soda) seemed to be the best substitutes for salt, while still giving comparable results and remaining physically and economically

A 40-cubic-foot soda kiln.

suitable for the studio potter. The byproducts of soda ash and baking soda are carbon dioxide and water vapor, which are safer and less damaging than the hydrochloric acid and sodium chloride fumes given off during the traditional salt glaze firing.

Using an existing hard brick, 35-cubic-foot downdraft salt kiln, I introduced soda ash in place of salt. The general results of orange-peel surface and gloss were comparable; however, pots located near the salt port showed a yellowish, glassy buildup not present in normal salt firings. Clay body tests indicated the presence of sodium chloride vapor left over from previous salt firings. The problem then was to determine the extent of contamination. Results from chemical analysis of samples taken from different areas of the kiln indicated that only the firebox area was causing this contamination. Because of these tests, I determined that replacing the firebox and bag wall would eliminate further contamination from sodium chloride.

Contamination areas from sodium chloride would be different in each kiln, depending on the firebox location and where the salt entered and deposited itself. However, before rebuilding an existing salt kiln to fire sodium carbonate, an analysis from various areas inside the kiln had to be obtained. Once these contamination areas were located, the time and cost of building a new kiln was eliminated. It is important to note that each kiln left a distinct pattern of unvolatized sodium chloride spread. And no one rule could be made to cover all situations.

To insure a more accurate observation of the effects of sodium carbonate, I decided to rebuild the old kiln in its exact dimensions. A standard, high-quality type firebrick was used as the main refractory. I retained the four natural drafts, inspirating burners from the previous kiln. The new firing chamber was coated with a wash of 85% calcined alumina plus 15% sagger clay to protect the bricks from the corrosive effects of sodium vapor glazing. I added to the kiln a Maxon Premix burner/blower unit as a fifth burner to help in the volatilization and dispersion of the sodium carbonate vapors. The Maxon Premix burner/blower proved

Dry sodium carbonate being fed into the burner/blower unit.

A soda kiln with the burner/blower unit in operation (side view).

so efficient that only 4-1/2 pounds of sodium carbonate were needed to produce a good orange-peel effect throughout the kiln. To achieve the same effect, 35 pounds of salt were needed in the old kiln without the burner/blower unit.

The firing procedure was comparable to that used in the old salt kiln, but when cone 9 was reached, the soda ash was fed through the Maxon Premix burner. The total 4-1/2 pound batch was slowly introduced over a 90 minute period. The soda ash had been previously ground to pass through a 60-mesh screen to facilitate rapid volatilization. The materials entering the kiln through the fifth burner were deflected to prevent direct contact with the pots. This was accomplished by extending the bag wall. After a series of firings, I noted that the best effects were achieved when the vapors were completely contained within the kiln by closing the damper. Because soda ash volatilizes at a higher temperature and with less vapor pressure than salt, it was necessary to introduce the soda ash in such a way as to insure more efficient volatilization. The Maxon burner unit increased the temperature at which the material volatized, as well as helped disperse the vapor throughout the kiln. After subsequent tests, it was determined that due to the low vapor pressure of sodium carbonate, two

ports of entry for the vapors (one on each side of the kiln) distributed the volatilized material more efficiently.

Whether or not a burner/blower unit is used, it is important to note that only the vapors reach the ware and not any unvolatilized material. When unvolatilized soda ash strikes the ware, the yellowish buildup described earlier occurs. In further testing, I observed that sodium bicarbonate seemed to be slightly more active in volatilizing than sodium carbonate. However, if a burner/blower unit was utilized, there was no

Soda kiln cone viewing port during firing.

The soda kiln after firing (front view).

appreciable difference between these two materials.

In conclusion, I am convinced that soda ash firings can and should replace salt firings. I have been able to duplicate the orange-peel texture and the various other characteristics of salt firing. Glaze and slip colors were generally brighter in the soda ash fire, and yellows and copper reds were more easily developed. These brighter glaze effects may be due to the absence of chloride and hydrochloric acid vapors in the kiln atmosphere. Sodium carbonate vapor glazing requires somewhat more working knowledge of the material and its characteristics than the traditional salt glazing, but the results are at least as good as salt and may offer an even broader range of color

Inside the soda kiln target brick (right side) on top of the bag wall deflected sprayed sodium carbonate.

Close-up of the inside of the soda kiln and the target brick (right side).

Close-up of the soda kiln cone 10, cone 11, and cone 12.

possibilities. Sodium carbonate vapor glazing is more than just a substitute for salt glazing. In addition to its favorable effect on glaze colors, it is noncorrosive to metals and nonpolluting in the atmosphere.

✳   To obtain the complete research papers contact Scholes Library of Ceramics, New York State College of Ceramics at Alfred University, 2 Pine Street, Alfred, NY 14802-1297, PH: (607) 871-2950. Jeff Zamek/Sodium Carbonate Vapor.

Soda Kiln Firing Update

From 1972 through 1974, a series of soda kilns were fired at Alfred University College of Ceramics. During the two year period, many methods were used to introduce sodium carbonate and sodium bicarbonate into the kiln during the firing. Since that research (Soda Firing Part 1., Soda Firing Part 2. Alfred University), many soda kilns have been built and fired. From the new kilns, several common elements were found to produce uniform textured soda glaze fired pots.

Objective

The primary goal was to duplicate salt (sodium chloride) vapor glaze in ware stacked throughout the kiln. To accomplish this objective it was necessary to devise a kiln firing system that would disperse sodium carbonate as a vapor within the kiln. The vapor would then react with the alumina and silica on vitrified clay surfaces to form a sodium, alumina, silica glaze. The kiln, clay bodies, and firing procedures should consistently produce a uniform orange-peel glaze effect on all exposed clay surfaces.

Kiln Size

It was found that a 20 to 40 cubic foot interior kiln stacking space produced the most even coverage of soda vapor on the ware. Kilns smaller than 20 cubic feet were too small to consider because of time and labor needed to build and fire a small kiln for an insufficient stacking space. Kilns over 40 cubic feet were too large for the even dispersion of the sodium carbonate. Sodium chloride (salt) travels much more forcefully and will spread throughout a smaller or larger kiln better than sodium carbonate. In kilns larger than 40 cubic feet, the fired results produced non-uniform coverage on pots. (Most pots looked like they were fired in a wood/salt kiln, showing signs of flashing on the exposed clay surfaces.)

Kiln Construction

Hard-brick interior kiln construction and salt refractory casting mixtures did

A 22-cubic-foot cast catenary arch soda kiln (four forced air, natural gas fired burners).

A cantenary arch soda kiln – rear burners, kiln stack and damper.

best in durability during the life of the kilns. A dense brick or cast mixture also has the benefit of holding salt on its surface, which volatilizes during the next firing. Sprung arch or catenary arch kilns did best because their shape helped circulate the sodium vapor atmosphere. Over each firebox, at the highest possible level, a salting port was left open (the hole was about the size of a kiln post, 2-1/2" x 2-1/2") where an angle iron full of sodium carbonate could be passed through and dumped into the firebox.

Sodium Compound

Sodium carbonate or sodium bicarbonate (which turns into sodium carbonate at 850°C) light powder was used for the new series of soda vapor firings.

Method of Introducing Sodium Carbonate

The kiln was brought up to the maturing temperature of the clay body and an angle iron of sodium carbonate was passed through the salting port. It was then turned over and the sodium carbonate dropped into the firebox. At no time was the pottery exposed to sodium carbonate directly. The sodium carbonate was to be exposed to the clay surfaces only as a vapor. The average amount of sodium carbonate used was one to two pounds per cubic foot of kiln size. Draw rings of clay where placed throughout the kiln and pulled out during the additions of sodium carbonate to check the progress of vapor coverage.

Soda ash on an angle iron introduced above the kiln firebox.

An angle iron turned over as sodium carbonate volitalizes inside the kiln.

Each soda port receives equal amounts of sodium carbonate.

Draw rings showing the buildup of orange-peel soda glaze on the clay body.

Unloading the soda vapor kiln.

Example of pulling test draw rings from the kiln.

Clay Bodies and Glazes

The best orange-peel surfaces were from porcelain clay bodies and stoneware clay bodies. The maturation of the clay body was a critical factor in the development of an orange-peel sodium, alumina, silicate, glaze. When sodium carbonate was introduced into the kiln, a reducing kiln atmosphere fluxed the clay body surface slightly, causing a better soda glazed surface. It was possible to develop good or-ange-peel textures on clay bodies below cone 9 (2336°F) provided the clay body was mature and vitreous and sodium carbonate was released in vapor form in the kiln.

Clay bodies and glazes containing talc, dolomite, magnesium carbonate, or any form of MgO didn't take a good glaze and were dry, dull, and bubbled. Light stoneware clay bodies showed the most effects from flashing and irregular patterns of soda and reduction atmosphere. The use of silica sand 65x- or 85x-mesh in the clay body (5% to 14% based on the dry weight. of the clay body formula) increased the orange-peel surface. Overall, the clay body formulas that produced good sodium vapor glazed surfaces had high amounts of flint 200x-mesh (10% to 25% based on the dry weight. of the clay body formula) in the clay body.

Color in Sodium Vapor

Coloring oxides could be mixed into the sodium carbonate before it was introduced in the kiln. Metallic coloring oxides can impart a color to the sodium vapor as it reacts with exposed clay surfaces during the kiln firing. However, a percentage of the unvolatized material remained in the firebox area of the kiln, effecting the vapor glaze color in future firings. White or light colored fired clay bodies offered the most distinctive surface areas for colored vapor glazes.

Blue soda orange peel – 1% to 3% cobalt oxide added to sodium carbonate.

Red soda orange peel – 1% to 4% copper oxide added to sodium carbonate (red in reduction atmosphere, green in oxidation atmosphere).

Brown soda orange peel – 1% to 5% red iron oxide added to sodium carbonate.

A gray soda glaze was most easily achieved through the use of a light firing clay body (low iron content in clay body) and rapid cooling of the kiln.

Borax (1% to 8%) added to sodium carbonate decreased the orange-peel effect and promoted a smooth unbroken gloss glaze surface but also contaminated the firebox areas of the kiln which could have influenced future glaze firings.

Summary

Sodium carbonate didn't cover pots as uniformly as sodium chloride when volatilized, causing dry or unglazed sodium vapor areas on the pots. To achieve complete vapor coverage throughout the kiln atmosphere, the damper was opened and closed when introducing sodium carbonate into the kiln, then several loads of sodium carbonate were placed into the kiln when the damper was shut.

For best results, the sodium carbonate was dropped in small amounts from the highest point above the firebox in the kiln. Greater volatilization resulted when

Soda vapor fired cone 10 porcelain form with copper slip design.

Soda vapor fired cone10 brown clay form with yellow slip design.

Soda vapor fired cone 11 bowl with green slip design.

Soda vapor fired cone 10 pitcher with yellow slip design.

Soda vapor fired cone 9 bottle.

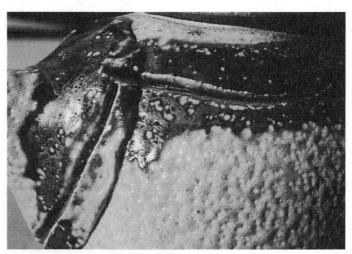

Gray clay body soda vapor orange-peel (close-up).

Brown clay body soda vapor orange-peel (close-up).

A soda fired (sodium carbonate) platter, diameter 15", black clay body, cone 9 r.

the material had a longer distance to fall before dropping to the firebox floor. At no time during the firing should unvolatilized sodium carbonate contact kiln shelves or pots. Increased sodium vapor coverage resulted when the material was placed in the kiln in small amounts (greater surface area for volatilizing) when the clay body reached maturity. To insure added kiln life, shelves, posts, and bag walls were lightly coated with calcined alumina kiln wash to retard sodium vapor buildup as practiced in common salt firing.

Sodium carbonate generally produced a higher luster glazed surface than sodium chloride. Glaze colors tended to be brighter, with more intense copper reds and yellows. The vivid glazed surfaces were possibly due to the glaze forming in an atmosphere free of hydrochloric acid and chlorine gas, byproducts of traditional salt glazing.

As with salt firing, creating a reduction atmosphere in the kiln before the introduction of sodium carbonate converted any ferric iron compounds in the clay body to a ferrous state. The clay surface became more vitreous, dense, and less porous which produced a better surface area for the sodium vapor to react with the alumina and silica in the clay body.

Chapter 20

Dendritic Slip Decoration

History

One of the most fascinating decorative techniques in pottery is the application and visual design effect of dendritic slips. The term dendritic describes tree-like, fine line dark patterns of slip applied on a contrasting light color clay background, resulting in what looks like a detailed network of tree branches. Dendritic slip decoration was originally used on some groups of mocha ware which were a type of refined, functional, red earthenware. The name is derived from Arabian mocha stone which has a similar "tree" or tentacle pattern.[30] Mocha ware was produced for more than 165 years in Britain, and to a lesser extent in North America and France. In later periods, white earthenware was also decorated with distinctive dendritic design patterns. British mocha pottery was exported as early as the 1770s.

The term mocha ware was used to indicate an extensive array of colored slip designs ranging from slip marbling (differently color slips mixed together on the clay surface) to uniform precise checkered patterns of slip trailing on pots. Each piece was thrown and when leatherhard, turned on a lathe where it was trimmed down over its entire surface to produce a thin uniform pot. Some ware had a decorative textured design impressed in the moist clay or variations of colored slips applied in exact patterns on the pot's surface.[31]

Mixing and Applying Dendritic Slip

Traditional dendritic slip effects were produced on low-fire white or red earthenware pottery. The techniques can readily be applied to any temperature range ceramic surface, but three main elements should be in place regardless of kiln firing temperatures.

1. A reliable clay body formula.

2. A base wet slip formula that fires to a color that contrasts with the dendritic slip. For example, if the base wet slip color is white, the dendritic slip could be black. It's critical that the base wet slip fit the clay body without cracking or peeling during the application, drying, bisque firing, and glaze firing stages. (A wet slip is classified as water clay(s) and/or other ceramic materials that can be applied to wet or leather-hard ware, resulting in a colored clay fitting the underlying clay body.)

3. A dendritic slip formula.

---

30. *An Illustrated Dictionary of Ceramics*, by George Savage and Harold Newman, p 194, Van Nostrand Reinhold Pub.

31. Cited in an article by Jonathan Rickard, "Slip Decorated Refined Earthenware" p.183, *The Magazine Antiques*, Aug. 1993.

Clay Formula
Low-Fire Red Clay Body Formula, Cone 06-Cone 04

Redart	55
Cedar Heights Bonding clay 50x-mesh	9
Thomas ball clay	17
M44 clay	7
Custer feldspar	6
Goldart stoneware clay	3
Flint 200x	3

Mix dry materials with water until the proper forming consistency is achieved. Cover the moist clay completely with a plastic sheet for one or two days. Wedge the clay thoroughly before using.

Base Slip Formula (wet application)
White Slip Cone 06-Cone 04

EPK	30
Thomas ball clay	25
M44 clay	10
Goldart stoneware clay	5
Flint 325x	20
Superpax	10
Bentonite	2

Yellow Slip Cone 06-Cone 04

Add 10% Mason stain Titanium Yellow #6485.

Weigh out the dry materials. Add water to achieve a specific gravity of 1.350, then place the wet slip through an 80x sieve three times. The slip is now ready to apply on a wet to leather-hard clay body.

Dendritic Slip Formula
Black Slip

Manganese dioxide powder	20 grams
Water	29 grams
Apple cider vinegar	29 grams
Tobacco	1 cigarette (king size)

Blue Slip

Cobalt carbonate	5 grams
Water	29 grams
Apple cider vinegar	29 grams
Tobacco	1 cigarette (king size)

Green Slip

Copper carbonate	5 grams
Water	29 grams
Apple cider vinegar	29 grams
Tobacco	1 cigarette (king size)

Mix all ingredients. Break open and add the contents of one cigarette to the slip (don't use the cigarette filter). Age the slip for 24 hours, then place the liquid through a 100x-mesh sieve three times before using. Discard any material left on the 100x-mesh screen. The shelf life of dendritic slip is two weeks. After that the properties of the growing tree patterns rapidly decline.

Glaze

Clear Glossy Cone 04

Ferro frit #3269	89.5
EPK	8.5
Flint 325x	2.0
Bentonite	2.0
Red iron oxide	1.0
Epsom salts	.5

Mix the dry materials and add water to achieve a specific gravity of 1.350. Place the wet glaze through an 80x-mesh sieve three times. The glaze is formulated for dipping, pouring, or spraying. Additions of 2% CMC (based on the dry weight of the glaze formula) allow brushing applications.

Applying Dendritic Slip

After the pot is thrown, hand-built, or otherwise formed, apply the base slip to the moist and leather-hard clay surface as soon as possible to insure a stronger bond between the slip and clay body. While the base slip is still wet, immediately dip a soft bristle brush in the dendritic slip mixture (dendritic slip settles very fast so constantly stir the brush in the slip jar). Fill the brush with a small

Dendritic slip designs spread out in the base slip after application.

Vertical dendritic slip application to wet base slip.

amount of the watercolor-consistency dendritic slip then barely touch the surface of the wet white slip with the brush. The dendritic slip will flow off the brush onto the base slip, leaving a pattern. A tree-like tentacle decoration can be devel-

Dendritic slip brush application to the base slip.

Detail of the "dripping" dendritic slip technique.

oped by holding the pot on the vertical. Concentric ring patterns can be obtained by applying dendritic slip to horizontal pot surfaces. Keep in mind that the wetter the base slip, the greater the dendritic design grows.

Bisque Firing and Glazing

Let pots dry thoroughly after the application of the base slip and dendritic slip. Then bisque fire the pots to cone 06 (1830°F).[32] Ceramic materials, clays, glazes, and slips work best when they are fired over longer periods of time to their recommended temperatures. Bisque kiln firings for average size functional pottery (3" to 16" high, 1/4" to 1/2" thick) should take between eight and ten hours to reach cone 06. Once the pots are removed from the bisque kiln, apply the clear glaze by dipping, pouring, spraying, or brushing. Fire the glaze kiln to cone 04 (1940°F). Glaze kiln firings should take ten to 12 hours to reach cone 04. Unload the glaze kiln when the pots are cool to the touch or below 200°F. The fired clay body should be dark brown/red in color with a white or yellow background slip color and the dendritic design. The complete design will be covered by a clear transparent glossy glaze.

Once-Fire Raw Glazing

An alternative method of glazing is to once-fire the pots. The clay body, base slips, dendritic slips, and the glaze are also formulated for once-firing or raw glazing. After the pot has been formed and allowed to dry to the leather-hard stage, trim the pot or apply any handles. Apply the base slip to the leather-hard moist pot. The dendritic slip should be applied immediately to the still wet base slip. When both slips are dry to the touch and the clay is completely dry, the pot is ready for glazing. The glaze can be applied by dipping, pouring, spraying, or brushing. Place the bone dry pots in a glaze kiln and fire to cone 04 in ten to 12 hours.

Horizontal fan pattern of dendritic slip application on wet base slip.

---

32.   All temperature references to cones are based on Orton Pyrometric cones heated at 270°F per hour.

Why It Works

The magic of dendritic slip seems to be in how it grows and spreads on the surface of the wet base slip. A very interesting aspect of the original formula devised by John and Richard Riley who produced Mocha Ware (or Tree Ware) from 1802 to

A once-fired, cone 04/electric, yellow base slip plate 10" diameter.

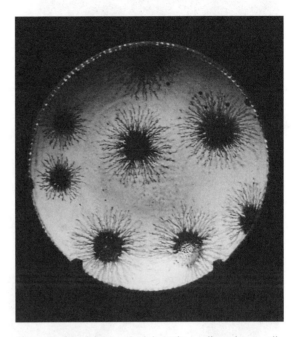

A once-fired, cone 04/electric, yellow base slip plate 8" diameter.

A once-fired, cone 04/electric, yellow base slip tea set.

A once-fired, cone 04/electric, yellow base slip bottle 7-1/2" high with dendritic slip design and clear glaze.

Close-up of the brown dendritic design on the bottle.

Close-up of the brown dendritic design on the plate.* Dendritic pottery and photographs supplied by Joel Huntley, Wisconsin Pottery. Additional photos by Robert Tobey.

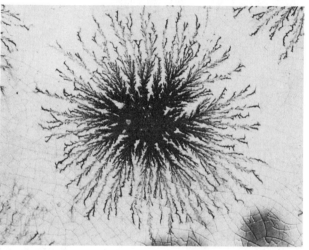

A once-fired, cone 04/electric plate 6-1/4" diameter yellow slip with brown dendritic design.

1828 was the inclusion of tobacco leaves, hop extract, and urine. Such ingredients supplied the acid base to the slip formula or "tea" as it was called. The brown, blue, and green color of the slip was produced by adding either manganese dioxide, cobalt oxide, or chrome oxide.[33] For aesthetic reasons, modern potters have replaced

---

33.   Cited in an article by Jonathan Rickard, "Slip Decorated Refined Earthenware" p. 187, *The Magazine Antiques*, Aug. 1993.

A once-fired, cone 04/electric, yellow base slip bottle 9-1/4" high with brown dendritic slip design.

the urine with apple cider vinegar, but the same principles of slip dispersion still apply to current formulas. The dendritic slip forms into tree-like patterns in the base slip because of the capillary action of the dendritic slip suspended in the base slip and gravity acting with the pH difference between each slip. Because dendritic slip is an acid with a low pH and the base slip is alkaline with a higher pH, the simple chemical reaction between the two causes the distinctive branch effect in the slip.[34]

Current Use of Dendritic Slip

Joel and Debra Huntley, owners of The Wisconsin Pottery in Columbus, Wis., are the foremost practitioners of this almost lost decorative technique inspired by 17th, 18th, and 19th century folk pottery. Their entire line of pottery is produced by hand, capturing the skill and feeling of the original pots. Joel has worked to improve each step in the production, application, and firing process. As with most ceramic related techniques, it is the subtle techniques at each level that make the big difference in the final pot. While I worked with Joel adjusting the original formulas, the procedures of mixing, aging, and applying the slip was a time-consuming hit-or-miss process that Joel expertly accomplished over two years. The Wisconsin Pottery currently produces 50 to 60 dendritic slip pots per week.

---

34. *The Observer's Book of Pottery & Porcelain*, by Mary & Geoffrey Payton, p.114 Frederick Warne & Co. Ltd. Pub.

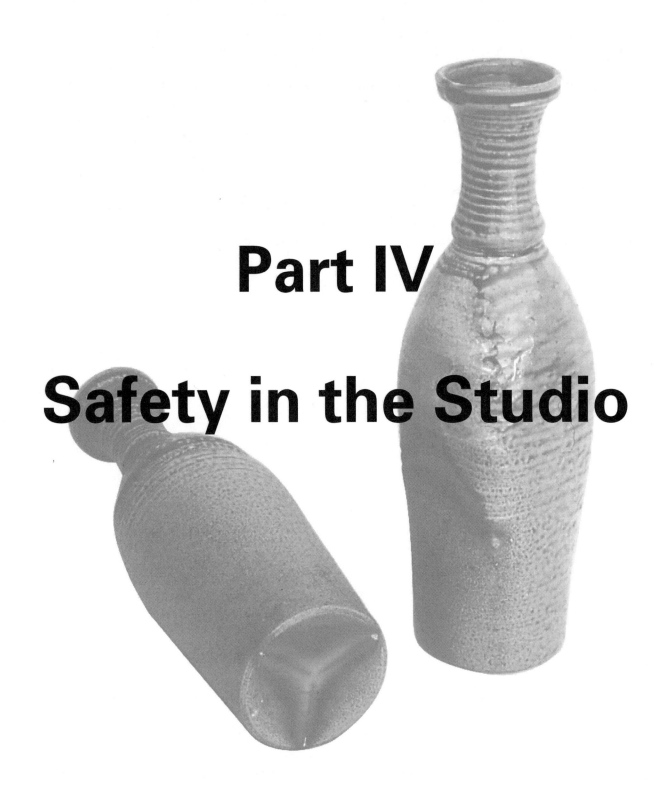

Part IV

Safety in the Studio

Chapter 21

Is Barium Carbonate Safe?

Is barium carbonate safe? Yes. Provided you don't eat it or directly inhale this white powder. Knowledge of the material, especially in the raw form, is vital to your health and safety. That is the short answer to a controversial issue raised by many in the field of ceramics.

Barium carbonate has a long history of use in clay bodies, glazes, and casting slips. It serves several functions when used in clay bodies or glaze formulas. Regardless of its history, many potters remove barium from their studios, fearing its toxic potential. As the general population has become more aware of health and safety issues, every material is more closely examined for potentially harmful effects. Understandably, potters don't want to jeopardize themselves when handling ceramic raw materials. They also don't want to place their customers at risk when using fired clay and glaze products. With such legitimate health and safety concerns, why use barium carbonate?

Facts about Barium Carbonate

The actual material used in clay and glazes is never found in nature in its elemental form but is mined from barite ore that contains barium sulfate. Barite is a naturally-occurring mineral used in the oil and gas drilling industries. About 5% of barite is processed into barium carbonate, barium chloride, and barium hydroxide. Barium carbonate is used in the manufacture of glass for television and computer screens because of its capacity to absorb x-rays generated when the image is produced. Barium carbonate is also blended with iron oxide to form ceramic magnets used in many products. Various industries in the U.S. use approximately 50,000 tons of barium carbonate every year.[35]

Barium Carbonate in Clay Bodies

You have probably noticed surface deposits of white powder on exposed parts of common red building brick. The soluble salts in the clay migrate to the brick surface, crystallizing and causing white scumming. When barium carbonate is added to the clay body (1/4% to 2% based on the dry weight of the clay body), it reacts with calcium and/or magnesium salts found in clays. It changes them to calcium carbonate and barium sulfate which don't produce soluble salt scumming. By eliminating soluble salts in the clay body, subsequent firing discoloration is reduced. Some red earthenware clays are more susceptible to soluble salt problems, but even so-called clean clays can occasionally have high levels of troublesome salts. Consequently, barium car-

---

35. Toxicology and Carcinogenesis Studies of Barium Chloride Dihydrate (Drinking Water Studies) U.S. Department of Health and Human Services (CAS NO. 10326-27-9) pages 13-16.

bonate is found in many different types of clay body formulas.

Barium Carbonate in Casting Slips

Ball clays used in casting slip formulas sometimes contain soluble salts. If the ball clay was left untreated, it would require excessively high amounts of deflocculent to transform it into a casting slip. Barium carbonate reacts with soluble salts found in clays, changing them into insoluble barium sulfates which reduces the deflocculent requirement for the slip. In low-fire white clay bodies where the amount of ball clay can be as much as half the clay body formula, the level of barium carbonate required can be .03% to .05% based on the dry weight of the clay body formula. The actual amount used depends on the soluble salt levels in the clay. In stoneware and high iron content casting slips, barium carbonate is needed to facilitate good casting properties in the slip and can be as high as 2% based on the dry weight of the clay body formula.

Barium Carbonate in Glazes

Barium carbonate can be classified as an alkaline earth that is very refractory. Small percentages in low-temperature glazes result in dry matte fired surfaces. At higher temperatures, barium carbonate is mostly known for producing soft, buttery glaze textures. It can also yield intense blue colors when combined with copper in reduction glazes. Barium causes unique glaze colors and surface qualities that are very difficult to obtain when using alternative glaze materials.

Toxic Effects

Ingestion

The effects of ingestion take place when barium carbonate changes in the presence of stomach acid (hydrochloric acid found in the stomach), yielding soluble barium chloride. The first symptoms can be vomiting, skeletal and muscle twitching, or muscle paralysis. If ingested, small amounts of barium carbonate (13 grams) can be lethal.

Most barium that enters the body is eliminated within one or two weeks.[36] Barium doesn't accumulate in the body. Previous information about barium causing cumulative central nervous system damage is not supported by the Environmental Protection Agency's toxicological evaluation of soluble barium.[37] Common sense tells you it's not a good idea to rush into your studio and eat barium carbonate, but accidents do happen. How can you prevent an accidental dose of barium carbonate from being swallowed? First, always wear a dust mask when mixing barium in glazes. Second, eliminate eating or smoking in the studio to reduce the risk of ingesting any foreign substance, including barium. And last, store barium carbonate in a covered jar.

Inhalation

Breathing particles of any substance in the pottery studio should be prevented. Whenever clay and glaze materials are handled in the dry state, small particles can become airborne. Wear a dust mask when opening bags of dry material or mixing.

Potters have used barium carbonate in their studios for more than 40 years and have sold functional pottery containing barium in their glazes. Medical records don't show any reports of toxic reactions to barium carbonate used in pottery studios or toxic levels of barium released from

---

36.   Toxicological Profile for Barium; U. S. Department of Health and Human Services; Public Health Service; Agency for Toxic Substances and Disease Registry; PB 93-110658.

37.   Environmental Protection Agency report, Federal Register, Vol. 62 No. 2 Friday, January 3, 1997, pages 368-370.

glazes.[38] This lack of information might mean that potters receive toxic doses of barium carbonate in their studios but their symptoms (vomiting, paralysis, etc.) aren't recognized or reported. Another possibility is that potential toxic reactions concerning barium carbonate are not happening. The absence of evidence concerning potters' misapplication of the material is one factor in considering the continued use of barium carbonate.

An occupational exposure study reports no adverse health effects related to workers exposed to high levels of barium carbonate dust for periods of seven to 27 years.[39] Clearly such diverse information about barium carbonate is confusing to anyone contemplating using the material in their studio. However, protecting yourself from inhalation by wearing a dust mask is a precautionary step that removes short or long-term hazard due to inhalation and ingestion and thoroughly cleaning your studio regularly is a further safety measure.

Handling Barium Carbonate In the Studio

Essentially, the same safety precautions should be in effect when handling any raw material. Whenever possible, purchase clean unopened bags of raw material and store them in a place where they cannot be broken. As a safety and studio hygiene measure, place raw material bags in covered jars or heavyweight plastic garbage bags with a twist-top closure. During glaze or clay mixing, return any unused raw material to the covered jar or storage bag. In this way, bags won't break accidentally, causing small particles of raw material to spread throughout the studio. When opening a raw material bag or mixing dry materials, always wear a cartridge respirator or a paper dust mask. Extra paper masks should be kept in a sealed container and once used, should be discarded. Change the filters in cartridge masks regularly.

Mixing Barium Carbonate in Glazes

Barium carbonate has a limited solubility in pure water. Any solubility of barium carbonate in glaze water is marginal. Solubility varies with glaze water pH levels. If the glaze water is acidic (low pH levels), some barium carbonate changes to barium chloride with levels in the water of 15.3 ppm to 45 ppm. Such amounts are well below any toxic concern for penetrating the skin even with an open wound on the hand. While mixing a wet or dry glaze with your hands is not recommended, barium carbonate in the glaze will not cause a health risk if you don't drink large quantities of the glaze. Medical literature doesn't contain any reports of barium carbonate migrating through wounds in the skin as might occur in a glaze mixing operation. By way of comparing the relative risks in glazing operations, mixing highly alkaline and soluble wood ash glazes with bare hands is more harmful because of the health risk of skin irritation and/or burns. Regardless, wash your hands after any glazing operation.

Barium Release Levels in the Environment

In the past long-term exposure to low levels of barium was thought to cause health problems but the data does not support this belief. The National Toxicology Program Study by the U.S. Department of Health and Human Services conducted tests where they fed animals water containing up to 700 ppm levels of barium. At this level of constant daily consumption,

---

38. Eight databases searched, BIOSIS (toxicological aspects of environmental health), TOXLIT (toxicology literature), RTECS (Registry of Toxic Effects of Chemical Substances), and MEDLINE.
39. Essing, H.G.; et al. "Exclusion of Disturbances to Health from Long Years of Exposure to Barium Carbonate in the Production of Steatite Ceramics" (translated from German); Arbeitsmedizin Sozialmedizin Praventimedizin; Volume 11 No. 12, pages 299-302, 1976.

the water was considered safe to drink and did not produce harmful effects. The medical assumption in this method of testing is that animals respond similarly to humans. The purpose of this study was to predict the possible long-term daily ingestion of barium in humans.

In its different forms, barium is commonly found in food, water, soil, and even the air we breathe. It is one of the most abundant materials found in the earth – we are in a barium laden environment. The Toxicology and Carcinogenesis Studies Report issued by the U.S. Department of Health and Human Services states that the drinking water in some states can exceed 20 ppm of barium. This amount of barium reflects what people consume daily without ill effects; it does not tell us what amount greater than 20 ppm people could consume with no ill effects! Humans ingest barium on a daily basis. It is found in many foods including tea, coffee, and fruits. Dietary consumption of barium from foods is from 300 to 1,770 mg. per day. Barium is also found in bran flakes (3.9 ppm barium release), eggs (7.6 ppm barium release), sea water (5.2 ppm to 25.2 ppm barium release), beets (2.6 ppm barium release), and Brazil nuts (1000 ppm barium release). However, the chances of eating enough Brazil nuts to achieve a toxic level of barium are remote because your stomach and digestive system could not hold that bulk of nuts.

Barium Release Levels in Glazes

Barium carbonate decomposes when heated and changes to barium silicate or barium salts in the fired glaze, after which the glazed surface can be soluble when it contacts weak acids contained in foods. Release levels of pottery glazes containing barium can range from 0 ppm to more than 1250 ppm. However, many glazes tested are within the 20 ppm barium release ranges. It is always prudent and useful to test for barium-release levels on functional pottery glazes that come into direct contact with food or drink. Choose a laboratory that is familiar with the testing procedure. If the test is done correctly, the accuracy rate is 99%.[40] Commonly, high barium release levels in glazes can be substantially decreased by firing the glaze one or two cones higher in temperature or adjusting the glaze formula. If you are unsure of how to adjust the glaze, seek guidance. Experimenting on your own without a basic understanding of glaze materials can be fun but it can also be time-consuming.

As potters, we should educate ourselves about the safe use of any raw material in our studios. We should then use this knowledge to protect ourselves and our customers from the potentially harmful effects of the ceramic process. However, we are often asked to make decisions about ceramic materials based on incomplete facts. In the past unchallenged claims, unfounded dire projections, and generalizations about raw material hazards brought more drama to the issues than usable facts. In some circumstances, the information published wasn't relevant to how potters use the material. An ongoing effort to increase our knowledge of questionable materials will yield a realistic evaluation of their hazards. Many valid disagreements exist about which materials are truly dangerous and such differing opinions are necessary because they contribute to discussions, testing, and greater research in ceramic raw material toxicologies as they directly relate to potters.

The ongoing health and safety issues concerning potters' use of barium carbonate falls into two primary areas of concern: the ingestion/inhalation of the material in the studio, and its potential release in fired

---

40. For testing of barium release or other elements in glazes (i.e. antimony, manganese, vanadium, lead, etc.) send a fired sample of the glaze on a cup or bowl to Office of Sponsored Programs, New York State College of Ceramics, Alfred University, Alfred, NY, 14803, PH: (607) 871-2486, Fax: (607) 871-3469. There is a $30 charge per element tested.

glazes. To prevent inhalation/ingestion, wear a dusk mask when mixing or handling barium carbonate. It's that simple. The second area of health worry relates to the potential release of barium used in clay bodies, casting slips, and fired functional pottery glazed surfaces. The low percentages of barium carbonate used in clay bodies and casting slip formulas and its potential release is considerably below any level of concern. In glazes, the ideal situation is an inert, stable, nonleaching fired surface. In the real world, this situation isn't necessary for barium as it should be for lead and other heavy metals, which are highly toxic and can accumulate in the body.

With the level of barium release in some communities' drinking water approaching 20 ppm with no ill effects in the population, a 20 ppm or lower release of barium for functional pottery glazes should be a conservative goal. This amount takes into consideration various factors which can cause variable barium release levels in glazes such as glaze thickness, kiln firing atmosphere, endpoint firing temperature, time to temperature, refiring glazes, and marginal glaze testing inaccuracies. The drinking water study (Toxicology and Carcinogenesis Studies of Barium Chloride Dihydrate) is significant because it relates to a barium consumption level in water (20 ppm) that humans drink every day over a prolonged time. This is the closest approximation to people drinking or eating from a barium release glazed surfaces for an extended time. It also assumes the worst case situation where a glaze releasing barium will continue to release the same amount of barium every time it contacts food or drink

Barium carbonate is not an easy material to classify concerning safety issues. It requires respect and effort to understand how to use it safely. You can always take the recommendations of experts, but the real information comes from building a base of knowledge from many sources. Disregarding raw material warnings is irrational, just as believing in the poison-of-the-

month theory is excessive. Both extremes are inaccurate and offer ignorance instead of insight. You must do some hard work and study the literature and toxicity statistics on this common glaze material. On some level, you calculate the relative risk factor in all daily events. How dangerous is flying? Not as dangerous as driving to the airport. How dangerous is barium carbonate as used by potters? Not as dangerous as driving to your studio or as incurring back pain from lifting kiln shelves; or carpal tunnel syndrome from throwing, wedging, lifting; or retina damage from looking into a firing kiln without eye protection. Proper protection and knowledge will prevent accidents in these known potential areas of risk. The same principle should be applied to barium carbonate.

What To Do?

Consistently follow the health and safety guidelines listed in the chapter on studio safety. Wear a dust mask when mixing barium carbonate or any dry raw material. Keep barium carbonate in a covered storage container. Test barium glazes that come in direct contact with food. If the barium release level is higher than 20 ppm, adjust the glaze or test an alternative barium glaze. The barium release on many glazes can be substantially lowered by firing one or two cones higher (however, the glaze should be retested). Often the most efficient method is to obtain several barium glaze formulas that have already been tested for barium release levels.

Barium Carbonate Alternatives

Sometimes if less than 6% barium carbonate is used in high-temperature (above cone 6 or 2194°F) glaze formulas and it isn't needed to promote color or glaze texture, it can be removed without changing the fired nature of the glaze. In such situations, barium acts as a marginal flux. Its absence from the formula won't appreciably affect the fire glaze result. In glazes containing barium carbonate in amounts greater than 6%, barium probably contributes to unique qualities of opacity and glaze color and removing it would substantially change the glaze.

Strontium carbonate goes into a melt more actively than barium carbonate. It has been used in place of barium (3/4 parts strontium carbonate to 1 part barium carbonate) but it doesn't yield an adequate match in glaze color, opacity, and texture. Another ineffective barium carbonate substitute, barium sulfate (insoluble and nontoxic) which is the form of barium used for medical procedures, has not been an adequate alternative in glazes or clay bodies. Sulfate fumes released as it reacts with the increasing kiln temperature cause blisters or pinholes in glazes and bloating in clay bodies.

Acknowledgments

Ms. Bethany Clark, Research Assistant, Jeff Zamek Ceramics Consulting Services, Northampton, Mass., was outstanding in her efforts to locate published information on barium carbonate. Her efficiency and dedication contributed greatly to this article.

Ms. Donna L. Kurkul, Medical Librarian, Richard H. Dolloff Medical Library, The Cooley Dickinson Hospital, Northampton, Mass., for her time and effort searching the data for information on barium toxicology.

Lauren Proctor, M.D., Amherst, Mass., was very helpful in advising the direction and scope of research concerning barium carbonate ingestion.

Bruce Cowan, M.D., Easthampton, Mass., who was most interested in my research and directed my efforts in obtaining the relevant medical information.

Paul Berman, M.D., Easthampton, Mass., contributed his time in helping me focus my search for toxic reactions of barium carbonate in the general population.

Mr. Jerry Cartlidge, (retired) Alfred University College of Ceramics, Engineering Division, Alfred, New York. It was a pleasure to work with Mr. Cartlidge again after so many years. His knowledge of testing procedures was most valuable in understanding ceramic materials.

Ms. Cynthia Edney, analytical chemist, Alfred University College of Ceramics, Engineering Division, spent considerable time locating and interpreting current barium release test data for this article.

Mr. Jerry A. Cook, Technical Director, Chemical Products Corp., Cartersville, Ga. Thank you for supplying data and information on barium carbonate sales in the pottery industry.

Mr. Bruce E. Connolly, Public Services Librarian, Scholes Library of Ceramics, NYS College of Ceramics at Alfred University. Thank you for your efforts in locating past articles on barium carbonate. Bruce has always demonstrated an exceptional ability to locate ceramics-related source materials, often with short notice.

Mr. Rudy Kottemann, Chemical Products Corp., Cartersville, Ga., who helped me turn raw information into readable text.

Alfred University College of Ceramics, Art and Design Division, Engineering Division, teachers and support staff who have given their time and effort in training potters.

Chapter 22

Studio Safety

A major concern of all potters is the fundamental question of studio safety. No one wants to work in a potentially dangerous environment or expose others to uncertain materials. However, some studio potters are unfamiliar with the safe methods of storing and handling the raw materials that form the basis of their clay bodies and glazes. In any pottery making situation, there are procedures that will produce a clean, safe ceramics studio. Many of the steps are very simple and thoroughly effective in removing material-related hazards in the workplace. Most of the recommendations involve low-cost cleanup equipment and its regular use. Fear of the unknown is often what causes the most anxiety when working with clay, so the best tool for a safe studio is a basic knowledge of the materials and how to use them sensibly.

Is the Kitchen a Dangerous Place?

When walking into your kitchen to prepare dinner, do you consider all the potential risk factors involved in that everyday activity? Using knives to cut vegetables, improperly cleaning food preparation surfaces, and lighting the oven all expose you to risk from cuts, food poisoning, and burns. Yet you are careful using the sharp knife, cleaning the meat cutting table, and lighting the oven. Inherent in these daily activities is the assumption that you know what the hazards are and take precautions to prevent a serious injury. Understanding the process and tools of cooking a dinner reduces it to the safe and mundane level. The real risk from household activities comes not from lack of knowledge about dangerous conditions and activities in the home, but from disregarding known hazards of daily life. How many people do you know who suddenly decide to put their hands in a hot oven? People get burnt in the kitchen because they let their guard down and are careless, not because they are ignorant of the fact that the oven is hot. The same principles can be applied to operating a safe ceramics studio.

Is the Ceramics Studio a Dangerous Place?

What separates the household kitchen from the ceramics studio in terms of risks to your health? It is the level of knowledge on how to use each set of materials and tools correctly. All activity involves some degree of risk. Knowing correct information about a situation either reduces the risk level or enables you to decide if the risk is too great for the reward. Most of us determine that the reward of obtaining a meal prepared in our kitchen is worth the risk. We have made this calculation by learning about safe food preparation and the dangers of hot ovens and sharp knives. The same learning techniques can be applied to working in our pottery studios, with equally satisfying results.

Most people assume that the greatest danger in the studio comes from inhaling airborne dust particles released from the movement of dry clay. Yes, there is some amount of dry clay in the air in any studio (depending on how consistently the work areas are swept and cleaned with the proper equipment), but it isn't the only studio situation that involves risk. A basic understanding of all the potential safety issues is critical in preventing health problems. Knowing where the most likely problems in the studio will occur is essential. The emotionally charged issues such as lung disease (silicosis, kaolinosis, or any respiratory distress) are major areas of concern, but other areas of serious risk are less dramatic and are sometimes given almost no thought.

One of the major health risks potters face is back injuries from improperly handling and lifting clay bags and kiln shelves. Always lift heavy objects with a straight back and don't lean over to place shelves in the kiln. Don't stretch to pick up heavy glaze buckets, large containers, or a full box of pots. Place your feet near the object and lift while bending your knees. Try not to twist your body when lifting and have a clear path to your destination. Rather than lifting a heavy load by yourself, find someone to help you. It may save you many weeks of pain.

Back pain is often caused by working at a wedging table that's the wrong height. If the table is too low, you have to bend over to wedge the mass of clay, if it's too high you have to work harder and strain to move the clay. The wedging table should be level with where your hands fall at your sides. This height allows the use of your upper body weight rather than pure muscle power to move the clay.

The height of the potter's wheel in relation to the wheel seat is also critical in preventing back pain. Try to have the wheelhead and throwing surface level with the height of the seat. Sometimes moving the seat an inch up or down will place undo strain on the back tendons and ligaments. This also makes centering the clay easier because the upper body weight directed through your arms applies more leverage than muscle in moving the clay to the center of the bat.

Another leading cause of studio injury is carpal tunnel syndrome (CTS) which develops when too much pressure is exerted on the nerve that runs through the carpal bone in the wrist. When the nerve is compressed against the bone, the hand and fingers can be affected. Symptoms of vise-like pressure and tingling can frequently progress to permanent nerve damage. It can be caused by any type of redundant hand motion. Factory workers on the production line, typists, dentists, roofers, auto body shop workers, or anyone involved in any repetitive hand motion over a prolonged time can experience CTS. Carpal tunnel syndrome can be successfully treated if diagnosed early.

Potters can damage nerves in their hand from the repetitive motion of wedging clay or throwing pots. The best way to prevent this type of injury is to break up the work activities associated with making pots into small segments, minimize repetition, reduce speed, and rest your hands in all shop activities. Don't wedge 100 pounds of clay at once or sit at the potter's wheel making pots for hours on end. As a further example, throwing 12 pots on the wheel shouldn't be followed by making another 12, but by trimming leather-hard pots or loading the bisque kiln for the next firing cycle. Working in clay involves a series of separate tasks. Shifting from one task to another avoids prolonged repetitive motion situations.

Other hazards present in the ceramics studio also need to be recognized and prevented. When unloading the kiln, wear protective gloves. Many potters don't realize that the sharp edges of fired clay, glazed surfaces, and broken pottery shards can cause cuts. It's possible to cut yourself without feeling any pain because of the razor-sharp edges. Always examine any glazed surface for dangerous areas.

Whenever a pot gets fused to the kiln shelf, wear safety goggles and gloves before attempting to chisel or remove the shards. Often small chips of glaze and shelf will fly off the chisel. Don't attempt to pick them up with your bare hands as they can easily puncture unprotected skin.

Some potters have an allergic reaction to moist clay that comes in contact with their skin. Small bumps or irritation on the hands and forearms develop after working with the clay. Applying hand lotion to the arms before working with moist clay will often eliminate a sensitive skin reaction.

Under the right conditions, mold can occur in moist clay (which can increase plasticity). Mold can also grow in stored wet glaze containers. A few drops of household bleach per gallon of glaze will eliminate mold growth. Potters should use a dust mask when handling dry clay containing mold.

The processing and washing of highly alkaline wood ash (used as a glaze raw material), along with soda ash, pearl ash, and potassium dichromate can cause skin irritation to unprotected hands.

Wear the proper goggles or eye protection when looking into any kiln during the firing. Sunglasses won't stop exposure from infrared or ultraviolet light damage to the eyes. It is essential to wear shaded goggles even at relatively low bisque firing temperatures. After the firing, don't unload the kiln until the pots are cool to the touch. Many potters receive burns from hot pots, kiln shelves, and kiln posts in their rush to see the fired results.

It is not unusual for potters to have their studios in the basement. This popular work space can present several potential health concerns. Good cross ventilation is important when firing any kiln in an enclosed area. Opening windows and doors during the first part of a bisque or glaze firing can allow good ventilation in the basement. It is strongly recommended that venting systems be installed in all electric kilns. Electric kiln venting systems remove organic and carbonaceous material found in clay, sulfur in clay, wax resists on pots, and organic gums in glazes, during the firing.

Another factor that can affect the environmental atmosphere in some basements is the presence of radon gas. Radon below the basement floor can drift into the studio. In high levels over prolonged periods, this colorless and odorless gas can cause damage to the lungs. At extremely high levels, it is the equivalent of smoking one or two packs of cigarettes a day. If you work in a basement studio, purchase a simple radon test kit available at the local hardware store. The test results will indicate if there is any radon gas present in the basement and list the steps that can be taken to reduce or eliminate the gas.

Safe Handling Of Raw Materials

Any raw materials used in the ceramics studio should be handled with common sense and care. A clean studio with materials stored in properly labeled containers is a substantial step in developing a safe studio condition. When it's time to order raw materials for clay bodies or glazes, get a Material Safety Data Sheet (MSDS) for each material from your ceramics supplier. The MSDS lists the chemical product, company identification, composition information on ingredients, hazard identification, first aid measures, toxicological information, and other safety considerations when handling the material. Read each MSDS sheet carefully and note the storage and cleanup guidelines for that specific material. Some raw materials such as lead or lead frits, cadmium, and selenium, beryllium, uranium oxide, zinc chromate, zinc yellow, antimony oxide, chrome yellow, and vanadium compounds require extensive safety procedures. Except in highly specialized situations, they should not be considered for use in ceramics studios.

Under the U.S. Labeling of Hazardous Art Materials Act (LHAMA), commercial glazes must be evaluated for chronic toxicity and must be labeled to supply information on how to use the glaze safely. The label must also indicate if the glaze is food-safe. It is a good safety practice to read all the information supplied with the product. If you are uncertain about the glaze, call your ceramics supplier for further details. Often the supplier can offer specific practices and techniques in the proper use of the glaze. Ceramics suppliers are also a good source for safety goggles, insulated kiln gloves, and dust masks.

Clay Dust in the Studio

The most often asked question about studio safety is, "What amount of clay dust in the air is harmful?" The practical answer is to keep all work areas free from any airborne materials. It's not the clay floating around the studio that is potentially harmful. The nose and lungs filter most of these

Studio safety starts with a clean, well-organized work place.

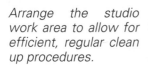
Arrange the studio work area to allow for efficient, regular clean up procedures.

large particles. It's the micron-size invisible particles that can get past our natural filtering mechanisms that can cause lung and respiratory irritation and possible permanent damage. Again, the best policy is to keep all levels of airborne material as low as possible. Some potters invest in room air filtration systems which can run into hundreds of dollars. Such units are a low price to pay for a higher degree of protection, but following proper cleaning procedures in the studio and a commonsense approach to working with dry materials will also be very effective in maintaining a safe work place.

Unfortunately, most of the current health and safety information is based on industry or mining operations where high concentrations and long exposure rates can be present in the workplace. It's impossible to calculate if similar conditions exist in any potter's studio, but the inhalation of large quantities of free silica found in some clays can cause silicosis after extended exposure. The cleaner the studio, the safer the studio.

Varying views are held on the potentially dangerous effects of any given ceramic material. Some experts speculate that the average amount of silica in the air when working with clay is roughly equivalent to playing baseball on a dirt field. Other authorities advise not to go into the studio unless it is maintained at "clean room" laboratory levels of purity. Somewhere between these two extremes, there is a practical approach to using ceramic materials in your studio. Research the available safety information from many sources to gain an informed viewpoint. Then go into your studio prepared to enact and maintain guidelines that will create a healthy workplace.

Safety Guidelines for the Ceramics Studio

* Always wear a National Institute of Occupational Safety and Health (NIOSH) dust mask when mixing dry glaze or clay body materials.

* Use a spray booth when spraying glazes and always wear a respirator with the correct filter.

* Always wear a dust mask in any studio cleaning operation.

* Don't use glass containers in the studio (they can easily break into sharp pieces).

* Never eat, drink, or smoke in the pottery studio.

* Don't store food in the studio.

* Always wet mop or vacuum (use a high efficiency HEPA filter in the vacuum) the studio floor every day to remove raw material dust.

* Store dry glaze and clay materials in sealed containers of double plastic bags.

* Clean up any raw materials spills on the floor or tables as soon as they happen.

* Place a doormat outside the pottery studio to catch dry materials.

* Wear a separate set of clothes in the studio and clean your studio clothes frequently.

* Clean your eyeglasses after leaving the studio.

* Wipe down work tables with a wet sponge before leaving the studio.

* Use a small particle air filtration unit in the studio to improve air quality.

* Keep infants and children under four out of the studio. Supervise children four and older at all times.

* Don't ingest or inhale any raw materials.

* Wear cotton clothing while firing kilns. Synthetics can easily ignite when exposed to direct flame. Clean your cotton clothes frequently (they trap clay dust).

* Wear protective eye goggles when chipping glaze off kiln shelves.

* Use extreme care when throwing pots (kickwheels have moving parts).

* Wash your hands before leaving the studio.

Chapter 23

Black Friday

After making pots for 20 years and teaching college ceramics for ten years, I decided I needed a change. Maybe it was the three-hour faculty committee meetings after teaching all day. Or my colleagues asking me why I wanted to "play with clay." I spent many months developing a plan that would get me out of the deeply worn pattern that had crept up on me over the years since graduate school. With some careful thought and a considerable amount of money, I moved from the city to the country. My new house had a sunny walkout basement which made a perfect place for my pottery studio. The space had good light and large windows opening on a grassy lawn edged by white birch trees. I equipped the studio with a wheel, wedging table, work tables, shelves, an electric kiln, and a glazing area stocked with raw materials. You would think the purchase of this property would be the one that changed my life, but it didn't bring about as big a transformation as my next purchase.

The New York city apartment house where I grew up and spent the my first 17 years didn't allow dogs. Cats, yes, but no dogs, probably because a dog has to be walked and the law of averages predicts that accidents would occasionally occur on the way to the street. During college, a dog was out of the question – it was difficult enough to take care of myself. After graduate school, my energies were spent learning to teach and accommodating my girlfriend (that's a whole other story that fortunately will remain only in my memory). So it was bad timing that left me dogless. In retrospect, my dogless years were soon to be balanced out by having too much dog. Which proves that if you wait long enough, things even out.

My change from "dogless" to "dogfull" started on a day when I had just finished making a set of nesting bowls in my studio and decided to take a break. While walking around the circle in front of my house, a very large black dog came running up to me. This turned out to be my future companion's brother or litter mate. My neighbor had purchased a six-month-old black Labrador retriever puppy. The dog looked almost full grown, with a massive head and exceedingly large feet. I couldn't believe how big that six-month-old dog was! After a few questions, I knew I had to get just such a dog. One of the questions I failed to ask was how much a dog that size would eat. I have since learned never to buy something large that has to be fed. Just ten minutes before my walk, I hadn't even considered getting a dog. But that's how things happen, right?

The trip to the dog breeder on that October morning found me in a rural driveway. I looked at two or three dozen black labs with a few chocolate ones scattered in. Most of the dogs were the short-legged Labrador hunting dogs often seen on outdoor clothing company calendars. However, a few dogs looked like they were on steroids or had strayed too near a nuclear power station. These creatures were taller, larger, and much bigger in every feature than their average-size companions. As I walked across the lawn, it became evident that my future giant dog was just waiting to be taken home. The only question was which giant would choose me to become its caretaker and friend.

As I found myself the center of attention in this group of dogs, one puppy came jumping up and knocked me over into a (thankfully) clean patch of lawn. It was just luck because when I looked around, there were many large mounds of...well you know. The strange thing about these lawn droppings was their size. They certainly could be mistaken as exiting from a cow. As my new friend licked my face with a meaty smell on his breath, I just knew we would be going home together. My companion was more than ready to go as I wrote a rather large check and was given his papers. He had championship parents who I met briefly while making the last arrangements for his adoption. The breeders, a nice couple, gave me a small bag of dog food, which lasted until we got to the car.

On the way home from the kennel, Robinson Crusoe came into my mind. Shipwrecked on a desert island, Crusoe finds a man washed up on the beach who he calls Friday. This was a perfect name for my new friend. I had visions of Friday watching me make pots and staying by my side as I worked in the studio. Well, visions was the right word for it because that's what they were – nice thoughts, but not reality based. Friday was always on the move, exploring, eating, excreting, and generally not at all like the quiet friend I had imagined for myself. He stayed in the ceramics studio with me until I caught him drinking out of the glaze buckets. It was time to "dog proof" the studio and get a personal trainer to work on his behavior.

Friday knew all the standard dog tricks – lie down, play dead, roll over, give me your paw, etc. It was just real life that gave him, or should I say me, problems. *His* real life was fine, *mine* revolved

around cleaning up after him and us going on long exercise walks. Somehow in my rush to get a dog, I neglected to research the Labrador retriever breed. They need lots of exercise and early training. However, they are gentle with children and have a good disposition. Maintaining his daily routine left little time for making pots.

By the sixth year of his life, Friday had slowed down to almost normal speed. He would sit by my feet in the morning while I had my coffee – a vast improvement over his past routine of pacing up and down the kitchen looking over his shoulder for the next drop of food.

Friday was solid black, almost blue black, and he shed many hairs into my newly thrown pots. After laying down on his side in the studio with that big pink tongue falling out of his open sleepy mouth, he would get up with clay dust on his side. I kept the studio very clean, but there was always a gray side to Friday. He was at his best in his resting or thinking position. His big brown eyes would follow the kickwheel around and around. Just looking at his eyes dart around made me dizzy. There's something to be said for a single digit IQ because he never found this activity (or lack of activity) too dull or boring. He was just glad to be with me. Thinking back, he was smarter than I since he was the one being fed, cared for, and had the run of the house and studio. All this for performing a few tricks. He led a wonderful, uncomplicated life and was a constant friend in the studio. I talked with him at length about the problems of making pots, glazing pots, and selling pots. Like a true friend, he listened intently and never once told me I should go into a more lucrative line of work.

When I planned a Florida vacation, I arranged to take Friday to a boarding kennel owned by friends where he had stayed before. On the trip to the kennel, he jumped and licked my ear all the way to the dog hotel. At the end of each kennel stay, he came back tired and sleepy but seemed to enjoy the new sights and smells of being away from home. Three days into my vacation, the kennel called me in Florida. I always called them to check on Friday, they never called me, so I knew it wasn't good news. They told me Friday had died. They had found him dead that morning. The veterinarian determined that Friday had died of internal strangulation. This potential problem is common in some breeds of large dogs, cows, and horses. When full of food, their stomach can flip over and close off their intestine. That morning I learned more about the internal plumbing of my friend than I ever wanted to know. I can't tell you the sorrow and ache in my heart. It's true in times of great loss that your heart does physically ache and hurt. I came home the next day.

My veterinarian suggested I have Friday cremated and keep his ashes. After ten years of being together almost every day, I just wanted to keep him around, so about two weeks later Friday did come home again. His ashes were in a small oblong tin box about the size of a grapefruit. I considered making a ceramic jar for his ashes but the box rested on a shelf in the basement studio. It did give me some comfort to know he was as close by as the basement. In fact, when a friend called several weeks later and asked about him I said that Friday was in the basement. After the phone call I realized I had forgotten to mention that Friday was dead.

Several months went by and every day working in the pottery studio, I would look up and notice the tin box on the shelf. While mixing glazes one afternoon, the thought that came into my head was one that many potters have had. In graduate school, the subject of bone ash had come up often. I had always wondered what sources of this high-temperature flux besides cow bones would work. As you've probably figured out by now, I was considering Friday in his present form (bone ash, calcium phosphate) to supply the bone ash requirement for my glaze. More specifically, I was thinking of glazing just one coffee cup for myself using Friday's bone ash as a glaze ingredient. The idea of having a part of Friday in my coffee cup would in some way keep him as close to me as he had been in the past.

Over the next several weeks, I mentioned this idea to some friends. After observing the look on their faces, I started being more selective about who I told. There was an interesting division among the group. Potters registered recognition and interest. Many expressed their relief because they had traveled the same mental and emotional path and had considered using the bone ash of a loved friend and companion. Nonpotters said (or probably thought) that integrating Friday into a coffee cup was morbid aberrant behavior on my part. They gave me either a blank or shocked look when I revealed my plans, but for the most part they were polite, allowing for my grief. My own feeling was that at some level you either intuitively make the jump or not. You either get it or you don't.

I took the tin down from the shelf and opened it to find a light gray powder. It was much the same as any other glaze raw material and it was easily measured out into a cone 6 electric, gloss black glaze formula I had developed several years ago when Friday was in the studio drinking from my glaze buckets. After weighing out all the other dry materials, I added water and ran the wet glaze through an 80x-mesh sieve three times. My bisqued coffee cup was on the work table and I first poured the liquid glaze into the cup, then poured out the excess. After letting the cup dry for a while, I dipped it into the liquid glaze for the outside coating and that was that!

Loading up the electric kiln the next day was interesting as I placed the cup on the kiln shelf and hoped for a good result. The kiln fired as expected and the cup was the first piece I looked for when unloading. There is a comfort in keeping loved ones close. As I write this at my kitchen table, my coffee is in a gloss black almost blue-black glazed cup.

Black Friday Glaze Cone 6/ox	
Nepheline syenite 270x	20
Whiting	15
EPK	18
Ferro frit #3124	20
Flint 325x	17
Bone ash (Friday)	10
Mason black stain #6600	12
CMC	1%

My coffee cup with Black Friday glaze (cone 6/ox).

Chapter 24

Conclusion

The most difficult part in advising people who are interested in ceramics is suggesting what they should do after they attend workshops, lectures, schools, or any other educational ceramics programs. Simply counseling them to continue their ceramics education is good advice, but should be qualified by also encouraging them to develop a mental attitude that will enable them to learn from every experience, good and bad. Everything changes in ceramics and knowing that, the student must utilize every circumstance to their advantage. When glazes run off the pot onto the kiln shelf, it can be a good opportunity to learn more about kiln firing and glaze chemistry. Or when a favorite raw material is no longer available, it might be time to experiment with other materials. The important realization is that nothing will stay the same. Rather than being upset by this fact, students can educate themselves in the various aspects of making ceramic objects so they can be ready for change and possibly grow from the experience. Many times, potters are locked into glaze formulas, clay body formulas, and kiln firing techniques that will become limiting and frustrating. Their written formulas might not change, their exact way of firing their kilns might not change, but over time, the raw materials in the formulas and the actual firing conditions in the kiln will slip away from them while they pursue methods that no longer work.

Most people learn about ceramics through teachers. Whether they learn at day camp, preschool, grade school, workshops, or graduate school, most of the population has worked with clay at some point.

However, not all teachers are skilled or dedicated to transferring ceramics information. It's the student's responsibility to take away useful insights from less than optimum learning situations. One of my first ceramics teachers in junior high school taught me an important lesson that I carry with me to this day. It occurred when I asked why the pots had to be bisque fired before I could glaze them. Why not just apply the glaze to the dry clay and do one firing instead of two? Suddenly, from across the room my teacher's voice yelled out, "Mr. Zamek, that is a dumb question. That is not how it's done." I immediately felt embarrassed in front of my classmates. I still remember a sick feeling in my stomach as I applied glaze to my bisqued pot. I never asked another question in that class. Why I didn't give up ceramics at that point is due to something I've come to appreciate and recognize in myself – persistence. Of all the factors necessary to become proficient in the field of ceramics, persistence will be the major attribute in your search for acquiring techniques and skills. I kept on making pots, kept on going through pedantic teachers, bad kiln firings, inconstant raw materials, my own mistakes, and eventually gained a certain kind of strength from plowing through the rough times. In short, it is important to take advantage of the good learning opportunities that come along, but it is critical to use and benefit from the bad times. Looking back, I sometimes smile to myself now when I once-fire pots using the knowledge gained after leaving junior high school. I think I've learned more about clay and glazes than my junior high teacher ever knew.

Students are always worried about asking dumb questions whether it be, "Can I use the clay after it freezes?" (yes, provided the clay is remixed and wedged again) to, "Why is porcelain white?" (porcelain contains kaolin, feldspar, flint, all of which contribute to the clay's white color). In fact, there are no dumb questions, only the potential for dumb answers. Don't be afraid to ask questions and look for a clear response, but also observe the way the teacher presents the information. Their concern and interest in you as a student will tell you more about them than their professional accomplishments or university ceramics degrees.

Why the emphasis on ceramics education and instruction? A diverse ceramics training – formal and informal – will enable you to express your artistic and technical concepts with greater accuracy and clarity. For example, learning throwing or hand-building techniques requires discipline but the end result is acquiring the tools to shape your own concepts into three-dimensional objects. Having the ability to throw a functionally correct plate on the potter's wheel and then trim, bisque fire, and glaze it to a successful completion is the framework for shaping your own ideas of how a plate should look and function. Practical ceramic skills go hand and hand with the ability to use what you have learned to give clay your own distinctive imprint. Throughout your ceramics experience you will gather small pieces of information about clay, glazes, kilns, kiln firing, and other related topics. At some point, a critical mass of individual bits of information come together, making for a greater understanding of all the factors involved with working with clay. Taking an aggressive role in your ceramics education will speed up the process. Be persistent in learning more about clay and glazes.

Part V

Clay Body and
Glaze Formulas

Soda Vapor Firing Clay Bodies Cone 9

Listed are clay body formulas that work well in soda firing (sodium carbonate) or salt firing (sodium chloride). They can be used for hand-building and throwing in oxidation and reduction atmospheres.

Cone 9 Light Brown	
Grolleg kaolin	25
A.P.G. Missouri fire clay 28x	25
Goldart stoneware clay	30
Tennessee ball clay #9	10
XX sagger clay	5
Custer feldspar	5
Silica sand F-65	4%
Grog 48/f	4%

Cone 9 White/Light Gray	
Cedar Heights bonding clay 50x	22
Goldart stoneware clay	19
Hawthorne Bond fire clay 35x	21
Tennessee ball clay #10	13
XX sagger clay	10
Flint 200x	9
Custer feldspar	6
Silica sand F-95	9%

Cone 9 Porcelain White	
Grolleg kaolin	50
Custer feldspar	25
Flint 200x	25
Bentonite B	2%

Cone 9 Dark Brown	
A.P.G. Missouri fire clay 28x	20
Goldart stoneware clay	37
XX sagger clay	15
Flint 200x	10
Custer feldspar	8
Redart	10
Grog 48/f	8%

Cone 9 Medium Brown	
A.P.G. Missouri fire clay 28x	23
Goldart stoneware clay	35
Cedar Heights bonding clay 50x	10
Tennessee ball clay #9	15
Redart	6
Custer feldspar	6
Flint 200x	5
Grog 48/f	6%

Cone 9 Black	
Goldart stoneware clay	50
A.P.G. Missouri fire clay 28x	20
Thomas ball clay	15
Barnard clay	5
Flint 200x	6
F-4 feldspar	4
Silica sand F-95	6%
Cobalt oxide	1-1/2%

Clay Body Formulas Cone 06, Cone 6, Cone 9

The clay body formulas listed are designed for throwing or hand-building forming operations. The cone 6 and cone 9 formulas can be used in oxidation or reduction kiln atmospheres, but there will be changes in clay body color due to the kiln atmosphere. It's always good practice to mix up a small test batch of any formula and note the results with your own glazes and kiln firing conditions. Clay body formulas are calculated to 100% batch weights. Coloring oxides, stains, grogs, and any clay body additives are listed after the 100% batch weight.

Cone 06 Low-Fire White	
Kentucky/Tennessee ball clay OM#4	50
Talc Nytalc 100	47
Whiting	3

Cone 06 Low-Fire Red

Redart	65
Goldart stoneware clay	10
Talc Nytalc 100	20
Kentucky/Tennessee ball clay OM#	5
Barium carbonate	1/4%
Grog 48/f	8%

Cone 6 White Stoneware

Grolleg kaolin	30
Goldart stoneware clay	30
Flint 200x	10
Nepheline syenite 270x	18
Tennessee ball clay #1	12
Bentonite	2%
Silica Sand F-65	6%

Cone 6 Light Tan Stoneware

A.P.G. Missouri fire clay 28x	15
Hawthorne Bond fire clay 35x	20
Tennessee ball clay #9	20
Foundry Hill Cream ball clay	15
Redart	5
F-4 feldspar	15
Flint 200x	10
Grog 48/f	8%

Cone 6 Brown Stoneware

A.P.G. Missouri fire clay 28x	15
Hawthorne Bond fire clay 35x	20
Tennessee ball clay #9	20
Foundry Hill Cream ball clay	10
Redart	10
F-4 feldspar	15
Flint 200x	10
Grog 48/f	8%

Cone 9 White Stoneware	
Goldart stoneware clay	15
A.P.G. Missouri fire clay 28x	15
Pioneer kaolin	10
EPK kaolin	18
Tennessee ball clay #10	20
Custer feldspar	12
Flint 200x	10
Silica sand F-65	5%

Cone 9 Light Tan Stoneware	
A.P.G. Missouri fire clay 28x	20
Goldart stoneware clay	50
Tennessee ball clay #9	15
Custer feldspar	8
Flint 200x	7
Grog 48/f	7%

Cone 9 Brown Stoneware	
A.P.G. Missouri fire clay 28x	20
Goldart stoneware clay	43
Tennessee ball clay #9	15
Custer feldspar	8
Flint 200x	7
Redart	7
Grog 48/f	7%

Base Glaze Formulas Cone 06, Cone 04

Base glaze formulas can be used with a wide range of metallic coloring oxides or stains.

Zam #1 Clear, Gloss	
Ferro frit #3195	80
Bentonite	20

Zam #2 Clear, Gloss	
Ferro frit #3195	63
Wollastonite	21
Flint 325x	8
EPK	8

Zam #7 Clear, Gloss

Ferro frit #3195	57
Wollastonite	19
EPK	8
Flint 325x	8
Barium carbonate	8

Zam #8 Clear, Gloss

Ferro frit #3124	78
EPK	9
Nepheline syenite 270x	13
Bentonite	2%

Zam #9 Clear, Gloss

Ferro frit #3195	65
Wollastonite	21
EPK	8
Flint 325x	6

Zam #13 Clear, Gloss

Ferro frit FB276-P2*	98
EPK	2
Bentonite	2%

*Ferro frit FB276-P2 can produce clear, transparent, glossy noncrazed surfaces in many glaze formulas.

Zam #3 Satin

Ferro frit #3134	60
EPK	20
Nepheline syenite 270x	15
Flint 325x	5

Zam #4 Satin

Ferro frit #3124	80
EPK	20

Zam #5 Satin

Ferro frit #3134	90
EPK	10

Zam #10 Satin

Ferro frit #3124	35
Ferro frit #3110	37
Talc	8
EPK	10
Zinc oxide	4
Flint 325x	6

Zam #11 Satin

Ferro frit #3124	40
Ferro frit #3110	35
Talc	8
EPK	9
Superpax	3
Zinc oxide	5

Zam #14 Satin

Ferro frit #3124	60
Kentucky Ball OM#4	20
Nepheline syenite 270x	15
Flint 325x	5

Base Glaze Formulas Cone 6

Zam #1 Clear, Gloss

Ferro frit #3195	50
Custer feldspar	21
Flint 325x	16
EPK	8
Whiting	5
Bentonite	2%

Zam #2 Clear, Gloss

Whiting	13
Dolomite	6
Nepheline syenite 270x	36
Flint 325x	33
EPK	6
Zinc oxide	6

Zam #3 Clear, Gloss

Whiting	18
Dolomite	6
Nepheline syenite 270x	37
Flint 325x	30
EPK	4
Zinc oxide	5

Zam #4 Clear, Gloss

Nepheline syenite 270x	20
Whiting	20
EPK	20
Flint 325x	20
Ferro frit #3124	20

Zam #5 Clear, Gloss

Ferro frit #3195	60
Flint 325x	22
EPK	12
Whiting	6
Bentonite	2%

Zam #6 Clear, Gloss

Nepheline syenite 270x	41
Zinc oxide	6
Whiting	16
Barium carbonate	7
Flint 325x	30

Zam #7 Clear, Gloss

Nepheline syenite 270x	31
Zinc oxide	6
Whiting	16
Barium carbonate	7
Flint 325x	40

Zam #8 Satin

Whiting	15
Nepheline syenite 270x	40
Flint 325x	38
EPK	7

Zam #9 Satin

Custer feldspar	37
Whiting	12
Zinc oxide	25
EPK	4
Flint 325x	22
Bentonite	2%

Zam #10 Satin

Nepheline syenite 270x	29
Magnesium carbonate	11
Zinc oxide	3
Gerstley borate	14
EPK	8
Flint 325x	35

Zam #11 Satin

Nepheline syenite 270x	31
Zinc oxide	6
Whiting	16
Flint 325x	40
Barium carbonate	7
Superpax	10

Zam #12 Satin

Custer feldspar	25
Dolomite	16
Whiting	3
Zinc oxide	3
EPK	18
Flint 325x	35

Zam #13 Matte

Nepheline syenite 270x	60
Dolomite	15
EPK	10
Flint 325x	15

Zam #14 Matte	
Nepheline syenite 270x	60
Dolomite	15
Kentucky ball clay OM#4	10
Flint 325x	15

Zam #15 Matte	
Nepheline syenite 270x	45
Whiting	18
EPK	20
Flint 325x	5
Zinc oxide	12

Base Glaze Formulas Cone 9, Cone 10

Zam #1 Clear, Gloss	
Custer feldspar	23
Tennessee #1 ball clay	22
Whiting	21
Flint 325x	34
Bentonite	1%

Zam #2 Clear, Gloss	
Nepheline syenite 270x	55
Flint 325x	27
Whiting	9
Magnesium carbonate	5
Gerstley borate	4
Bentonite	1%

Zam #3 Clear, Gloss	
EPK	10
Whiting	20
Custer feldspar	40
Flint 325x	20
Nepheline syenite	10
Bentonite	2%

Zam #4 Clear, Gloss

Custer feldspar	55
Whiting	20
Tennessee #1 ball clay	15
Flint 325x	10

Zam #5 Clear, Gloss

Tennessee #1 ball clay	17
F-4 feldspar	34
Flint 325x	27
Whiting	22

Zam #6 Clear, Gloss

Dolomite	5
Whiting	16
Custer feldspar	34
EPK	14
Flint 325x	31
Bentonite	2%

Zam #7 Clear, Gloss

Whiting	18
Dolomite	6
Nepheline syenite 270x	36
Flint 325x	30
EPK	4
Zinc oxide	6

Zam #8 Clear, Gloss

Custer feldspar	60
Whiting	15
EPK	10
Flint 325x	15
Bentonite	2%

Zam #9 Clear, Gloss

Ferro frit #3195	35
Custer feldspar	42
Flint 325x	13
EPK	6
Whiting	4
Bentonite	2%

Zam #10 Satin

Petalite	76
Talc	14
Whiting	3
EPK	7

Zam #11 Matte

G-200 feldspar	45
Flint 325x	5
EPK	25
Dolomite	22
Whiting	3

Zam #12 Matte

Custer feldspar	45
Flint 325x	5
Tennessee #1 ball clay	25
Dolomite	22
Whiting	3

Glossary

Author's note: The definitions listed here may differ slightly from other texts, but I've tried to offer an explanation on how the words were used in this book.

Alkaline earths – A group of nonmetallic oxides that can be used as fluxes in glazes.

Bag wall – An internal kiln wall protecting the pots from the direct flame path of the burners.

Bisque firing – A preliminary firing enabling the pots to become more durable for the glazing process.

Blister – A defect producing a sharp-edged "crater" effect in the fired glaze surface.

Bloating – The interior expansion or bubble in a vitrified clay body caused by trapped gases.

Catenary arch kiln – A kiln consisting of a self-supporting arch that doesn't require external support.

Casting slip – A mixture of clay, water, and deflocculent, and sometimes other ceramic raw materials, that produces a liquid clay body for pouring into molds.

Coefficient of Expansion – The degree of expansion or contraction in ceramic materials when heated and cooled. Materials with high coefficients of expansion will shrink or contract more than materials with low coefficients of expansion.

Crawling – A glaze defect where the molten glaze rolls back on itself exposing bare areas of the underlying clay. The boundary of the crawl often has a rounded edge. In some instances, molten glaze can slide off the pot, landing on the kiln shelf.

Crazing – A fine web or lines in the fired glaze.

Damper – A heat-resistant plate that can be moved in and out of a kiln stack to control escaping gases.

Deflocculation – Causes the particles in clay bodies to repel each other, increasing the moist clay's fluidity. Deflocculents are used in casting slips, causing the clay to become liquid without the addition of excess water.

Devitrification – The ability of a fired glaze to grow crystals upon cooling.

Down-draft kiln – Escaping kiln gases are directed up and then down to an opening at the bottom of the kiln.

Endpoint temperature – The highest temperature reached in a kiln firing.

Engobe – The term in some texts is used interchangeably with slip, but engobes contain higher amounts of clay in their formulas than slips. However, they still contain combinations of clay, water, and other materials that can be applied to a clay body for color or surface texture decoration.

Eutectic – A combination of two or more ceramic materials causing the lowest possible melting point.

Firebox – The interior part of the kiln into which the burners direct their flame.

Flocculation – Causes the particles in a moist clay body to draw towards each other, binding them together. A term widely used with casting slips but it can also describe throwing and handbuilding clay bodies' "tight" feel when being worked on the wheel or during the handbuilding forming methods. A properly flocculated throwing body will exhibit less moist slurry clay coming off in the potter's hands after pulling up on the wheel.

Flux – A ceramic material that brings into a melt other materials in a clay body or glaze.

Frit – Specific combinations of oxides that have been blended, fired to a molten state, cooled, and ground into a fine powder for use in glazes and some clay bodies.

Interface – The area where the clay body ends and the glaze layers begins on a fired ceramic object.

Jigger – A manufacturing process for the forming of pots. The inside of the pot is shaped by a mold which is turning on a wheel, the outside of the pot is carved by a template brought up to the surface of the turning clay.

Maxon premix burner – A burner/blower unit for kilns that can feed dry material and a gas flame into the kiln. (This unit was used in a series of soda firing tests to introduce sodium carbonate into the kiln.)

Overglaze washes – Metallic coloring oxides and/or stains mixed with water and applied over an unfired glaze surface.

Oxidation – Firing a kiln with excess air (oxygen) which allows any organic material in the clay body to burn off. In glazes, an oxidation kiln atmosphere can offer a different spectrum of colors as compared to reduction kiln atmospheres.

pH – A measurement of alkalinity or acidity in a solution.

Pinhole – A glaze defect producing a small smooth-sided round hole in the fired glaze surface, which, in some instances, will expose the underlying clay body.

Pyrometric cones – A combination of ceramic materials formed into cone shapes. Each cone is formulated to bend as specific temperatures are reached in the kiln.

Ram Press – A process patented in 1952 by Ram Inc. for the pressing of clay between two porous molds using air pressure through the molds to release the clay form.

Reduction – The decreasing of oxygen from ceramic oxides during the kiln firing process, causing a change in color of the clay body or glaze.

Refractory – Resistant to heat.

"S" shaped crack – Found most often on the bottom of wide-based wheel-thrown forms or forms thrown off the hump caused by improper coning up procedure before centering the clay.

Salt glaze – Traditionally, a pebble textured "orange peel" glaze formed on exposed clay surfaces when salt (sodium chloride) is introduced into the kiln during the last stages of clay body maturation. The salt is heated to a vapor that reacts with the alumina and silica in the clay body to form a sodium, alumina, silicate glaze.

Salt kiln – A kiln in which salt (sodium chloride) is deposited during firing, resulting in sodium vapor forming on all interior surfaces of the kiln.

Shivering – A defect where the fired glaze peels away from the underlying clay body, often looking like paint chips.

Sintering – The first stages of fusion where dry particles stick together before actual melting takes place in a clay body or glaze.

Slip – Water, clay(s), and other ceramic materials that help the slip fit in the application, drying, and firing process. The material combinations form a decorative liquid clay blend that can be applied to a clay surface.

Soaking – The process of holding a kiln at temperature for a specific period of time to promote glaze maturation.

Soda kiln – A kiln in which soda ash (sodium carbonate) or baking soda (sodium bicarbonate) is deposited during the firing, resulting in an "orange peel" sodium vapor glaze. Both sodium compounds are free of hydrocloric acid and chlorine when heated.

Short – A term applied to clay bodies in a moist state, indicating a lack of plasticity.

Sprung arch kiln – A cube-shaped kiln with a slightly rising arch on top. The kiln and arch are held together by an external framing material which is usually angle iron.

Thixotropic – A term widely used with casting slips, but when applied to throwing and handbuilding clay bodies, it is the capacity of the moist clay body to deform under pressure. This characteristic can take place when wheel-thrown forms have a gelatin-like consistency as pressure is exerted on the clay when pulling up a cylinder.

Underglaze washes – Metallic coloring oxides and/or stains mixed with water and applied to raw or bisque ware.

Vitreous – The glass formation in a clay body or glaze corresponding to low porosity in the clay body or glaze.

Vitrification – An increasing amount of glass formation in a clay body or glaze as temperature is increased.

About the Author

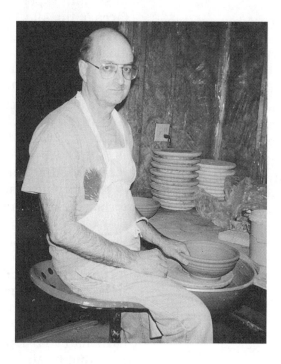

Jeff Zamek started making pots in 1968 and received a Bachelor of Science degree in Business from Monmouth Univeristy, W. Long Branch, New Jersey. He then attended Alfred University, College of Ceramics, Alfred, New York, where he obtained B.F.A./M.F.A. degrees in ceramic art and design, after which he taught ceramics at several colleges in the Northeast. He has developed clay body and glaze formulas for ceramics supply companies throughout the United States.

Zamek has written many articles for ceramics magazines and in 1983 launched his own consulting firm, Ceramics Consulting Services. He has worked with individual potters, ceramics companies, and industry sources in offering technical information on clays, glazes, kilns, raw materials, and ceramic product development.

Articles by the Author

"Methane Gas and Sewer Sludge: New Routes to Energy Efficiency in Firing Clay," *The Studio Potter*, Dec. 1984, Vol. 13 No. 1.

"Methane and Paper Sludge," *Ceramics Monthly*, June 1983.

"Sodium Vapor Firing Part 1," June 1973, "Sodium Vapor Firing Part 2," April 1974, Scholes Library of Ceramics, New York State College of Ceramics at Alfred University.

"Functional Pottery Sets" *Pottery Making Illustrated*, Summer 1998.

"Studio Safety: Assessing Risks" *Pottery Making Illustrated*, Summer 1998.

"Production: Mistakes to Avoid" *Pottery Making Illustrated*, Spring 1998.

"Education: A Lifetime of Learning," *Pottery Making Illustrated*, Winter 1998.

"Marketing: 12 Steps to Success" *Pottery Making Illustrated*, Oct. 1997.

"Avoiding Common Problems" *The Firing Line*, Winter/Spring 1997.

"Weighing the Benefits of Wet vs. Dry Clay" *Clay Times*, June 1996.

"Alternative to Salt Glazing" *Craft Horizons*, June 1973

Index

INFORMATION, COACHING AND INSTRUCTION

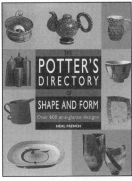

The Potter's Professional Handbook

A Guide to Defining, Identifying and Establishing Yourself in the Craft Community
by Steven Branfman
With detailed information and step-by-step guidelines for everything from shelf building to record keeping, this book is a comprehensive guide to building a professional life in clay by Steven Branfman, author of the best-selling Raku: A Practical Approach.
Softcover • 7-1/4 x 9 • 240 pages
100 b&w photos • 40 color photos
POTBUS • $29.95

The Potter's Directory of Shape and Form

Over 600 at-a-glance designs
by Neal French
This unique directory offers more than 600 immediate shape and design solutions for ultimate creativity. Quickly learn the four major shapes plus the extras such as lips, spouts, feet, and flanges. Get tips on making perfectly proportioned pieces.
Softcover • 9-3/4 x 7-1/2 • 80 pages
600 b&w Illustrations • 200 color photos
PDSF • $19.95

Mold Making For Ceramics

by Donald E. Frith
This is a must-have book for your library - the only book to demonstrate precisely the craft of making and using all types of molds - from decorative press molds to complex, multipart slip-casting molds. Two calculators are bound in as your special bonus. Originally released with a hard cover.
Softcover • 8-1/4 x 10-7/8
240 pages
16-page color section
MMCERS • $34.95

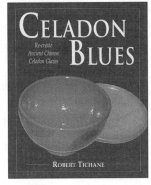

Ash Glazes

by Robert Tichane
The author takes the guesswork out of ash glazes, thanks to his exhaustive research and experimentation. The practical and usable information will benefit both the novice and experienced potter. Nearly 40 ash glaze recipes are included, as well as instructions for making synthetic ash glazes.
Softcover • 8 x 10 • 240 pages
300 b&w photos • 16 color photos
GLAZ • $24.95

Celadon Blues

Re-create Ancient Chinese Celadon Glazes
by Robert Tichane
Celadons—some of the most beautiful, subtle, and visually varied glazes—can be re-created with the guidance available in this terrific study from noted chemist and potter Robert Tichane. He shares the results of thousands of tests to help you achieve success with this notoriously fussy glaze.
Softcover • 8 x 10 • 240 pages
150 b&w photos • 16-page color section
CEBL • $24.95

Copper Red Glazes

A Guide to Producing this Elusive Glaze Effect
by Robert Tichane
Finally potters can master the ancient secrets of copper red glazing without expensive and frustrating experimentation. This is the most comprehensive book ever compiled on this fascinating and popular group of glazes. Even the beginning potter will gain insight into the problems encountered when making copper red glazes and benefit from the practical instruction offered.
Softcover • 8 x 10 • 312 pages
15 b&w photos • 50 color photos
CRG • $24.95

THE POTTER'S LIBRARY

Electric Kiln Ceramics

A Guide to Clays and Glazes, 2nd edition
by Richard Zakin
This inclusive guide will assist you in using the electric kiln to produce clear, brilliant colors and richly textured surfaces. Provides you with completely revised glaze recipes, information on commercial glaze for low fire and updated health and safety information.
Hardcover • 8-1/4 x 10-7/8 • 304 pages • 16-page color section • **EKC2** • **$39.95**

The Kiln Book

2nd edition
by Frederick L. Olsen
You'll find complete plans and instructions for building a kiln of any size and purpose in this informative volume. Plus, discover the principles of efficient design and information on refractory materials, building methods, flues, curved and common walls, bricklaying courses and arches.
Hardcover • 8-1/4 x 10-7/8 • 291 pages • **KILN** • **$40.00**

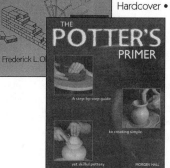

The Potter's Primer

by Morgen Hall
The compete potter's handbook! Get a solid foundation on numerous techniques. This inclusive guide runs the gamut, from selecting the right clays and forming techniques to throwing, turning, decorating, glazing and firing.
Softcover • 8-1/2 x 11 • 144 pages full color • **POTPRI** • **$24.95**

The Potter's Palette

A Practical Guide to Creating Over 700 Illustrated Glaze and Slip Colors
by Christine Constant and Steve Ogden
You'll never again suffer the uncertainty of mixing a color and getting an entirely different fired result. This reference walks you through glaze circulation, formulation and use. Includes color bars to show fired results.
Softcover • 8-1/4 x 10-7/8 • 80 pages color throughout • **POPA** • **$19.95**

Clay And Glazes for the Potter

by Daniel Rhodes
Discover the ins and outs of clay and glazes in this classic work. Rhodes will walk you through Raku, salt firing, fuming with metallic salts, overglaze processes, and the use of fibers and fiberglass in clay. A bonus detailed appendix includes 32 glaze formulas to experiment with.
Hardcover • 8-1/4 x 10-7/8 • 330 pages • 8-page color section • **CGFP** • **$31.95**

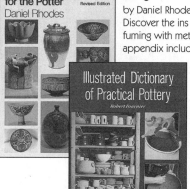

Illustrated Dictionary of Practical Pottery

3rd edition
by Robert Fournier
You'll be completely up-to-date on pottery issues with this revised edition. Discover changes in modern techniques and firing methods and learn about the newest materials. You'll learn about the latest warnings for lead compounds and asbestos-based materials as well as vital health and safety information.
Hardcover • 8-1/4 x 10-7/8 • 288 pages • **IDPP3** • **$34.95**
